ROD SERLING

ROD SERLING

◆

THE DREAMS AND NIGHTMARES
OF LIFE IN THE TWILIGHT ZONE

◆

A BIOGRAPHY BY JOEL ENGEL

CB
CONTEMPORARY
BOOKS
CHICAGO

Library of Congress Cataloging-in-Publication Data

Engel, Joel, 1952–
    Rod Serling : the dreams and nightmares of life in the Twilight
Zone / Joel Engel.
       p.   cm.
    ISBN 0-8092-4538-8 (cloth)
          0-8092-4075-0 (paper)
    1. Serling, Rod, 1924–1975—Biography.   2. Authors,
American—20th century—Biography.   3. Television
personalities—United States—Biography.   I. Title.
PS3537.E654Z63   1989
813'.54—dc20
[B]   89-17374
                                                    CIP

To my wife, France,
who makes all good things possible

CONTENTS

ACKNOWLEDGMENTS

To list all of the people and institutions without whom this book could not have been written, and to whom I owe a debt of thanks, would require more space than allotted here. But special acknowledgment must be made of the following: Dick Berg; Saul David; John Champion; Alden Schwimmer; the staffs at the Wisconsin Center for Film and Theatre Research and the State Historical Society's archives reading room, in particular Harry Miller and George Talbot; Randy Dolnick and Ronald Simon at the Museum of Broadcasting; William F. Nolan; Lieutenant General (ret.) Edward M. Flanagan; the Department of the Army; Barbara Hatch at the FBI; the Special Collections Department at UCLA's University Research Library; the Santa Monica Public Library reference librarians; Alan Landsburg; Buck Houghton; Martin Manulis; Jackie Cooper; Reginald Rose; Michael Zimring; Karin Horgan; Shirley Tabas; and Les Gilbert.

My most profound gratitude is extended to Robert Serling. His kindness, candor, insight, encouragement, and friendship were utterly invaluable.

ROD SERLING

PROLOGUE

This was a story right out of "The Twilight Zone": Rod Serling, the professional celebrity on any of a dozen television game shows, grotesquely mocks his lustrous past.

Submitted for your examination: a man who's dying inside. Not so many years ago, he rode the crest of a golden wave he thought would never end. He reveled in the loud acclaim of his greatness. But that was before giving birth to the Creation. Three years have passed now since the Creation refused to die. Each day he hears fewer whispers of his greatness, and those still heard cannot be believed from inside the private hell to which the Creation has doomed him.

The year is 1967. Here sits the most famous writer in the universe—the only writer in history whose name, face, and voice are as recognized as his writing. For the cameras he smiles and laughs, makes a joke, seems witty and engaging. But wit and laughter are growing more

1

difficult to conjure up all the time. At only forty-two years old, he feels ancient and obsolete. The deep, craggy lines of his once-handsome face are filled with heavy makeup—lines that wouldn't be there at all but for too much sun, too little sleep, too much despair.

Very soon, when this day of taping game shows ends, he will drive alone to his psychiatrist and attempt again to deny that the only applause he has heard for three years has been on these shows. He will try to believe that they still remember him for what he was, and he wants to forget that his best work now lies behind him. He will come to accept that what remains of his talent is now glaringly out of proportion to his fame. And he will cry to discover that it was his addiction to fame—and fortune—that cost him his chance at true greatness; he has traded distinction for celebrity. And then he will laugh again, bitterly: perhaps this is the story he will write to make them forget his mistakes. The sadness and poignancy appeal to him. He likes to tell stories in which character is revealed by stripping away layer after layer of pettiness and ego, leaving the protagonist naked, small, and vulnerable.

Portrait of a man who realized too late that talent does not alight forever, that money is a poor substitute for greatness, that fame is a prison, and that self-deception can be a deadly vanity. The few successes remaining to him in the final years of his life will be empty ones, devoid of joy and exhilaration. Like an impotent man whose sex drive continues to rage, he will be haunted by memories of his past splendor and tormented by each new mediocrity. The moral, ladies and gentlemen, because all stories have morals, is simply that everything in this universe comes with a price tag. Rod Serling went on a shopping spree. His last stop was the Twilight Zone.

1

WALKING DISTANCE

The jungles of Panama, through which the laborers
had hacked for fifty-one miles in order to construct
a waterway that would join the Pacific and Atlantic, had become the most disease-ridden region on earth.
For the previous ten thousand years, the mosquitoes that
swarmed there had tasted very little human blood, but
they now feasted continually. Yellow fever, malaria, and
typhoid ran rampant through the camps. And if the tropical diseases didn't attack the men, the wild animals
might. At least the wages were good and the work steady.

For Samuel Serling, the Panama Canal represented a
mighty adventure. This was, he knew, history in the
making. "A land divided, a world united" was the slogan of
the construction team. From his home in Detroit, Sam
had avidly followed newspaper accounts of the canal's
progress ever since ground breaking in 1906, when he was
thirteen. Even at that age, he had marveled at the engineering complexities inherent in building a lock canal
across an isthmus covered by dense jungles. Where
another boy might have believed the task was as simple as

clearing a vacant lot and shoveling out some dirt, Sam instinctively understood the challenges. His mind worked that way. He himself loved to tinker and construct small devices that amused him. He wanted to be an engineer. If only he had been able to stay in school, he would have made a good one. His curiosity was immense, his intelligence quick. But his poor, Lithuanian-born father asked him to quit before high school graduation and get a job; the family needed the money. But what about his father's brother, the one here in Detroit, who'd struck it rich in America? Wouldn't he give them the money so Sam could continue in school? Don't even ask, his father said. Bitterly, Sam accepted his fate but spent the rest of his life a little ashamed, and very sorry, that he'd never gone to college.

If he couldn't be an engineer, he at least wanted some sort of job that allowed him to use his mind. Just being told what to do without making any independent decisions bored him to desperation. But without even a high school education, none of the jobs for which he could qualify allowed him that small pleasure. One day while running an errand in an office, Sam noticed the boss's secretary making some relatively unimportant decision on paper. Compared to the mind-numbing jobs he had had, her latitude to effect such decisions took on magnified importance. That she also resided in the front office, with the powerful, made the job all the more attractive. Her assumed salary superiority was not as important, although he considered that too. The very same night he enrolled in a secretarial school. He was the only man.

In those days male secretaries were about as plentiful as female business owners. That didn't bother Sam Serling in the least. He felt it gave him an advantage, because he believed he was smarter than any woman. Within a few months he had learned to type 120 words per minute on those primitive typewriters and to take shorthand skillfully enough not to miss a syllable, no matter how quickly the boss dictated. Now he had a real skill and could sell it to the highest bidder.

Sam went to work for a small business in Auburn, in west central New York. Handsome and well-dressed, he had no trouble meeting young women—like Esther Cooper, the daughter of Lithuanian immigrants who had done well in the grocery business, operating a small chain of stores in that region of New York. Esther herself had been born in Russia and came to the United States at age three. Without the hint of an accent, she spoke well and intelligently, complementing her good looks. She and Sam were soon engaged to marry.

Esther's father, no doubt the most well-to-do man in the history of his family, did not particularly relish the idea of his daughter marrying below what had become her station. Nor did he like that Sam was firmly to the left of Reform Judaism, while he and his family remained devoutly Orthodox. He had a fondness for Sam, however, that outweighed these objections. He found him bright, energetic, eager to learn. A young man like that could learn the grocery business and help it to prosper further. And when Sam agreed that he and Esther would keep a kosher house, the wedding date was set.

Sam had a surprise for Esther. "For our honeymoon," he told her, "we're going down to Panama." He may as well have said Tahiti or any other tropical locale. All Esther knew of Panama was that ever since they met Sam had talked passionately of the incredible project being undertaken there. It sounded pleasant, if far away. But that wasn't the real surprise.

Sam, who certainly didn't have the money to spend on such an exotic vacation, had signed on as a stenographer to Colonel G. W. Goethals, the man in charge of the canal construction. It was a well-paying job, one filled with challenge and excitement, and promised a real future. Maybe, he explained, he would be able to become an apprentice engineer and learn through experience what he lacked in education; at the very least it would likely be the adventure he hoped for. Esther could not argue. Nor would she let her father.

By the time the newlywed Serlings arrived in Panama

in the fall of 1915, a Panamanian freighter had already passed once from the Atlantic to the Pacific through the Canal. Now the fine work had to be completed, and that would take up to six more years.

The first night in their cramped, moldy, ramshackle apartment, the Serlings heard a muffled cry from the closet. They opened the door to find a shoe box in which a newborn had been abandoned. The black-skinned infant, whom they turned over to the American authorities, would come to represent how each of them viewed their two years in Panama. For Sam the child was an affirmation of the pioneering spirit he felt a part of; after all, his days were filled from early to late with transcribing the minutiae of this emerging engineering miracle in this incredible jungle wilderness. Even though soon after their arrival a fantastic landslide had dumped thousands of tons of dirt and jungle into the structure, closing it to through traffic for most of their two-year stay, Sam still felt the joy of daily creation. He witnessed the evolution of the project as it progressed from thought to paper to fact, from abstract to concrete. History in the making.

For Esther, however, the baby was simply a reminder of the daily desperation and poverty that surrounded them— realities her husband ignored—and of the emptiness of not yet having her own child. But raised to be quiet and submissive, Esther accepted this disparity as her lot, perhaps even her fate.

Had she not contracted yellow fever, their lives might have turned out very differently. Certainly by 1917 the disease was supposed to have been mostly eradicated through the efforts of the army physician and sanitation expert William Gorgas, who spent years exterminating the type of mosquito that carried the virus. Esther Serling's case was a fluke.

She became very ill with the fever and hovered near death. That she pulled through was probably due more to constitution and luck than to any treatment she received. But when she did regain her health, she noticed that her husband seemed much more attentive, less focused on himself. If she wanted to go home, he said, they could.

The Serlings arrived back in Auburn in the fall of 1917 to discover that Esther was pregnant. For Sam it was more a shock than a joy. Now, with a child on the way, he would be forced to accept his father-in-law's offer of a career in the family grocery business. They moved to Cortland, where Mr. Cooper gave him the smallest store in the chain to manage. The very idea of working in retail hurt him. Although he loved Esther dearly and even happily anticipated the birth of his first child, he felt he was a prisoner of circumstances, his mind wasted. And when the United States entered the First World War, the patriot could not even join the army and fight the enemy, as he was soon to be a father. That disappointed him as deeply as his stifled ambitions. (The army briefly considered drafting fathers with only one child, and Sam grew excited in anticipation of being sent overseas to fight. But the war ended before the plan became operative.)

The birth of their son, Robert, was difficult for Esther. According to the physician, her reproductive organs had been weakened by the tropical disease and the boy would be her only child.

For the next six years, the Serlings prospered financially and became firmly of the middle class, 1920s style: day maids and even an occasional cook took care of their housekeeping chores, and there was money to play in the raging bull market. Although Sam never completely forgot that he was just the manager of a grocery store and not engaged in a more creative or intellectual livelihood, the three of them were reasonably happy and content. Hard-earned but steady money, and the easier life it bought, would do that.

In early 1924 Esther's father moved Sam to the family's Syracuse store, where the old man needed him more. By summer Esther had missed enough menstrual periods to know the doctors had been mistaken; she was thirty-two at the time. It was, of course, a surprise for all of them, but hardest on Bob. He was a bright child but lacked the sort of ebullient personality that would endear him naturally to people. And having had his parents to himself for six and a half years—in an era when there were very few only children—he had grown very close to them. The thought that he'd now have to share them with an invader, one who'd likely take most of their attention and time, hardly appealed to him.

The new baby was due on or about Christmas Day. To make up for their possible absence, and probably also to ease the pain of forcing a sibling on Bob, Sam and Esther bought him a Lionel electric train set and placed it wrapped in a huge box under the Christmas tree. Even though she had grown up in an Orthodox home, Esther had long since abandoned any attempt at remaining observant. Sam's secular beliefs dominated the house. Virtually the only vestige of Judaism that could be seen or felt was cultural, in the discussion of Jewish-related issues. Ever since Bob had been born the family had celebrated, along with all of their gentile neighbors, the pageantry of Christmas; not to have done so would have been to isolate themselves socially. Perhaps if all other things had been equal a few decades hence, the Serlings might have celebrated Hanukkah instead, but in the 1920s the holiday commemorating the retaking of the Temple of Jerusalem from the Syrians had not yet acquired the sort of festival atmosphere it eventually would in American Jewish life.

Bob awakened Christmas morning to find that his parents had left during the night for Good Shepherd Hospital, where his brother, Rodman Edward, was born. Alone with the maid and his new, shiny red electric train set, and excited and impatient, Bob could not wait for his father. He put together the circular track and lined up the engine, baggage car, and two passenger cars. Unsure of himself, he shoved the rheostat. The train began circling too fast, went out of control, and crashed.

"My first realization that I had a brother," Bob remembers, "was that I hated the little son of a bitch 'cause he'd wrecked my train."

Shortly after Rod's birth, Sam investigated a business opportunity that would allow him to get away from his father-in-law and brother-in-law. With the little bit of money he had saved the previous eight years, Sam bought from them the Cooper Meat Market in Binghamton, population seventy-five thousand and located seventy-two miles south. The remaining three Serlings stayed behind in Syracuse in case the venture failed, while he moved himself and operated the business alone. Within a year he arranged for his wife and two sons to join him. Soon he bought a house on Bennett Avenue, in the decidedly middle-class west side of town.

Binghamton, the seat of Broome County, sits almost on top of the Pennsylvania border at the confluence of the Chenango and Susquehanna rivers, a geographic location that made it the area's major shipping center for agricultural and industrial products produced in the region. Shallow, green mountains separate the area from the famed Finger Lakes region. The city planners, more than one hundred years before, had seen to it that all main arteries led to the courthouse square, hub of the four-block-radius business district, and Court Street (where Sam Serling situated Serling's Sanitary Market, his new name for the old Cooper Meat Market). On the west side of the Chenango is the primary residential area where the affluent middle class lived then and still live today. To the north was an ever-growing enclave of white European ethnics—Polish, Russian, Czech—who had come to Binghamton in search of work in the area's numerous factories. Binghamton for decades had had a reputation as one of the foremost shoe-manufacturing areas of the country (as well as a leader in cigar making), but the immigrants of the first decades of the twentieth century came primarily because of one man, George F. Johnson.

Johnson had left school at age thirteen, in 1870, to work in a boot factory in his hometown of Milford, Massachusetts. Later his interest in the business led him naturally to Binghamton, where he took a job at the Lester Brothers Company boot factory. His energy and ideas were soon noticed and taken seriously. In 1884 he convinced his employer, Henry Endicott, to build a new factory outside the Binghamton city limits, in what became known as Lestershire, on the then-radical theory that large manufacturing concerns ought to be removed from the crowding and congestion of a bustling town. (Within a few years Lestershire would be incorporated as Johnson City.)

In 1892 Endicott appointed Johnson production and sales manager and seven years after that sold him a half interest in Lestershire Manufacturing Company. Johnson assumed the task of reorganizing the company after a lean decade that had caused shakeout in the industry. "Cut out the frills and unnecessary costs and give the workers an incentive to produce—put them on piecework at a decent rate," Johnson said, stating his goals and philosophy.

Two years later the partners formed Endicott-Johnson Company and built a leather tannery in a village to the west of Binghamton that in 1906 would be incorporated as Endicott. (Endicott, Binghamton, and Johnson City are today referred to as the Tri-Cities area.) Coupling E.J. with the manufacturing capabilities of the old Lestershire Company made them one of the largest shoe manufacturers in the Northeast.

By the time Johnson became president of Endicott-Johnson Company in 1920, he had been able to put into practice his plan of providing his workers with quality homes at affordable prices and extremely modest interest rates. Many of the homes—solid, usually unadorned, but far from tract reproductions—are still standing today and sell for prices that would have amused Johnson. When the company later incorporated, he also established a profit-sharing system.

With at least a half dozen factories in the immediate area, Endicott-Johnson had become one of the largest shoe manufacturers in the country under Johnson's brand of benevolent paternalism. He provided free medical care for his employees and furnished each of their children with a free pair of shoes every Christmas. He gave numerous banquets and parties, all free, and built recreation centers and parks, with free boating and swimming privileges. The George F. Johnson Pavilion, erected during the Depression, attracted famous-name big bands; for a buck, Binghamtonians could dance all night to Tommy Dorsey's band, featuring Frank Sinatra, his Adam's apple quavering in his skinny neck. Binghamton boasts the largest collection of operating merry-go-rounds of any city in the world—six of them—all donated by Johnson, who never charged anyone a cent for a ride.

Both Johnson's and the company's reputation grew internationally. Immigrants, especially Eastern Europeans, would land at Ellis Island not knowing a word of English but with hand-drawn signs hanging from their necks: "Which way, E.J.?" Friendly customs and outreach workers would make certain to get them on the proper train to Binghamton.

Most of them settled in close proximity to each other, in an area of town that soon became known as First Ward. While they huddled closely for a sense of safety, somewhat bewildered at first by their new country and language, they were desperate to assimilate into American culture, even at the cost of abandoning many old-country customs. They insisted that their children be educated in the public schools with other American kids, even if they were occasionally horrified by the relative rebelliousness of their sons and daughters as they became Americanized more quickly than their parents.

There is every reason to believe that this "worker's paradise" profoundly affected Rod Serling's eventual *weltanschauung*. Because he was exceptionally bright, observant, and impressionable, the cultural phenomenon taking place in his hometown made several distinct impressions, all of which would later find numerous avenues of expression, both in his work and his philanthropy.

For one, he clearly understood that these immigrants who streamed into Binghamton by the thousands during his early life were drawn as much by America's Bill of Rights as by the promise of gold in the streets. Well before even the arrival of the first refugees fleeing Hitler's Germany, Sam had provided his sons with a sense of perspective, explaining with passion that such rights were privileges not available just anywhere else and for which millions had died. And when these escapees did begin arriving in Binghamton, Sam would rage to the boys about the evils of Nazism and the coming war that would inevitably determine the fate of the world. Consequently, both boys had an unambiguous perception of America's beneficence as the moral and spiritual leader of the world. These early impressions remained an influence on Rod throughout his life; though he detested mindless jingoism, he never abandoned his deep patriotism.

Sam pledged his passionate allegiance to Franklin Roosevelt—"God, how I love that man," he would say as they sat around the radio to hear FDR's fireside chats—but remained firmly Republican. Right there in his own backyard as a daily reminder was the vivid representation of the best of both political ideologies, Endicott-Johnson Company. This was compassionate capitalism, and it stood for all that was good in America. Consequently, Rod grew to believe that profit-oriented industry and the nobility of the common worker are not mutually exclusive, that one does not have to suffer because of the other; every job, no matter how menial or exalted, had dignity. He saw that Johnson was beloved by his employees and that Johnson loved them; Johnson's gains were their gains and vice versa. He saw that even during the Depression, when men in other parts of the country went begging for work, Binghamton remained relatively unaffected, because Johnson insisted on operating on smaller profit margins or cutting back on everyone's hours rather than firing some of his workers. (He also shrewdly built one whole factory dedicated to making soldiers' boots.) Of course, if there had been mass layoffs at any of E.J.'s factories, Rod's own father's business—and in turn his family—would have suffered; that was obvious, and Sam, like all other small-business owners in town, was grateful to Johnson for his policies.

Rod Serling's own life could hardly have been more removed from the daily struggles that the Eastern European immigrants faced. His world, with few exceptions, stayed insulated from most harsh realties, and his childhood, on the surface at least, appeared almost as idyllic as he made it seem in later dramas. "In the strangely brittle, terribly sensitive makeup of a human being," he later remarked, "there's a need for a kind of geographical womb to crawl back into—and that's your hometown."

"Rod's memories of Binghamton were far greener than mine," Bob Serling says. "Far greener."

It is only with a type of psychological microscope that a subtext of quiet fear and anxiety can be seen to share that geographical womb with Rod Serling's green memories.

Without question, Rod got everything he needed, if not everything he wanted. From birth, his energy and personality dominated the home in a way that Bob's never had. He was unarguably adorable, as well as outgoing, endearing, and beguiling. "Rod was very charming from the time he was a baby. Everybody would make a fuss over him," notes Ann Goodman, a Binghamton neighbor and close friend of Esther Serling. "He was the type of boy whom people would just love on sight of him."

As is often the case with a physically appealing child who also happens to be bright and precocious, Rod attracted people to him by sheer force of personality. He received constant praise, even adoration, and soon found difficulty living without them. He wanted everyone to like him, and virtually all who met him did. So on those occasions when he did not enjoy the type of admiration he had come to expect, he actively pursued it, as though performing for applause. Goodman says that he sought gestures of love from everyone. With a huge smile that somehow conveyed a sense of wit and joy, adults especially found it hard to resist him. And if the smile failed to win them over, his natural gregariousness allowed him to talk his way into practically anyone's affection.

Talking, he had learned as an infant, when his early verbal skills rewarded him with kisses and praise, was an easy way to make friends. He was curious about everything anyway and liked to hear himself think. His soliloquies had attained legendary status in the Serling family by the time he was six. Bob Serling recalls one particular car trip to Syracuse from Binghamton. Before leaving, his parents discussed how to keep Rod from driving them crazy with his constant chattering for the three hours it took to cover the seventy-two miles; it had happened more than once before. Forced to share the back seat with him, Bob had a vested interest in the solution. Sam suggested that the three of them remain completely silent. Surely, he predicted, if Rod had no one to talk to, he would have to be quiet.

"So help me God," says Bob, "he did not stop talking from the time we left our house till the time we pulled up in front of my grandfather's house" in Syracuse. As his parents grew more hysterical in the front seat and Bob more irritated in the back, Rod jabbered the entire way. He commented on whatever he saw. "Look at the cows, the cows have four legs, the cows are eating the grass, then the grass turns into milk, and the farmers squeeze the milk out of them. Hey, Dad, have you ever milked a cow? I'd like to milk a cow. . . ."

"He's gotta be quiet some time, doesn't he?" Sam asked.

Not as long as he occupied center stage.

The inadvertent but unmistakable message delivered by friends and family was that Rod had been blessed and that Bob was just another unremarkable child. "I think Bob suffered from that," Goodman reflects. "He was the victim of Rod's popularity." Possibly because he was so much younger than his brother, Rod never tried to deflect some of the spotlight from himself onto Bob.

Bob Serling chose his career based on the belief that he had not had conferred on him, as his brother obviously had, the minimum requirements for stardom. Unlike Rod, Bob knew he did not have the technical skills, the physical strength or appearance, or the maturity to turn his "fantasy careers"—soldier, airline pilot, naval officer, football player, baseball player—into reality. He knew from the age of twelve that the only way he could live out these fantasies would be to write about them. "I wasn't going to be famous myself, but I was going to associate with people who were famous and important and brave—by being a newspaper reporter," he says. (He would often attend college football games, writing his own accounts of them, which he would compare to the next day newspaper stories.)

Bob, like his brother, succeeded in achieving his goal. Bob understood exactly what his limitations were, and Rod understood exactly what he could not live without—attention. As an adult, Bob recalls, Rod would suffer "total, absolute panic depressions" when he did not get the recognition or praise he believed was due him.

Esther was concerned about the effects of the inevitable comparisons between her sons and purposefully tried to devote more of her time to Bob. This plan backfired. Her subtle arching away only made Rod more intent on receiving her full attention. As Goodman remembers, "She was scared to death that Rod was going to be spoiled. And his father did spoil him."

"We both had idyllic childhoods," Bob says, "but I don't think I was as happy a kid as Rod."

Sam "worshiped Rod," says Suzanne Fischer Hersch, Rod's closest female friend through high school.

Miraculously, Bob appeared not to be overly affected by the inequities. The two boys became close friends, despite their considerable age difference, and played together constantly. Not until later, when Bob went off to Antioch College in Ohio as Rod entered junior high school, did their sibling rivalry begin. "Rod was into bebop music, and I had acquired this tremendous love of classical," Bob remembers. "I think he thought I was a pompous, pseudo-intellectual ass, playing Beethoven and Wagner. He'd say, 'You're not sincere; you don't like that classical junk. You're just showing off.'"

Had Bob been unable to handle, at least outwardly, his younger brother's gifts, the Serling family life may have been considerably less sunny than it seemed. But with apparent harmony at home and Sam's income adequate to sustain the trappings of a middle-class existence in the 1920s and 1930s, the Serlings lived very well. The food on their table was plentiful, and the talk was about current events and issues, not monetary problems. (Sam had consistently noted that the meat section of his market was the only profitable section and had phased out his retail groceries to concentrate on selling wholesale meats. As a high school student, Rod delivered meat around town in his father's truck.) The boys had bicycles and the newest toys, and their friends were always welcome. Esther cordially ushered the kids into the house, showed them the refrigerator, then left them alone. It was an atmosphere of trust. There were even occasional trips to New York City for the weekend, staying in hotels, eating dinner at fancy restaurants, seeing Broadway shows.

Every summer the Serlings vacationed for two months at one of two lake resorts. When Rod was very young, they went to Owasco Lake, located in the Finger Lakes region near Auburn. Unwilling his whole life to take extended vacations, Sam would drive up only for the weekends, while the boys remained at the lake with their mother and her sister Ada Robbins, who lived with her husband, Albert, in Syracuse. Later the family relocated to a more upscale resort area, Saratoga Lake, north of Schenectady. There they stayed with Betty—Esther's other closest sister of the eight—and her husband, Ed Rosenthal. Bob was friendly with their oldest son, Bob, and Rod with their youngest son, Lewis.

Ada saved Rod's life at Owasco. The cottage they shared stood fifty yards of green lawn away from the lake, which then had a three-foot cement retaining wall that allowed the kids the freedom of unsupervised play. Rod, about three, had wandered off by himself. Trying to balance himself on the top of the wall like a tightrope walker, he slipped and fell into the lake. No one had seen him. Ada and Bob, however, heard the curious splash and instinctively ran over to the water. By the time Ada got there, Rod was floating face down in the lake, motionless. Like Rod, Ada couldn't swim, but she immediately jumped over the wall into the water and lifted him out. At first, as they pushed on his stomach and chest, he didn't move; then suddenly he vomited a bellyful of the lake and let out a cry. From that moment on, Ada had her brother-in-law's undying gratitude.

Throughout his career, Rod Serling rarely wrote convincingly or insightfully about women. In none of his memorable dramas did he invent a memorable female character, not one who was anything more than a caricature of his idealized notion of a woman. The women had no substance to them, as his men often did. Even in "Patterns," his breakthrough drama, the ambitious woman is an ambitious *wife*; she's anxious for her husband's betterment. Clearly, Serling did not feel comfortable with his knowledge of the female viewpoint. No doubt this is at least a partial reflection of his home life and relationships with his parents. The fact that he called his mother "Dearest," after the mother in *Little Lord Fauntleroy*, tells much about the way they viewed each other.

The quintessential Norman Rockwell wife and mother, Esther Serling was passive, tolerant, and careful to avoid confrontations that might lead to angry exchanges. As a result, even at seventy years of age Bob Serling did not know where his mother had stood politically—or whether she even had voted. Her role was peacemaker in the house; she'd be crushed each time Sam got mad at one of the boys, and she worked constantly to smooth sore feelings and tensions. "She was so without fuss or bother or anything—just a very nice lady," says Ann Goodman. While there was much to love in her, the respect in the family went to her husband. "Mother was a typical loving housewife and a great mother and very doting," says Bob, "but Dad had the brains."

Sam was interesting to his sons. Passionate in his beliefs, he conveyed his impressive knowledge and opinions eloquently, using a broad vocabulary gained in part from flipping through dictionaries and writing down words; it was a pleasure to hear him use the language. Unlike their mother, who adhered to convention, Dad could be spontaneous. On the way to pay a visit to Aunt Ada in Syracuse one Saturday afternoon, the Serlings' 1927 Jordan broke down in Cortland. Garages were not open on weekends, so Sam had the car towed to the nearby Packard dealership, the only open store in sight. Told he'd have to wait until Monday for repairs, Sam eyed a seven-passenger limousine on the showroom floor. Several minutes and a few thousand dollars later, the Serlings drove off the floor and into Syracuse in style. Esther was tolerantly amused, the boys wild with amazement.

When they arrived back in Binghamton, they discovered the limo had to be squeezed into the garage slowly and carefully, with barely an inch of clearance on each side. Even then the car's tail stuck out into the backyard. The inconvenience wouldn't bother him, Sam said, but Rod and Bob raised hell because they couldn't ride their bikes in or out of the garage. Without a word, Sam backed up.

The next day he came home with several planks of lumber, some hinges, nails, and other assorted hardware. Within a week he had built an incredible, Rube Goldberg–like device that enabled him to pull the Packard limo all the way into the garage while still allowing the boys to park their bikes. Utilizing the height of the nearly two-story garage, he built a ramp that jutted from the side and front of the entrance. The boys rode up the ramp onto a platform suspended by adjustable chains; once on top, they lowered themselves into the basement on a collapsible ladder Sam had also designed and built.

Years later, when his heart kept him more sedentary, Sam devised an automatic sprinkling system for the backyard, which he could turn on from the upstairs porch. He also invented the prototypical doggie door. Just about the time Sam's heart virtually confined him to his chair, the Serling's toy Boston bulldog, Toni, developed a poor bladder. Unable to get up from his chair as often as she requested, Sam rigged a system of pulleys that attached to a small door within the rear door of the house. Instead of using a flap that swung both ways, he inserted a piece of metal that could be lifted upon command. When Toni whimpered, Sam reached back to pull the lever. The dog then ran out the back door. When she wanted to come in, she whimpered outside his window until she heard the door rise.

Another of his ideas, never created, was a hot dog in the shape of a hamburger. The favorite American food, he said to the boys one day, is a hot dog. They sell it at ball games, serve it at picnics and barbecues. Everybody likes to eat a hot dog. But the one bad thing is the shape of the roll. It's impractical. It's oblong, and mustard gets all over your hand. The hot dog never really fits inside. Then the roll breaks and the hot dog slips out. Sam wanted to invent what he called the "frankburger," which would have the taste of a hot dog with the convenience of a hamburger.

In many ways, Sam Serling had the sort of loony tendencies attributed to fictional absent-minded professors and inventors. What differentiated him from caricature was his respectability—he submerged his own passions in favor of being a breadwinner. Given his druthers, Sam would have holed up in a small room and allowed his imagination to run wild, letting imagined necessities mother a spate of inventions. When, in 1941, his meat market earned the Serlings only a bare living, he sold their Bennett Avenue home and moved them into a three-bedroom apartment on Chapin Street. With Bob gone, he explained, they no longer needed such a large house. In truth, as Esther admitted to Bob years later, they could have continued to live in the old house only at the expense of Rod's college education. It was crucially important to Sam that his sons not live with the regret he carried; inside his butcher's body beat an engineer's heart. "If only I could've gone to college," he told his sons, "then I could've made something out of myself. The meat business? Not for my boys."

Rod cherished the knowledge that his father, underneath that patina, was a cauldron of wackiness, and he admired and respected the strength that kept his father true to his family obligations; he too acquired that trait. His mother did not have to sacrifice any of her ambitions to be a good mother; her ambition *was* to be a good mother. His father had to sacrifice much.

Living in west Binghamton and attending Alexander Hamilton grammar school, West Junior High, and finally Binghamton Central High School, Rod had schoolmates and friends who were most often children of successful, well-educated, and professional people. They considered the American Dream a part of their birthright. In the 1930s, at least in Binghamton, young people still believed that rebellions took place only in history books. A halcyon innocence pervaded the town and washed over Rod Serling's life and dreams.

Far from rebelling against adult authority, Serling made a specific effort to endear himself to adults. "People would always pat him on the head," Ann Goodman remembers. "He just loved it." His childhood friend Jim Haley recalls when Serling, about age fourteen, visited his home after school one day. Haley's father, a dentist, came in, and Rod, in perfect seriousness, said to him, "Hi, doc. How are things at the office?" Dr. Haley's lower jaw dropped. No one that young had ever asked him about his business or personal affairs. Rod was, without question, the type of boy every parent approved of: a good student, active in the debate and drama clubs, a Boy Scout, a Red Cross member, editor of the school newspaper, president of the class; he was unfailingly polite and unceasingly cheerful. He even came home from his only trip to summer camp carrying a trophy that proclaimed him best camper of the year.

Lloyd Hartman, his high school debate coach and the faculty adviser to the school paper, which Serling edited as a senior, remembers him as perpetually having a "big grin on his face. He spoke to everyone in the corridors. He was a likable kid, and everybody liked him. Everyone knew who he was, too. He was such a happy-go-lucky guy."

Helen Foley, who taught him English in junior high school, recalls his "beautiful smile, beautiful coloring. He had black curly hair, rosy cheeks, and white, white teeth. He was a darling. Always smiling."

Serling invariably presented himself as confident and self-assured. He always had a joke to tell and laughed easily at anyone else's attempts at humor, which is the prevailing image of him most of his childhood friends retain to this day.

Yet he also had a touch of Peck's bad boy, or even Eddie Haskell in him: his smile often hid disquiet and anger. And he was not quite always unfailingly polite. Ann Goodman remembers the time she left the teenage Rod to babysit her toddler. Who better to watch her Leslie, she thought, than that perfect young man? Yet when she came back into the house for something she had forgotten, she heard him yelling at the baby with an unexpected tension in his voice, "You son of a bitch. You go to bed and go to sleep."

Rod Serling and Binghamton were perfect for each other. Each projected a persona that gave little hint of the ironies hidden beneath. A sublayer of subtle but insidious anti-Semitism affected all Jews in Binghamton's small-city "perfect harmony," including the Serlings. Likewise, Serling's care-free, buoyant, easy-going exterior hid a very real sense of desperation. (Throughout his life, in scripts, stories, interviews, and correspondence, all forms of the word *desperation* appear with frequency and regularity, as in, "I need this desperately.") Binghamton and Serling were, in significant ways, mirror images.

It is clear from his later works that Serling's imagination was greatly shaped by the thousands of hours he spent at the movies as a child and adolescent. He liked to go at least once a week, regardless of what played—from cowboy-and-Indian shoot-outs to Preston Sturges comedies, Busby Berkeley musicals, and Howard Hawks adventures. The magic was in the dark, fixating on heroes and villains and imagining himself as their characters. He projected himself onto the screen, pretending to be not just the character but Rod Serling playing the character. "We both fantasized a lot," says Robert Serling. "I can remember the two of us wearing cowboys' guns and hats in the kitchen. We'd get out my dad's liquor shot glasses and pour ginger ale in them and sit there like a scene out of a western. We'd go to movies together and come home and act out the parts. I can remember acting out *Dr. Jekyll and Mr. Hyde* the first time we saw it, in 1933, the one with Fredric March. I got some plastic teeth, and Rod and I figured out what kind of concoction from my chemical set would foam up in the beaker, like the one we'd seen in the movie."

Actors were the center of attention, as Rod wanted and needed to be. Whether on the stage or screen, the leading men—Gary Cooper, Clark Gable—commanded you to look at them. "He loved acting, loved the spotlight, loved the limelight," his brother notes. Acting, he could see, was a fantastic way to occupy center stage. He started out playing a few roles as a young child in local theater groups. One of them was an Elmer Rice play, *Counselor at Law*, in which the only other child was his friend Sue Fischer. Then came junior high school and high school dramatics. He was in at least a dozen productions in all. In none of them did the audience ever forget the Barrymores.

He did have a great talent for mimicry, though, and was able to reproduce almost precisely the timbre and tone of foreigners speaking English. And he told wonderful jokes that relied on exact reproduction of dialect; Germans and Japanese, particularly during World War II, became his favorite targets of nasty jokes. When a "Jap" spoke in the joke, he squinted his eyes and bucked his top teeth.

Once, while home on vacation from Antioch, Bob received a call from someone he particularly disliked. The young man had an irritating, high-pitched voice that Bob hated as much as he did its owner: "Bobby, how are you? Please, while you're in town, have dinner with me."

No matter how persuasively Bob turned him down, the young man persisted. Finally Bob invented some ridiculous excuse, and the young man hung up. A few minutes later, Rod appeared with their father.

"You're not gonna believe this—that idiot Tom called me," Bob said. "I couldn't get rid of the bastard."

At that, Sam Serling began laughing so hard he put his hands on his knees. Bob realized he'd been had by his little brother. "I didn't know before then that he was that good," he says. "He was perfect."

Serling understood there would be no leading roles in his future, and it caused him considerable anguish. In the thirties, leading men weren't five feet, five inches tall; they were six feet plus. No one knew Alan Ladd stood on a soapbox, and Al Pacino and Dustin Hoffman wouldn't show up for another thirty or forty years. Dark and handsome—or at least cute—Serling was; tall he was not.

And if he couldn't be the leading man, then he wouldn't settle for character parts. After all, like short boys, character actors never got the girl. Convinced that only small girls would go out with him, he confined his amorous quests to them. In turn, they often thought him just "cute." Even Sue Fischer, as close to a real girlfriend as Serling had through high school, seemed less interested in him romantically than he was in her. Jim Haley recalls that Serling tried to finagle—to no reward—some time alone with his younger sister, Eileen, by "allowing" Haley to ride his new bicycle, thereby getting him out of the house. Although she too was short, Eileen didn't respond to his overtures. Already feeling constrained by his size, Serling possibly projected an unthreatening, brotherly facade, making it difficult for girls to take him seriously. Certainly his constant cheerfulness was hardly perceived as sexually alluring; he may have been, and was, immensely likable, but that was hardly the same as sexy.

Throughout Serling's life, his small stature remained as much of a burden, and sometimes an embarrassment, as it was then a motivating factor. While some short men prefer to fade into the background, Serling chose to be the focal point and constructed his whole personality around that decision.

He attempted to cover his deepest insecurities with perpetual jubilance. If he were really so happy and confident, why begin a lifelong habit of making self-deprecatory comments, calling attention to what he believed people already were thinking about him as a way of defusing their perceived criticisms? *I'm aware of these things, and I'll call attention to my failings before you do.* He would refer to himself variously as short, Jewish, aging, untalented—all words revealing the depth of his self-consciousness.

In high school Serling continually placed himself in situations that allowed immediate confirmation of people's opinions of him. He ran for class president and won—a confirmation. He told jokes; laughter was a confirmation, silence a criticism. And he joined the debate club, which judged him directly on his performance.

Interestingly, Serling exhibited a trait in his formal debates that subtly betrayed his persona. The intramural debate format allowed an affirmative and a negative speaker. The affirmative speakers recited from notes, following a prepared logical argument on a particular topic. The rebuttal was, naturally, ad-libbed. Lloyd Hartman, his high school debate coach, remembers Serling as lacking the discipline to be lead-off speaker, who had to have done his homework to build logical arguments. However, "he just loved to pick up somebody else's argument and create a new argument opposing it."

The original argument made, Serling would approach

the lectern, often with a big grin on his face. Helen Foley, who coached him in junior high debates, says the bravado "made up for his stature. He pretended he wasn't scared." This was the entertainer in him, the ham appealing for chummy support. "Gee," he'd say, "this is a real nice high school. I've never been here before. You kids are all so great." If the students weren't yet disarmed enough, he might take some of his allotted time to tell a funny story or joke. Only then would he begin to rebut: "That was a terrific argument you came up with, but there were *just a couple* of little points. . . ."

His rebuttals were usually devastating, all the more so considering that they'd just come out of this ingratiating person. And that was the point: underneath the sunny disposition was an argumentative soul who had the eloquence and facility to cut someone down to his own size. Shirking the affirmative for the rebuttal, he was more interested in tearing down than creating and most interested in having the last word—not being brought down himself.

Serling's intense need to be accepted—and consequently his feeling that he never would be—was heightened by the brand of amorphous anti-Semitism that ran through Binghamton as quietly as an underground river. Whether he ever consciously decided that, yes, he was the direct victim of discrimination, the effect on him and other Jews in town became all the more insidious for its completely unsentimental nature. This was not a virulent, hate-seething mob. Theirs were not opinions. These were "facts." Jews are: Communists; rich; greedy; sexy. Even as a childhood friend and army buddy of Serling noted, "Jews are party people." In short, Jews are different from you and me.

While no cross burnings, Torah destructions, or other blatantly violent acts were committed until the 1950s, there were some isolated incidents. "It was pretty bad here in the thirties," Sybil Hullman Goldenberg remembers. "It was covert but definitely there. You could absolutely feel it. I only knew something was strange because I couldn't get into the clubs that the other girls were in."

In polite Binghamton society, one did not speak of these things. But the hundred or so Jewish families in town felt a sense of necessarily being herded. Like any racial or ethnic group in the midst of WASP America, where even Catholics could be blackballed from a high school sorority, the Jews tended to band together. A community developed around the Jewish Community Center and a reform synagogue, both of which they all contributed to build.

"We all hung out at the JCC," says Goldenberg. "My association with Rod was because we were both Jewish kids growing up in this Jewish community. We went to Sunday school together."

Neither Rod nor Bob had a bar mitzvah, although both, as a gesture for their mother, were confirmed in the synagogue. Had it been up to Sam, it's likely neither would have ever attended even Sunday school. The Serlings did not have Passover seders after leaving Syracuse, where Esther's father always led the services. Occasionally, though, the family, at Esther's urging, did attend synagogue on Rosh Hashanah and Yom Kippur, the holiest days of the Jewish year. Bob Serling recalls one year sitting next to his father, who had been ignoring the prayers to fixate instead on a nearby couple.

"He was a money-grubbing bastard, and she was a social-climbing bitch, and my parents hated them," Bob says.

Through his gritted teeth, Sam whispered, "Look at that hypocritical son of a bitch, praying for more money."

Sam Serling set an example for his sons. A thirty-second degree Scottish Rite Mason, certainly unusual for a Jew, he also belonged to the Shriners and the Elks. "I don't choose my friends for their religion; I choose them for the kind of people they are," he told his sons. "I'm not a good Jew, but I think I'm a good person. If you want to be very religious, that's up to you. My own philosophy is, I take people for what they are, not where they go to pray. I have friends who are Jewish, Catholic, Protestant, atheist, what have you. And I love them all."

Other Jews in the community, Goldenberg notes, developed a sense when growing up, "that you're really not the same as everyone else. Like you didn't date non-Jewish kids." A feeling of discomfiture pervaded. She recalls that most Jews in the community believed they should not seek to transcend their Jewish community boundaries too exuberantly, "because the reception was icy." The Binghamton Club would not accept Jewish members, and even IBM, which got its start in the Tri-Cities area, would not hire Jews.

Neither would the City Club or Binghamton's country club accept Jewish members, says Patricia Hamlin Be-Gasse, a Catholic who knew that at least one high school sorority would not accept her because of her religion.

While never ashamed of his Jewish background, Serling felt it was important not to be categorized as a Jew, and his cultural education, however deep it went, was largely unintentional. Because Sam was not a Zionist and not at all religious, there would have been no other reason to talk about Jewish life and Jews and what it meant to be a Jew had it not been for the events in Germany. He understood Jewishness almost solely because of his father's regular tirades about Hitler and the growing Nazi threat.

Then in his junior year of high school, Theta Sigma fraternity blackballed Rod Serling, the Jew. He was temporarily devastated. Before, being Jewish had never been more than a simple fact, like having black hair. Now it had become a hindrance. Vern Hartung, a high school buddy who later was in the service with Serling, contends that many people had no idea Serling was Jewish (just as many friends in his adult life would not know of his Unitarianism). That's how convincingly he "passed." Serling, however, should have known better and not been surprised. But he had kept hidden in a purposeful ignorant bliss that suited his needs. "It's not like you went and made an effort to get into these things," Goldenberg says. "You weren't invited to join." Rather than belong to either of the two all-Jewish fraternities, both of which would have accepted him gladly, Serling decided not to belong to any fraternity.

"It was the first time I became aware of religious differences," he later remarked. If so, his realization was likely a case of naïveté of choice—choosing not to see that which was so evident to others. Coincidentally or not, that same year Serling ran for school president and was elected. (In those days, Binghamton Central had too many students to accommodate them all at one time, so the day was divided into morning and afternoon sessions; "Roddy" Serling won election as president of the Morning General Organization.)

Rod Serling had gone to a Sunday movie matinee with Sue Fischer on December 7, 1941. Both were high school juniors. Shortly before the feature ended, the projectionist stopped the film, and the manager ran to the stage in front of the screen. "Ladies and gentlemen," he said, "the Japanese have ferociously attacked our military at Pearl Harbor in Hawaii. We know only that there has been much damage and a great loss of life."

Few in the theater that day did not appreciate the ramifications of this news. For the previous two years the United States had been on the brink of being drawn into the events in Europe. This catastrophic event surely would propel America into a world war.

At the time, Fischer did not believe that the announcement had had such a startling effect on her friend. She remembers that the two of them returned to her house afterward and told her mother, who at first did not believe them because they tended to create "fantastic stories." "She didn't even react," says Fischer, "because she was so sure this was another one."

Rod, however, had apparently been greatly affected. He would later claim to have run away to Canada, even before Pearl Harbor, in an effort to join the Royal Air Force, for whom he could fight on the British side. He told *Seven-*

teen magazine in 1963 that the RAD "sent me home after a hot meal and [gave me] the following advice: 'Come back when you grow up, sonny.'" This too is likely to have been a fantastic story.

The truth is that Serling really did want to quit school soon after Pearl Harbor and enlist in the army. War has traditionally been the arena in which young men prove themselves, and for Serling, the temptation to prove himself in such a clear-cut fashion was enormous. He credited his civics and history teacher, Gus Youngstrom, with talking him into graduating. "Remember," Serling quoted Youngstrom as saying in the same *Seventeen* article, "that you owe a debt to your parents. They need you also. And your country needs you—not just for now but for the future. War is a temporal thing. It ends. An education doesn't."

The following September, in the *Panorama*'s very first issue of the new school year, editor Rod Serling published his own editorial:

> It seems rather apparent that as the term progresses, students generally show a noticeable lack of interest in what's happening in this war. The conflict itself, on other fronts, is treated with almost indifference as an abstract occurrence with little importance. The war on the home front too can be fought much more effectively than we are doing it. For example, the sale of war stamps is far lower here in school than should be expected from a student body of over 1500 students.

> No one expects to be fanatically overzealous concerning our war effort, but what is expected, and what has every right to be expected, is a change from this state of almost semi-apathy so apparent among the majority of us. In other words, let's merely get more war-conscious.

> It's not a hard thing to do, either. It's merely a matter of reading up on the news, knowing what's going on, of purchasing war stamps and bonds as often, and in as large a quantity as we are able to, and of assisting whenever and

wherever it is possible in civilian defense, scrap and rubber drives, and war charities. These things represent the major requisites for being war conscious.

We can feel sure that those men in the fox holes on Bataan, the marines at Wake and the Solomons, and the gobs at Midway and the Coral Seas were all pretty much war conscious. Certainly if they were, the students of Central can snap out of their lethargy and take a little interest in what is going on themselves.

Written only a month after the Allies landed on Guadalcanal in the Solomon Islands, the editorial understandably omitted any mention of battle sites in North Africa and the Atlantic. It was fitting, therefore, that the South Pacific should be where Serling found himself little more than a year hence, experiencing the terrifying realities of war that would forever change him.

2

REQUIEM FOR A BOY

Rod Serling graduated high school—ranked 35th out of 180—in late January 1943 and was inducted into the army the next day. Although he would later tell numerous interviewers that he enlisted, the truth is he was drafted. His eighteenth birthday had come the month before and with it his draft notice. It's certainly possible that he had intended to enlist and was not given that opportunity because of the early notice. However, just a few months before he had received his acceptance to Antioch University and had indicated to his family that he planned to enter the university as a freshman.

On February 3, he and his Binghamton friends Vern Hartung and Joe Levine, along with a couple of thousand other inductees, boarded a troop train bound for Fort Niagara. Virtually the first soldiers they saw upon disembarking were paratroopers in their spiffy uniforms, shiny black boots, and official jump jackets with parachute wings on them. Immediately on reaching their barracks and throwing down their belongings, Serling said to Hartung, "Let's join 'em." There was a gleam in his eye, an excitement. Paratrooping was about the most dangerous assignment in the army, and only a very few got their wings. Hartung had wanted to be an air cadet, but as Serling pointed out to him, the cadets accepted ROTC graduates first and had an interminable waiting list. Hartung said no to the paratroops, and Serling stomped out of the barracks to sign up by himself. A few minutes later, Hartung followed.

Patriotism reached an all-time high during World War II. The Germans, fighting for Nazism, seemed clearly evil, and after their domination of Czechoslovakia few doubted that they wanted world domination; the Japanese achieved equal status in the Allies' eyes after Pearl Harbor. Therefore, there was the usual competitive jockeying not just to see who would go to fight but also how that fighting would be done. The paratroopers were glamorous, and even ordinary foot soldiers of higher rank stood in awe of them.

Serling was sent down by train to Camp Toccoa, Georgia, where the paratroop volunteers were screened for their fitness and desirability. Physicals, interviews, and scrupulous testing followed, as the regimental commander, Colonel Oren Haugen, personally handpicked the couple of thousand men; he accepted only about one in eight. This was a seller's market. Paratroopers, despite the inevitable danger they faced, were considered the elite.

The other reason to join an airborne unit was that every paratrooper knew that the men fighting on both sides of him qualified as the best the army had; they knew they could count on each other. Less important, a paratrooper earned about double what an ordinary foot soldier made. To the basic pay, about twenty-one dollars a month, the army added an extra fifty for jumping, considered hazardous duty.

"I never could understand why he went in," says Bob Serling, whose military duties were confined stateside because of his poor eyesight. "The only thing I could think is that it was one more challenge. The best way to get Rod to do something was to tell him he couldn't do it. I think he was trying to prove himself to his peers. . . . He had a streak of daring, a desire to do something no one else was going to do."

Colonel Haugen interviewed every man personally. "Why did you volunteer to be a paratrooper?" he asked. The correct answer—the one Haugen wanted to hear— assuming the volunteer passed the physical examination and psychological profile, was the one Kenneth Haan (who was later in Serling's platoon), from Detroit, gave: "Because I want to get the best training possible."

Although Serling gave the same answer, Haugen rejected him because of his size. When he looked up on the bulletin board to find his name omitted from the acceptance list, he was devastated—as he always was when rejected. He wanted this as badly as anything he'd ever wanted. Walking straight into Haugen's office, he pleaded his case, still to no avail. He threatened to sit forever unless the colonel changed his mind. Any man who wants it this badly, Haugen figured, is welcome in my outfit. "But you still have to make it through jump school," he warned, "and most guys don't." Serling smiled. He was now a member of the 511th Parachute Infantry Regiment of the Eleventh Airborne Division.

Basic training took three months at Fort McCall, North Carolina. Although small, Serling surprised most people with his strength, quickness, and agility. He had not been particularly athletic while growing up, but his naturally powerful physique suited the specific rigors of army life; he excelled at calisthenics and endurance.

Jump training at Fort Benning, Georgia, took the better part of a month. To qualify, each man had to make five jumps. Much of the training was arduous and frightening, in part because the job was inherently a difficult one and also because some men necessarily had to be weeded out—to ensure the regiment would not waver during combat. All were gung-ho, and a sense of competition arose among them. None wanted to fail.

After fundamental study, the first jump, in many ways the most frightening of the training jumps, was from a tower three hundred feet tall. Each man was drawn to the top on wires, then cut loose with the chute already open. It took a combination of skill, guts, and poise to land properly from that height and in such close proximity to the metal tower—and many were not able. Their legs, ankles, and, in some cases, wills were broken.

By the end of the month only about 1,800 men, including Serling, had passed the training successfully, their sense of elation tempered by the knowledge that sooner or later they would be performing the most dangerous feats in combat. In a battle zone that is anything less than totally secured, paratroopers floating to earth at twenty miles an hour become fat targets for enemy fire.

Serling felt enormous pride in having earned his paratrooper's wings. When the regiment was granted a two-week furlough after being sent back to Camp McCall, he immediately went home to show off the crisply starched uniform that bore the wings. He walked up and down the streets, knocked on the doors of friends and classmates, and even visited teachers at Binghamton Central High and West Junior High. Virtually the entire town knew that Rod Serling, hometown boy, had distinguished himself.

The vision of Serling as a paratrooper surprised most Binghamtonians; the regular army would have been one thing, but the paratroopers were quite another. They thought of Serling as a cute little boy, not capable of or disposed to jumping out of planes. "He definitely wanted you to know what he'd done," Jim Haley says. "Seeing him in that paratrooper outfit—he almost wore his patriotism on his sleeve."

The advanced training at Fort McCall was even more difficult than the initial paratroop training. Each man made another couple of dozen practice jumps, including one at night. Serling and the rest of his demolitions platoon made more jumps than that, since demolitions soldiers often need specialized skills that the majority of paratroopers never use. He made thirty-seven practice jumps in all.

Buoyed, perhaps, by his successes—certainly he now felt he was the equal of any man in camp—he signed up to box, representing the 511th against the other divisions when they moved to Camp Polk, Louisiana, for maneuvers. Boxing appealed to Serling. He was a big fan of both Ernest Hemingway and Jack London, authors who had written about boxing, the manly art, in a way that seemed to glorify the man-against-man combat. Besides affording him another opportunity to prove himself, boxing literally placed him center stage, where he became the entertainment, the focus of attention.

Moreover, boxing provided him with something else: "Like Hemingway, Rod was macho," says Dr. Ernest Pipes, Serling's pastor years later at the First Unitarian Church in Santa Monica. "They both had some deep center of self-doubt" that boxing seemed to assuage.

Over the following months at Polk, Serling, at 118 pounds, had eighteen fights and won the first seventeen. He learned quickly from a few lessons, given by an ex-professional who had had sixty-eight fights. Serling's speed and strength were impressive, and, not coincidentally, the competition in his weight class, the lightest, called "catchweight," was poor.

In his eighteenth and final official bout, for the catchweight division championship, Serling got his face pummeled by a far superior and more experienced boxer, who was later rumored to have been a professional. Knocked out cold, his nose broken in two places, he finally opened his eyes to see Vern Hartung. Assigned to different battalions—Serling the first, Hartung the third—the two friends had not seen each other since arriving at Toccoa, several months before. Hartung had sneaked out of work detail to attend the fights, unaware even that Serling had been accepted as a paratrooper. "I took the sponge away from the handler and dabbed him in the face," Hartung remembers. "He looked at me and said, 'You goddamned bastard. Where've you been?' He had a real need for recognition. He didn't care whether he got his brains knocked out or not."

In January 1944, the regiment received a final two-week furlough, and Serling took his final tour of Binghamton as a boy. He would never again see his hometown through the eyes of an innocent. Three months later he boarded a troop train going north. No one knew yet whether they were going to Europe or the Pacific. Only when they woke the next morning in Oklahoma did they surmise that they were Pacific bound.

The SS *Sea Pike*, which the 1,800 men of the 511th boarded on the Sacramento River about forty miles north of San Francisco Bay, was an old Henry Kaiser–built cargo ship converted to a troop carrier. Remarkably, they made the sixteen-day trip to Oro Bay, New Guinea, unescorted, without a single navy cruiser for protection. There were concerns, naturally, that an entire airborne regiment could be wiped out by a single torpedo attack from Japanese submarines, but these worries were quelled by assurances that the speed of the *Sea Pike*, capable of up to twenty-one knots, rendered it invulnerable to submarine attack.

The speed of the ship notwithstanding, there really was substantial reason for worry: every man on board understood that the Japanese knew their position. The second day out on the high seas, a radio picked up one of Tokyo Rose's infamous broadcasts. "Welcome 511th parachute infantry on the *Sea Pike* to the Pacific theater," she said. "We know that you're on your way to Oro Bay, New Guinea, and you'll be there in about sixteen days. You will be attacked by submarines." Although no submarines attacked, they sighted several subs trailing the ship from afar.

Many of the men felt seasick the entire journey, and for those who didn't, the pervasive smell of oil and metal could be as nauseating as seasickness. Few if any of the soldiers had ever been to the South Pacific before, and they were unprepared for the beauty of the night sky in the southern hemisphere. The moon appears brighter there than anywhere else in the world, and the stars seem almost to descend on anyone looking up at them. On the evening the ship crossed the equator the regiment held a celebration. Serling acted as emcee until the army chaplain, who didn't appreciate his off-color jokes, cut off his microphone. By the time the regiment reached New Guinea in late April, Serling was one of the more popular men. Even to those few who did not like him, his exuberance made him well known.

Six months earlier, there had been intense fighting in the jungles near Milne Bay, where the *Sea Pike* and other troop ships disembarked. The American Thirty-second, aided by the Australians, had driven the Japanese much farther north. Now that part of the island was serene except for the ferocious, disease-carrying bugs, which would not be deterred by clothing, and Serling, like others, contracted malaria. Although he responded well to treatment, he would need to be hospitalized again fifteen months later for recurrent symptoms.

The men spent the following months basically in waiting, except for occasional jungle maneuvers. Serling got lost on one and had to spend the night alone in the jungle. When he emerged the following day, he wore a sheepish grin and explained his actions only with a shrug of the shoulders. He soon transferred from demolitions to S-2, an intelligence company (S stands for staff, while 2 means intelligence of the enemy). His platoon's eventual assignment in battle was to bring back as much information on the enemy as possible from the papers many Japanese soldiers carried on them, as well as from field interrogations of prisoners made with the assistance of two Hawaiian-born Japanese who stayed with the platoon.

The different companies had made their way inland from Oro Bay and made permanent camp at Dobodura, a large airplane strip. Using grass and logs from chopped-down trees in the nearby mountains, the men erected huts and settled in for a hot, humid, and boring six-month wait before seeing action. At the time, no one had guessed for sure that they would be going to the Philippines, which had not yet been invaded by the American Sixth army.

Intending to break the monotony and tension, Serling seemed perpetually to be joking. Richard Loughrin, assigned to F Company, remembers standing in formation as a C-47 transport plane carrying some important military man prepared to land. Over the roar of the plane and the indifferent silence of the men who had had to form dozens of times for just such arrivals, he heard Serling pretending to talk the plane down in made-up German: *"Vos is das in kress und schver der hungter fasse mit bitte kritte ditte. . . ."* Then Serling switched into a pseudo-Japanese dialect: *"Yaga tsuku dicki taka badada. . . ."* It wasn't exactly Jack Benny, but given the circumstances, Serling impressed Loughrin as "one of the funniest guys I ever heard. I thought, 'I'd like to know this guy. He's got a real sense of humor.'"

Loughrin struck up an easy conversation with Serling, and their resulting friendship sparked him to transfer to Serling's S-2 company. He, Serling, and several other men— "people who could talk on more than one subject"— formed a small group that met occasionally to discuss philosophy, literature, and metaphysics. Loughrin named them the Dobodura Chapter of the New Guinea Literary Metaphysical Philosophical Discussion Society of the Old Men of the 511.

A fireside discussion one evening turned to their future after the war. "Dick," Serling said, "do you realize the millions of words that are used everyday in radio? Somebody has to write those words. And that's what I'm going to do. I'm going to be a radio writer."

This is apparently the earliest proclamation of Serling's intentions to write, and it may have been just the idle words of a soldier waiting for the war to begin, knowing he might never again see his home. The statement certainly does not reflect any passion—only the pragmatic

awareness of a young man who knew, from his high
school newspaper days, that he had at least a modicum of
ability to string words into sentences and sentences into
paragraphs, and that if he did indeed make it through the
war intact he would eventually need a trade.

Any passion he then felt for writing was expressed in
poetry. He worked several days on the poem "Paratroops,"
which reflected his pride in the paratroopers:

> Take courage and deviltry,
>   cockiness, guts
>   —mix 'em in with a gang of right guys,
> Give 'em wings and boots
>   call 'em Paratroops
>   let 'em jump with a chute from the skies. . . .
> We're good and we know it,
>   We have and we'll show it,
>   there's paraguys fighting this war.

Seeing the positive reaction from his comrades, he
mailed the poem off to his brother, who had graduated
from Antioch and who had been a reporter for United
Press before enlisting when the war broke out. Two weeks
later Serling received the disappointing reply. Bob, understandably, hadn't thought much of his literary effort and
explained, "You weren't meant to be a poet, Rod." He was
unaware both that Rod looked up to him and that his
words would be taken so seriously. Kenneth Haan, assigned to the same platoon, recalls that Serling was stung
by his brother's criticism.

Some time later, Serling decided to box again, only this
time he challenged a heavyweight from another regiment—"Kelly, a great big rough, tough guy from service
company," Haan remembers—a man who had won fight
after fight in his own division. Both men put on the gloves
under the guise of it being instructional—Serling said he
wanted to learn from the master—but the event really
became an exercise in sadomasochism: Serling, at maybe

five feet five and now 115 pounds, tried to brawl with a six-foot-two, two-hundred-pounder. "OK, Rod, hit me now," the soldier said, flicking off Serling's punches as though they were merely pesky insects. Then he'd take a full swing and knock Serling on his butt. "Kelly seemed to get a kick out of popping him good," Haan says.

The fight, such as it was, was reminiscent of scenes in at least fifty films. Shaking his head to clear out the cobwebs, Serling would grin and get back on his feet—the feisty little guy intent on proving his manhood. Each time he was hit flush, Serling would wince, fall down, roll over, smile, get up, and raise his gloves. Unlike in the cinema, the bully received no poetic comeuppance; Serling did not teach him a lesson in the end. And whatever it seemed he was trying to prove, only his foolhardiness showed.

The regiment watched the fighting in the Pacific shift farther north and west. By summer it became clear that their first combat engagement would be in the Philippines. What they could not see was the intricate decision-making process that would bring the war to the seven-thousand-island archipelago.

In the early 1930s America had been beset with domestic difficulties brought on by the Great Depression, and the awful memory of World War I—"the war to end all wars"—still burned strongly in the minds of most citizens. So when Japan began making its first aggressive moves in Asia, the average American wanted to grant unconditional independence to the Philippines, which had become an American protectorate in 1898 under the Treaty of Paris that ended the Spanish-American War. There were no obvious benefits in the natural resources or trade of the Philippines, and being committed to protecting the islands against the aggressive Japanese was an obligation few wanted. President Herbert Hoover vetoed a Congressional act that would have granted complete independence to the islands after ten transitional years of self-rule under American watch because, he said, it would have saddled the United States with responsibilities but no power. A similar bill, subsequently passed in 1935, was signed by Franklin Roosevelt, then accepted by the Filipinos.

The fear of Japan was still prominent in 1935 when Roosevelt sent General Douglas MacArthur to the Philippines as a military adviser to establish defensive forces. The following year MacArthur was elected field marshal of the Philippines Commonwealth army. But Japan's attack on the Philippines at the same time as Pearl Harbor threw the country into war. Japanese troops swarmed over the islands in huge numbers and launched a pincer offensive on Manila, attacking from both the north and south. MacArthur's 80,000 men (65,000 of them Filipinos) were hopelessly overwhelmed and withdrew to the Bataan peninsula and Corregidor Island. From there they guarded the strategically important Manila Bay; but when no reinforcements arrived, the Japanese took Manila in early January 1942, following brutally protracted action. Roosevelt ordered MacArthur to Australia in order to take command of the Allied forces in the southwest Pacific. Reluctantly, the general left Corregidor but not before making his famous proclamation, "I shall return," a solemn oath to the Filipino people he loved that the United States would not desert their country.

It took MacArthur two and a half years to return, and he nearly missed the opportunity at that. The view from Washington, shared by Admiral Chester Nimitz, commander of the Pacific's naval forces, was that the Philippines were not strategically important and ought to be left alone. They wanted to employ the manpower and materials to invade Formosa and then the mainland of China. MacArthur was outraged, and in a historic meeting between him, Roosevelt, and Nimitz at Pearl Harbor, he threatened to resign.

"Come on, settle down, Doug," Roosevelt said.

"I will not," MacArthur insisted. "I made a pledge to the people of the Philippines, and I intend to keep that pledge."

In the end, ostensibly to prevent MacArthur from resigning at a crucial point in the war (and perhaps with reelection in mind), Roosevelt resolved the conflict in Mac-
Arthur's favor.

The Japanese heard through their intelligence sources
that the Allied forces would be concentrating on the
Philippines. This came as somewhat of a surprise because
Japan believed that the air strikes the Allies had been
leading against the Japanese troops on Mindanao, one of
the chain's largest islands, would be the extent of the
Allied interests in the Philippines. They may have believed that Roosevelt, who had been assistant secretary of
the navy under Woodrow Wilson, would side with Nimitz,
who they knew preferred Formosa as a target for an all-out
offensive. Surprised or not, they re-directed the majority
of their remaining naval forces to engage the Allies in the
Philippines, convinced that the battles there would be the
turning point of the war for control of the Pacific.

On October 20, 1944, several divisions of Allied liberation forces landed on Leyte, an island in the middle of the
chain. In a naval engagement then called the fiercest in
the history of the oceans, the Allies, under naval Commander (later admiral) William "Bull" Halsey, drove the
Japanese forces across Leyte and into the mountains.
With the immense beachhead thoroughly secured, the
Eleventh Airborne Division, including Rod Serling's 511th
regiment, completed their week-long journey from New
Guinea and landed on the east side of Leyte, at Bito Beach,
where they set up camp. They spent eight relatively tran-
quil nights there, hearing only an occasional distant
mortar round from the mountains where they would soon
face their first combat.

This was a fearful time for many of the young men.
Word had spread that the Japanese troops had been di-
verted from all over the Pacific to concentrate on Leyte.
While the soldiers were, probably to a man, anxious to
finally get involved in combat, the anticipation of impending combat, combined with what had seemed to be

endless days and months of waiting, created its own brand of dread and anguish. They developed a let's-get-it-over-with-already attitude.

The regiment ate a large Thanksgiving meal, Thursday night the twenty-third, then boarded amphibian craft on Friday morning to traverse a river that normally would have been crossed by a now bombed-out bridge. On the other side they loaded into troop trucks for the short ride inland to Burauen, a small town in the foothills of the mountains, and camped the night. On Saturday morning they began a march into the mountains, there to engage the enemy in what would be the longest thirty days of their lives—no matter how long they lived.

Even without the gruesome fighting, the conditions were appalling. The plans called for the regiment to march across the mountains, flushing out the remaining Japanese who had fled from the Allied offensive, and come out on the other side, thirty-five miles away, at Ormoc Bay. An infantry unit, they carried with them only rifles, machine guns, and mortars—and very little food; they would be supplied on a daily basis by supply planes dropping crates down to their positions. But on December 8 Japanese paratroopers flying over from Manila jumped on division headquarters at San Pablo airstrip. The Japanese planes looked exactly like American C-47s, and as they flew overhead American soldiers lining up for chow hardly paid attention. Suddenly the Japanese paratroopers began bailing out—the first time the enemy had actually jumped on the Americans. By the time the attack was repelled, three days later, the Japanese had knocked out many of the single-motor L-4 and L-5 planes intended to resupply the 511th troops trailing over the mountains, leaving only about a dozen intact. In poor weather these Cubs could not fly well at all.

Between the rain and the fog, on most days the 511th went without food. During one ten-day stretch several platoons had to catch rainwater in their ponchos and eat whatever apparently edible roots they could find. Several almost died, and many others were left vulnerable to such jungle diseases as malaria and dysentery. When the L-5s did drop supplies, it often became a battle between the Americans and the Japanese to see who would get to them first. Americans would locate a drop sight and find only broken crates, the contents missing. "If I ever get back to Binghamton," a voraciously hungry Serling said to his platoon, "I'll never pass a Dinty Moore's again."

Ironically, at least four men brought into the field hospital had been killed by these falling boxes. One of them was Melvin Levy, probably Serling's closest friend in the platoon. Levy, a corporal, had hated the mud almost worse than the fighting, and he cursed it constantly. At first the cursing had been good-natured—he was known among the platoon members as a comedian—but it soon became real. The mud was a symbol of his hunger: there was mud because there was rain, and the rain fell from a foggy, gray sky that kept the planes from dropping his food. Each time he lifted his boots from the brown goo that sucked him down, he damned the wet earth.

The radio operator finally announced on December 10 that they would be receiving a drop, and when they heard the drone of the engines overhead, there was a loud celebration. "Scorecards, getcha scorecards," Levy joked. "You can't tell a Piper Cub from an L-5 without ya scorecards."

Then he instinctively fell in behind a tree with two other men lined up for cover. Four planes came buzzing in at about six hundred feet, while the men cheered as the tiny red and green chutes attached to the cargo crates opened. More of them came now, falling in clusters—bigger crates, without chutes, carrying fifty-pound boxes of K rations, maybe a hundred of them. A few of the boxes fell dangerously close, and when Kenneth Haan turned to the man behind him to say, "That was close," he found Levy dead on the ground, his head bashed in by a crate of food that was supposed to fortify him.

Serling had lost a dear buddy to an accident that seemed all the more tragic for its absurdity: in the middle of a goddamned foot-rotting jungle, surrounded by men who would just as soon cut out his heart as eat dinner, a box of food caves in his skull. He didn't know whether to laugh through his tears or cry through his laughter. Here was final confirmation that death is waiting around every corner and that God or good or righteousness or fairness has no say in who lives or dies—not in war, at least, and perhaps not in peace either. His strong sense of irony, so essential to his best writing, may have been born at that moment.

He helped bury the body near where Levy fell and formed a Star of David on the site with twigs. Later, when they had the opportunity, Serling and several other men returned to dig up the body for shipment home, a procedure reenacted many times for many other bodies.

The nature of the fighting into which the 511th had been thrust was particularly ferocious—true jungle warfare for which their training in the pine forests of Georgia and North Carolina could not have prepared them. Even their maneuvers in New Guinea had provided woefully inadequate preparation. The jungles of Leyte would not permit a patrol to scatter out over a hundred-yard radius, as they had practiced; they were forced to bunch closely together, making them easy targets for a successful ambush. More important, what were supposed to have been scattered and disorganized pockets of resistance turned out to be virtually a full division of Japanese soldiers. And with their supplies chronically low, the Americans had to wait for an opportune moment to shoot or lob grenades.

For the most part, it was nighttime combat—and almost every night. The platoons would advance during the day, usually encountering only sporadic fire, then bivouac for the night in foxholes. At some point after dark they would hear the Japanese commanders hollering their orders. The voices would come first from the left, followed by a response from the right, then the bushes would move. "You knew then they were coming," Haan remembers. Hand grenades, thrown when they estimated the Japanese had drawn close enough, were the Americans' best weapons. Many of the Japanese attacks were made by banzai soldiers, who would scream as they advanced with bayonets. When the Americans heard the advancing screams they'd climb to the top of the foxholes and fire point-blank.

The fighting and screaming and explosions would last all night, and in the dark the soldiers could hear the moaning of an enemy soldier who had been hit but not killed—or was it a buddy who lay dying? With several platoons firing from all around, it was impossible to tell how many had been killed until daylight. "Who knew who was going to make it one more day, one more hour?" Richard Loughrin reflects. When they were pinned down for more than a day, a shifting wind might carry the smell of decaying bodies into the foxholes.

Many of the men who fought at Leyte and survived, like those involved in the jungle horrors of Vietnam, have spent much of their lives trying to forget what they experienced there. The soldiers, young men, could feel their humanity, their identities, stripped away by the mud, the slime, the constant fear of and hatred for another race of men who had also been reduced to obeying only the laws of the jungle; they grew up too fast. Not only had the numbers of the enemy been much greater than they had expected but also the type of violence they encountered was much more uncivilized than any of their preconceptions of war. This was hatred and anger personified. If it moved, you shot it or it would shoot you. Even when they had the rare luxury of sleep, most of it during the day, they could not escape the fear and dread, which infected their dreams.

The mornings brought the men a sense of exhilaration. Finding themselves alive and more of the enemy dead, and having stories to swap, instilled in them a peculiar joy. Everyone, without exception, had made kills. "I got five." "I got seven that I know of." "I think I killed ten." Whatever was in front of them. These were their bragging rights. On one particularly gray and rainy morning, forty-three enemy bodies were counted on the perimeter, the highest one-night total of the battle. (In all, at least four thousand Japanese died during the one-month period.)

Even the severely wounded Japanese had to be taken seriously. "If they could get you first, they would," says Jerry Shea, a member of Serling's platoon. "They were fanatics. You had to be careful counting bodies." At least one of them had exploded a grenade with an American standing over him, killing them both. The bodies were searched for any intelligence they might be carrying, and in the thirty days of the march to Ormoc, only one prisoner was taken by Serling's S-2 platoon. He had been wounded in an artillery barrage but refused to give any information.

As the troops—their number diminished by about 15 percent—marched out of the mountains, where transportation took them to division headquarters, they were exhausted, starving, and emotionally numb from the stunning intensity of the previous thirty days. Fittingly enough, this was Christmas day—Rod Serling's birthday. Serling wrote eloquently about his "Most Memorable Christmas" for a *Good Housekeeping* article by Gerald Walker in December 1963. That morning, he recounted:

A long line of men rested along the sides of a jungle trail— gray jump suits blending with gray-covered beard; tired inward-looking eyes reflecting nothing. A nineteen-year-old second looie got to his feet and spoke. "All right—on your feet. Let's move out."

We rose—the packs, the ammo belts, the weapons, all fused to us like extensions of our bodies—and plodded through the ankle-deep mud—a long line of dirty, bearded samenesses.

And then somebody far up the line stopped dead. A whispered message started down the ranks. Each man froze and held his breath because any whisper from up front might mean a machine gun or a pocket of Japanese or mines or any one of a dozen other reminders that there was a war here. But this particular message was an incredible jar to memory—a reminder of a different sort. The man in front of me whispered, "It's Christmas."

I continued to lift my feet one after the other, and suddenly I wasn't aware of the cold rain or the mud. I gave no thought to the sickening ache deep inside the gut that had been with me for so many days. Someone had just transformed the world. Those two words reminded me that people still lived and that we did, too.

Then a scratchy, discordant, monotone voice way up front started to sing, *O Come, All Ye Faithful*. Somebody else picked it up and then we all sang. We sang as we walked through the mud. We sang as we led the wounded by the hand and carried the litters and looked back on the row of handmade crosses left behind. We sang, *O Come, All Ye Faithful*. It had come—the Holy Day. The day of all days. It *was* Christmas.

Besides professing a reverence he did not feel for Christmas as a religious holiday, Serling's memoir illustrates his characteristic tendency not to detail the horrors of combat he and his comrades had faced for the previous month. Except for a single phrase, "fierce daily fighting," early in the piece (not quoted here), he chose not to convey the experience he had endured, only the aftereffects on the regiment's spirit and psyche. Equally dispassionate were two phrases in his first draft of the story, both edited out of the published version by *Good Housekeeping*: "[War] is separated into moments of survival and the passage of time is unheeded except to chronicle the fact that some have lived and some have died. . . . We had come up as fresh initiates in the art of war, and were now dirty postgraduate men taught wisdom by the impatient teacher that is conflict."

Neither did his letters home mention any fighting, fear, grief, despair, hunger, pain, desolation, depression—sensations he and all of his company had known intimately. He did not note that he had lost nearly eighteen pounds from a frame that had weighed only 118.

In fact, for the rest of his life he spoke only on rare occasions about any of his war experiences. He felt, as he wrote in the first paragraph of the reminiscence, that he would never be "fully understood by those who have not lived with the tension, the violence, the anguish of war."

(During a party almost twenty years later, one six-year-old boy asked Serling about his experiences in World War II. Gravely, Serling said that his company in the Philippines made one memorable combat jump; all jumped successfully, except for one coward. "He froze as he hit the door. The sergeant finally had to kick him out of the airplane. Even that didn't do any good. He twisted as he went around and grabbed the sill, holding on for his life. The only way the sergeant could get him to let go was to take his boot and stamp the guy's fingers until he couldn't hold on anymore." The boy's eyes opened wide. "Jesus," said Serling with a wide grin, "my fingers were sore for a month." Another time, Serling told his brother in a suitably grave voice: "You know, Bob, many times there was nothing between me and that cold jungle floor but a thin native girl.")

Even with his buddies from the 511th, a few of whom he continued to see throughout the years—men who certainly had shared with him the "tension, the violence, the anguish of war"—he communicated only briefly, if at all, about the experience that had changed them all so drastically. While that sort of quiet endurance of pain may have been a form of machismo before Leyte, Serling's reticence following the battles on Leyte and the upcoming one on Luzon and for the rest of his life owed less to bravado than to trauma.

Driven by trucks back to Burauen after hiking out of the Leyte mountains, the 511th was given a Christmas dinner—canned boneless turkey, whose richness, compared to their spartan diet of the previous thirty days, made most of them sick. Nonetheless, the meal almost instantaneously revived their spirits enough to vocalize to their commanders what many of them had been complaining about privately: they were paratroopers, not ordinary foot soldiers, and all those months of jump training were being wasted. Slogging through the jungles of the

Philippines in hip-deep mud was hardly the glamour they'd envisioned when they signed up for the paratroopers. If they'd wanted that, they would have joined the regular army.

Charles Feuereisen, an S-2 man from another company, had heard his fellow soldiers complain and felt the same. So when he and a comrade were assigned to handcarry the intelligence materials the S-2s had gathered to division headquarters at Tacloban, he decided to convey their feelings to General MacArthur. Surprisingly, perhaps, MacArthur's aide de camp agreed to grant him an audience—provided he report first to the quartermaster for a shower and fresh uniform.

Feuereisen was led into a large room filled with American and Australian generals and colonels. Rather than return his salute, MacArthur, dressed in an immaculately tailored tropical worsted uniform, came over graciously and shook the private's hand. "I heard you've engaged the nip," MacArthur said.

"That's right," Feuereisen replied.

"Well, what did you think of him."

"I didn't think much of him, sir."

"The nip is a damn fine soldier," MacArthur said. "But we're better."

Then Feuereisen presented the 511th's complaint. "Can you tell us, sir," he asked, "when we're really going to get a jump in, so we can show our training?"

In response, MacArthur took him to a wall map of the islands and pointed to some strategic airfields on nearby Mindoro Island. "We're all very proud of you men, and I want you to tell the regiment when you get back that as soon as we take these airfields we'll be able to get a jump. You'll be attacking Luzon."

The general had been forthcoming, treating him as a man of distinction. Feuereisen couldn't resist asking MacArthur why the Eleventh had not been getting the sort of publicity and notoriety that other airborne units, namely the 101st and 82nd, had been getting in Europe and North

Africa. *Stars and Stripes*, the military newspaper, and the general circulation newspapers in the States had not been carrying stories of the Eleventh's exploits. "I'd get letters from people back home who said, 'You guys aren't in any kind of war,'" Feuereisen recalls. "No one had ever heard there were any paratroopers in the Pacific. The Eleventh Airborne was like an unknown outfit."

MacArthur argued that the element of surprise was more important than the publicity, that winning the war with as few casualties as possible was his main objective. He cited Tokyo Rose's welcome to the men on the SS *Sea Pike* as a situation that could have been avoided with tight lips. As Feuereisen notes, MacArthur had fewer casualties per one hundred men than any other general in the army.

Had the 511th made its first jump before the battle of Leyte, it's likely they would have been more excited about finally being able to jump. Now, having already faced horrible combat, they were also frightened and apprehensive. The regiment began training almost immediately for Luzon by making sand tables of the drop zone and readjusting their strategies according to the terrain. The soldiers knew that they were about to engage in the decisive battle of the South Pacific; there would be a winner and a loser, and the line between them would be devastatingly clear.

The first paratroopers from the Eleventh jumped on Luzon January 31, 1945, about sixty miles south of Manila, and began marching north, while simultaneously two cavalry divisions landed at Lingayen Gulf, north of Manila, and began driving south. Serling's 511th jumped at Tagay-tay Ridge, about thirty miles south of Manila, three days later. The drops were made from only five hundred feet. The chutes no sooner opened automatically on the static line than they were on the ground—giving the paratroopers three seconds of sublime fear; but MacArthur's intelligence reports had been correct and there was no ground fire directed at the paratroops. In contrast to the jungles of Leyte, Luzon was a full civilization, with paved roads and accessible towns. The objective was to march toward Manila—where the Japanese had already butchered at least 100,000 Filipinos, making it the second worst city, behind Warsaw, in all of World War II for civilian mortality—and ostensibly drive the enemy north, into the clutches of the other companies that had cut off their retreat to the north. In many ways, the pincerlike strategy was very similar to the one that had captured Manila for the Japanese three years before.

Serling's company was assigned to recapture the Church of Our Blessed Lady, a nearly two-hundred-year-old chapel on a knoll on the outskirts of Manila, which the Japanese had been using as a stronghold from which they could cover the Manila highway. In a brutal predawn raid that followed a stealthy climb up the side of the mountain to the chapel, dozens of men were killed, but once again Serling escaped serious injury or death, although a Japanese soldier had pointed his rifle at Serling with the clear intent to kill. Close enough to see the barrel from which would soon come the bullet to end his life, Serling experienced the stupefied and anguished sensations of a condemned man—until an American soldier behind him shot and killed the enemy.

The nature of the combat was different from that on Leyte. Instead of hand-to-hand fighting, where in the moonlight a soldier might see the face of the man he just killed, mortars and large millimeter guns were doing most of the damage. Having lost Leyte, which they knew they had to win in order to defend Manila, the Japanese were now facing certain defeat unless they could repel the attack with a brutal counterattack.

To make their last stand, the Japanese set up what became known as the Genko Line (named for the Japanese field general in charge of engineering their incredibly elaborate defense system, including linking many of Manila's huge mansions—which themselves acted as fortresses—together by a series of underground tunnels) south of Manila, near Nichols field. The Genko Line was an astonishing display of firepower—guns of all types beside each other in ground emplacements, some of them three- and eight-inch naval guns that had been taken off ships sunk in the harbor. At first sight of the formidable and imposing contrivance, one of the American field commanders sent a radio message to division headquarters advising Bull Halsey where the Japanese fleet had assembled: just south of Manila—on land.

After marching in cold numbing rain thirty or so miles northward from Tagay-tay Ridge, most of the division, including the 511th, had to crawl on their bellies across Nichols Field as the big guns, aimed horizontal to the ground, blew death over their heads. Their job was to swarm over the Japanese troops operating the guns and get to Manila.

"I was bitter about everything and at loose ends when I got out of the service," Serling later said.

No wonder. For someone as obviously sensitive as Rod Serling, the bitterness was all around. Word had come back from the first cavalry and paratroop units in Manila that the devastation in terms of human life surpassed anything they imagined. The retreating Japanese, angry at apparently losing the war, vented their frustrations on the Filipino people, committing incredible acts of violence without provocation. Inside the walled city, for instance, the Japanese herded several hundred Filipinos into a room measuring ten feet by ten feet by twenty feet, then sealed the door shut. Days later, when the suffocated and crushed human bodies began to decay, the gases from the corpses caused an explosion, blowing the door off its hinges. Other reports mentioned that nuns and priests had been crucified on the crucifixes in their churches and that Filipino women had had Japanese bayonets plunged into their vaginas and ripped upward to their necks.

Even in the war's silver spots were dark linings. The Japanese had held 2,147 slowly starving civilians—most of them Filipino but also many American nurses, nuns, priests, and missionaries—at Los Baños prisoner-of-war-camp for three and a half years. In what was probably the most daring rescue mission of the war, at least in the South Pacific, special-forces guerrillas lay in quiet on the perimeter of the camp for a few days, while antitank vehicles also moved into position and waited for the signal to attack. The signal came at seven o'clock on the morning of February 23, when 511th B Company commander John Ringler's parachute opened. The special-forces guerrillas, the tanks, and the rest of B company assaulted the 247 Japanese holding the camp as most of them took their morning exercises. Thrilling, glamorous, and successful, it was an incredible operation that justified, as if any justification had been necessary, why these men had joined the paratroopers. Yet the mission's success was eclipsed when the Japanese, angered by the camp's liberation, tortured and burned to death anyone in the nearby town of Los Baños whom they suspected of complicity with the Americans—and they suspected nearly everyone.

Was this victory? Serling might have asked. Were these truly moments of glory to be savored? It would seem that similar thoughts during the war must have sharpened his sense of irony, for in his later works such Pyrrhic victories figured importantly. Many of his main characters would receive exactly what they believed they wanted, only to find that attainment has changed them; they did not know how to value what they had until it was lost to them. Almost always, the fruit of victory that his characters tasted was self-knowledge.

The brutality of the war and his role in it altered the preconceptions of victory, bravery, and heroism that Serling had brought to the paratroopers. Dozens of his teleplays and film scripts would be written around the same theme of cowardice. In "The Sergeant," his first produced show (another writer actually adapted his story), an American sergeant in the Korean War sends his demolition squad to blow up a bridge, a mission that would have been

successful if the sergeant himself had not suddenly
screamed out and alerted "the Reds" to their well-hidden
position. The four survivors out of forty, busted and
bandaged in a field hospital, fantasize what their sadistic
revenge would be if only the sergeant were there—if only
he had survived. With bandages everywhere but over his
eyes, the sergeant is just then wheeled into their room as
the doctor and nurse discuss the head surgery he's destined for the next day. When one of the men painfully
drags himself across the floor to choke the sergeant—the
sergeant's eyes staring up less in terror than in resignation
and relief—the doctor comes in and, in melodramatic
fashion, proves to the men how the sergeant had been
"hurt in the mind" by his previous tours of duty; he had
finally cracked from the fatigue and cold and fear and the
numbness from seeing his men blown up. As in "Company
of Cowards," a screenplay Serling wrote a few years later,
the message is twofold: one, that those who haven't experienced "the province of combat" should not judge the
actions of those who have; and two, cowards are sometimes not as cowardly as they appear.

Serling's record at this point in the war is nebulous and
somewhat contradictory. But reflecting on the most repetitive of his personality themes, it's difficult not to specu-
late that he began to suffer a crisis of self-confidence. On
patrol one afternoon, a mortar cap sent small fragments
into Serling's wrist and knee. The injuries may have been
painful, but they were not at all deep; he received first-aid
from a field medic at the site and required no hospitaliza-
tion. Curiously, the army has no record of Serling being
wounded, although he was awarded a Purple Heart for this
injury, nor do any of his comrades in arms remember any
type of injury. Only the Veteran's Administration corrobo-
rates the injury, yet its records show that he had been
injured in Leyte—a virtual impossibility. Serling himself
wrote to an old army buddy in 1961 that the injury
occurred the day after Colonel Haugen was shot by a
sniper (he died weeks later from the wound), in early

February, on Luzon. Further, while the V.A. notes that the two wounds were merely superficial—leaving no lasting damage to "deeper structures, only one scar the size of a dime on the dorsum of his wrist and another one-and-a-half inch by one-eighth inch scar just below and to the right of the knee cap"—for whatever reason, it was determined that only the wrist injury, and not the knee, was service connected.

In dozens of newspaper and magazine interviews Serling gave, particularly early in his career, he mentioned a "severe shrapnel wound" in the knee, a claim he also made to his brother, who had no reason to doubt him; when Rod played paddleball or tennis too long and too hard, blood would leak through the trusslike bandage he always wore to protect his knee. Bob Serling believed that the blood came from the wound, as did others who played with Rod. His wife, in at least one magazine interview, stated that of the two wounds, the knee was the "serious" injury and caused him a lifetime of trouble.

What is known for sure, according to army records, is that he was missing from his combat platoon for at least two months, when he joined an army service unit. These noncombat assignments range from the quartermasters' duties to filing clerk. Serling was given a desk job at division headquarters for April and May 1945. In the battles for control of Luzon, American casualties mounted at an alarming rate, and company commanders removed soldiers from their combat positions only for good cause. When at the same time, for example, George Doherty, from the 511th's G company, asked to join the combat photographer's team and stay with his platoon, his commanding officer refused his request because of a combat troop shortage. So for a soldier to be reassigned a noncombat service unit job would have likely required a proper reason.

Severe, debilitating depression would have been a good one. Serling told both interviewer William F. Nolan and actor Earl Holliman in 1959 that he began writing "as a therapeutic necessity" after the war. About eight years after that, Serling told an audience of single parents from a group called Parents Without Partners that writing his feelings at this time of crisis made him realize that he wanted to be a dramatic writer. He indicated to the group that he was assigned to write as a specific form of therapy and explained that he worked out on paper what he could not otherwise make sense of internally. In the absence of either an army psychiatrist or psychologist, a chaplain in the field hospital would have assigned him that duty. The chaplain probably would have noted that Serling had been the editor of his high school paper and might have seen some of the articles Serling had written for the small newsletter published irregularly by the 511th. He might then have suggested Serling write out his feelings on paper without regard to form or content, just as catharsis. As a writer, Serling's best and most believable stories centered around characters resolving their consciences, their compulsions and impulsions.

It's possible that the macho Serling was embarrassed by his wound, which could have seemed to him about as critical as a hangnail. Compared to the other men he had seen with limbs blown off or worse—and considering the countless hundreds stacked like wood on morgue trucks or evacuated to hospitals in Australia and New Guinea— he would have felt astonishingly lucky. At the same time, the slightness of his injury would have highlighted his true vulnerability: men who are wounded for the first time, however slightly, are often surprised and terrified by the awareness that yes, this can actually happen to *me*.

Like all paratroopers, Serling had believed himself to be superior to the average man—braver, more powerful, better able to cope. Finding that that wasn't necessarily so may have been very difficult for a young man who had always harbored such an enormous need to prove himself. In World War II, particularly for the elite paratroopers— and certainly for Rod Serling—shell shock was not considered a legitimate excuse for missing action. This chink in his armor of bravado likely remained with him the rest of his life, and it could explain why he rarely discussed the war—or why in the retelling he casually invented his wound to be more serious than it had been.

When he rejoined his company, Serling never mentioned the disability that had kept him from combat for more than two months. In the commotion of the war, his absence may have gone unnoticed by the other soldiers, who themselves had been coming and going. The wound he suffered had not been one to share. (Twenty years later, when he was undergoing analysis three times a week, he would still find psychotherapy—i.e., what he considered personal weakness—an embarrassing subject.)

Serling ran into his old friend, Vern Hartung, who'd been selected to make a jump at Aparri, in northern Luzon. The objective of the jump was to land behind the retreating Japanese forces, rumored to number in the tens of thousands, and keep them from evacuating the island. It appeared to be a suicide mission, and Hartung was scared. The night before the jump, "I was all shook up," Hartung says. Serling gave him a drink, then put his arm around him. "Don't worry, Vernie," he said, "I'll be praying for you." This was a graver Rod Serling than even five months before, when he likely would have made a joke rather than promise a prayer. (The paratroopers encountered almost no resistance in Aparri and took as prisoners only two slave laborers from Taiwan.)

There was still some mopping up to be done in various places around the islands, most notably in the Malepunyo mountains, where the remnants of General Fujishigi's Eighth Tiger Division ferociously defended the Batangas province. In one memorable combat encounter, a patrol sent into the mountains to set up observation posts found a cave out of which came a Japanese soldier, clad only in a loincloth and waving a white flag. Just as the Americans prepared to accept his surrender, three more soldiers came running from behind him, throwing hand grenades that killed several Americans.

But Serling had missed most of those battles, and by the time he got back to his combat outfit, there was less concerted resistance. Late in the spring, however, his platoon was still exchanging very heavy groundfire at the same time that an American C-47 flying overhead dropped some supplies. Included in the drop were copies of the *Stars and Stripes*, quoting Douglas MacArthur as announcing the end of all Japanese resistance. "I hated the son of a bitch that day, and I'll hate him till the day I die," Serling told his brother.

They may have been able to laugh at the "son of a bitch's" blowhard claims, but if that was MacArthur's best face, how bad was it really going to be when they invaded Japan? The optimistic estimates were that in facing upwards of forty full Japanese divisions a million men might die. On June 21, the Americans had retaken Okinawa, making it just a matter of time before they subdued the remaining Japanese forces there and moved on to Okinawa, and from there to Honshu and Kyushu. No one knew what kind of elaborate surprise—à la the Genko Line, or worse—the Japanese would have in store for them when they arrived. Both the Japanese and the Allies knew the invasion was inevitable. Months before, American B-24 bombers had rained incendiaries over Tokyo, starting fires that killed more than one hundred thousand people.

Witnessing the Japanese penchant for brutality and revenge these past months made the Americans more than terrified of the inexorable future, which grew closer with a full-scale American air war on Honshu and Kyushu in early July and on Tokyo a week later. If the Japanese had fought this hard on these small Pacific islands, how would they be in their own homeland? They would soon find out; the 511th was given a drop zone in Kyushu. Most faced the inevitable with quiet, frightened resignation.

The Japanese government had rejected the Potsdam Declaration calling upon the country to surrender, even after U.S. planes dropped leaflets over Hiroshima on August 4 that warned, "Your city will be obliterated unless your government surrenders." And on August 6, when the *Enola Gay* dropped its ten-foot-long, nine-thousand-pound "Little Boy," four square miles of Hiroshima were indeed obliterated. One hundred thousand Japanese died immediately; another hundred thousand would eventually die of burns and radiation sickness. It was a measure of the military's stringent secrecy measures that no rumors of American atomic power had reached the troops who would have assaulted Japan.

"I'll tell you one thing, the day they dropped the atomic bomb on Hiroshima was the happiest day of my life," Jerry Shea recalls. His thoughts echo the elation of probably all troops destined to invade Japan.

Three days later "Big Boy" was dropped on Nagasaki, and a day later Japan finally surrendered.

On August 28 the paratroopers of the 511th boarded troop transport planes for the flight to Okinawa and then on to Yokohama. Serling's flight was delayed on the apron. With the war finally over and spirits again high, Serling reassumed his role of entertainer. In a heavy German accent, he pretended to be the German emigre actor Albert Basserman as a Hershey bar salesman: "Vit each and ev'ry Hershey bar vit nuts, ve give von free Brownie camera." Viewed in context—a plane filled with giddy young men who had survived several brutal battles and no longer had to face a certain nightmare—this was funny stuff. "He'd have everybody roaring with laughter," Peter Hurst, a medic who had been on both Leyte and Luzon, remembers. "He was an enormously amusing man."

Serling's company landed at Atsugi Airport in Yokohama. The sight of the defenses the Japanese had built around Atsugi—tunnels, bunkers, gun emplacements, and hundreds of trucks lining the streets—temporarily dampened their high spirits. It seemed that the estimate of a million casualties was indeed an understated figure.

When they got to Yokohama, the town was deserted, creating an eerie landscape similar to the one Serling created in the pilot for "The Twilight Zone," in which a man (played by Earl Holliman) can't seem to locate any

other human life. Like many of the other soldiers, Serling
jumped into one of the empty trucks and began joyriding
around the streets of Yokohama. They honked their horns,
waved and shouted happily. The spontaneous demonstra-
tion was an expression of joy, but the Japanese perceived it
as a hostile act.

As the Americans soon discovered, the Japanese greatly
feared the American occupation troops, believing that
they would decapitate the men after raping the women
and beating the children. In fact, acting on MacArthur's
orders, if not their own morality, the Americans committed no confirmed acts of vengeful violence during their
occupation in Japan. As their fears slowly abated, the
Japanese became "extraordinarily friendly," Hurst recalls.
In Morioka, where Serling's regiment was stationed, the
citizens even helped the Americans build a rope tow up
the side of a hill, so they could ski in the coming snowy
months.

Just weeks before the Americans and the Japanese had
been mortal enemies. Even now they would have been
waging bloody war on this soil if the United States had
not—irony again—dropped the two bombs that killed
several hundred thousand people. (Serling's regiment
helped clean out the elaborate underground tunnels
loaded with dynamite that the Japanese had constructed.)
No doubt this remarkably elastic change in attitude and
action had a lifelong effect on Serling, as it did, both
positively and negatively, on any other soldier with a
minimum of perception and awareness. With his literary
and cinematic idealism, Serling often asserted that the
reasons nations fight wars and citizens fear each other are
bred in ignorance, not reality. Naïvely, though, he would
either miss the point or forget that had the situation been
reversed, the Japanese, based on their actions in Korea, the
Philippines, and China, would not have been as benevolent or decent in victory. And in fact in later years, when
Serling began supporting nuclear disarmament, he separated himself from the majority of his ex-comrades in
arms.

Two weeks after they arrived in Japan, Serling received word that his father had died. He was crushed by the news and angry that the Red Cross had botched the task of delivering the message in time for him to make the funeral, which had been held the week before. "Dad's passed away, and I can't get there," he cried to Vern Hartung, the only other man there who had known his father. Without the finality of the funeral to make the death concrete, or his family to share the grief, his feelings remained jumbled and largely unresolved. Even after witnessing so much death that last year, he had developed no mechanism with which to cope. Serling's sense of desperation only increased. Not until he was able to visit the cemetery did he begin to come to grips with his father's death.

"How was the funeral?" he bitterly and ironically asked his brother.

As Bob Serling later explained to him, their parents had been driving from Schenectady to Syracuse in the 1940 Oldsmobile Sam had just bought. It was Labor Day. Sam and his brother-in-law Ed had become partners in a jewelry store in Schenectady that Ed would operate. Sam pulled over to the side of the road and asked Bob, Ed's oldest son, to drive, explaining that he didn't feel well. He got out of the car to walk around to the passenger side and dropped dead on the side of the road.

Sam Serling, like his son Rod, who took up the habit during the war, smoked three to four packs of cigarettes a day. Like his son would twenty years hence, he continued to smoke that much even after he was advised by his doctors to give it up for his heart's sake. Sam was fifty-two years old when he died, and like his son he knew that the men in his family had a predisposition to die early from heart failure. The factor they didn't share was that, unlike his son, Sam had to worry constantly about his younger boy being killed or maimed in the South Pacific.

"He was proud of Rod, but Rod being a paratrooper hurt him badly. He knew Rod was in combat. He worried everyday," Bob Serling recalls. "Mother felt nothing would happen to him. Dad was more realistic. He worried more.

He better understood the implications of that kind of conflict."

Rod Serling was certainly sensitive enough and intelligent enough to surmise that his being a combat soldier might have contributed to his father's early death. Yet he also knew that his father's patriotism made Sam more proud than worried.

In October Serling briefly entered the hospital again for symptoms of malaria. After rest and treatment he took up residence with other troops in an old cavalry barracks in Morioka. Everyone huddled around small brazier stoves to keep warm when the weather turned cold in the winter. Their years of war and training behind them, the young American men had a palpable need to be boys. When they weren't sleeping, they often fought, usually good-naturedly, just to let off steam. The medics patched soldiers who had fallen down and injured themselves while drunk. And Vern Hartung recalls passing Serling coming out of a geisha house on a hill in Morioka. They had their picture taken together in front.

It was snowing the early January day Serling shipped out for home from Yokohama Harbor. The sign on the side of the ship where the troops waited before walking across the gangplank said, "Stateside Express." This was supposed to be the happiest day of his life, the day he had dreamed of while dodging sniper fire, banzai bayonets, mortar shells; the day he thought he might never live to see. Yet he was not exultant, nor even mildly excited. Too many dark thoughts crowded out any emotion but relief. Yes, he could go home, but too many others could not. He crossed the gangplank filled with equal parts grief and anguish.

"Hey, you don't look so happy for a guy who's going home," said a sailor who directed him to his quarters.

"Hell, I'm the happiest goddamn guy aboard," he said, an ironic smile on his face.

"I doubt it," the sailor said.

"I doubt it, too," Serling muttered.

3

A MOTH TO A FLAME

Serling returned from Japan in late December 1945 and was discharged by the army January 13, 1946. His service to the United States fell twenty-one days shy of three years. But like most other young men who experienced the war in the South Pacific, he had aged much more than just three years. As he later conceded in an interview, the war remained forever the emotional low point of his life: "I was convinced I wasn't going to come back," he said.

Admittedly bitter and depressed, Serling could not even return to the Binghamton of his boyhood to salve the emotional wounds. Following Sam Serling's death, Esther had wanted, indeed demanded, to move into Bob Serling's bachelor apartment in Washington, D.C., where he had taken a job as a reporter with United Press International. "I was a fat, happy, twenty-seven-year-old having the time of my life," he says, "and she announces she wants to come make a home for me." Without her husband to play wife to, and her children to mother, Esther had no identity. She was caught as poorly prepared to be a widow at age fifty as

64

she was surprised to have to be. She could not even write out a check by herself. Fortunately for Bob, her sister Betty convinced Esther to move to Schenectady with her and her husband Ed.

Everything had changed in those three years. His mother gone, Serling no longer had roots in Binghamton, except for the strongly romantic images of the place he had lived in before the war changed him—images he would retain and idealize the rest of his life. Jim Haley remembers seeing him unexpectedly one day after the war, standing on Court Street in front of the Security Mutual Building, staring straight up at the most famous (neoclassic) architecture in Binghamton. Other times Serling would knock on the door of his old house on Bennett Avenue and ask the new owners for a quick look around— "just to see what you've done with the place."

The gentle memories of his childhood contradicted the war's bitterness and his father's sudden death, making Binghamton seem all the more like a storybook land, and he expressed that mythic sense often through his later work. In "Walking Distance," one of his best "Twilight Zone" episodes, a successful man (Gig Young), the same age as Serling when the show aired, accidentally falls back in time to his childhood hometown, where he tries to recapture his youth. "And perhaps across his mind there will flit a little errant wish, that a man might not have to become old, never outgrow the parks and the merry-go-rounds of his youth," Serling said in his closing narration. The resolution of that struggle—of having to own up to the responsibilities of adulthood—was the very conflict he now faced after the war.

This untethered sensation, almost of homelessness, became a seminal influence on him. Given his enchantment with Binghamton and his state of mind at the time of his discharge, had his mother still lived there it's possible he might not have left his hometown to go to college at Antioch in the fall. The lingering depression obscured even his ambition and need for attention. Allowed to indulge those feelings in an idealized Binghamton, he, like other returning veterans in town, may have found it convenient to stay—and ended up staying too long.

Twenty years later, Serling translated this personal existential dilemma into a short-lived television series, "The Loner," in which Lloyd Bridges portrayed a former Union cavalry officer roaming aimlessly across the west in search of meaning. "In the aftermath of the blood-letting called the Civil War," entoned the narrator, "thousands of rootless, restless, searching men traveled west. Such a man was William Colton." Colton's search for truth was identical to Serling's after the war, and the blood-letting Colton had escaped might just as well have been World War II.

After staying on and off with his mother and Betty and Ed until the fall, he enrolled, under the G.I. Bill of Rights, at Antioch in Yellow Springs, Ohio, where his brother had gone to school. Despite his previously stated intention to write some of those "millions of words" that radio required, he majored that freshman year in physical education. He wanted, he said, "to work with kids."

"I never had a master plan that included a built-in compulsion to write," he later told an interviewer. "My interest had always been in the area of physical education. This was a pretty amorphous thing, not really thought out or planned—but it constituted some vague objective which, of course, the war put an end to."

His interest must have been very amorphous, considering he'd never participated in athletics before, with the exception of boxing in the army and pickup football games in the backyard. Bob Serling does recall one visit to Yellow Springs when he watched Rod play halfback in an intramural football game. Despite the bad knee, "he was so fast. He ran by me one time, where I was standing on the sidelines, and I swear I could feel the wind on my face."

That first year Serling fell in and out of love with regularity. Every time Bob visited, his younger brother had another girlfriend; after facing death in faraway jungles, he no longer feared the female as he once had. Now his natural charm poured from a ruggedly handsome—no longer merely cute—face, creating a much more potent combination to disarm the opposite sex. The war had taken his youth and made him look like a man. He had added almost thirty pounds to what had been an emaciated, hundred-pound frame in the Philippine jungles.

On one occasion Bob took Rod and his date to the Wagon Wheel restaurant in Springfield, nine miles north of Yellow Springs. "That was the night I realized how deeply his war experiences had been etched in his brain," Bob says. "He got bombed"—on Southern Comfort—"and started to fight the battle of Leyte all over again." Serling was hallucinating and screaming, "They're coming, they're coming through the doors. The Japs are coming."

Nothing that Bob or Serling's date or the restaurant manager did calmed him down. He was actually repulsed by them and evaded their advances, fearing they were Japanese firing at him. When they finally took him out of the restaurant, Bob drove him back to the dorm, removed his clothes, shoved him into a cold shower, and put him in bed. When Serling awakened the next day, he remembered nothing of the incident. Bob is convinced that his brother suffered the rest of his life from nightmares, and resultant insomnia, brought on by the war.

Antioch had been founded almost a hundred years before by Horace Mann, the renowned educator, who wanted to develop the students' complete personality, not just their intellect. To implement this goal, the work-study program was adopted. A student would alternately, for three- or six-month periods, attend classes and then work in a field related to the area of study. In the summer of 1947, at the end of his freshman year, Serling took a a counselor job at Camp Treetop, at Lake Placid, as a requirement of Antioch's field studies program. (The previous semester he worked at Herrick House, a halfway house in Bartlett, Illinois, for young cardiac patients.)

This experience as a camp counselor may have disabused him forever of the notion of "working with kids"—as it has many others—and sent him head-first into broadcasting, which still required that daily million or so words. When classes started again in the fall, he had changed his major from physical education to literature and language.

"I really didn't know what I wanted to do with my life," Serling told interviewer William F. Nolan. "But I felt a need to write, a kind of compulsion to get some of my thoughts down, so I began doing radio scripts." Years later he would note that he did not write as a result of any "massive compulsion. I don't feel, you know, God dictated that I should write. . . . [No] bony finger comes down from the clouds and says, 'You, you write. You're the anointed.' I never felt that. I suppose it's part compulsion, part a channel for what your brain is churning up."

"We all strive for identity, and writing offered me that," Serling told an interviewer.

Under the tutelage of Antioch's writer in residence, Nolan Miller, Serling churned out a series of short stories about his war experiences that were intended to comprise the chapters of a novel. These early efforts, in some respects, seem more assured than his professional attempts years later, when he dictated rather glibly into a Dictaphone rather than agonize over each word in the typewriter, as he did in college. (Miller likened the style of one of his earliest stories to a traffic jam.) Here, the power of his experiences splashed onto the paper; the first-person narrator's voice showed a preternatural maturity. In contrast to his paratrooper poem, he had clearly shed most of his emotional baby fat. This work was terse, hard-edged, and ringed with bitterness, detailing the deaths of many men (yet he omitted mention of his own brushes, including the shrapnel wound). When he exhausted his need to chronicle what he had seen, he turned to more clever tactics that nonetheless illustrated how much the war had affected his former bravado. Where once he had seen the battlefield as a personal proving ground, the horrors he experienced compelled him now to want to "outlaw war," as he noted in one imaginative paper, "Transcript of the Legal Proceedings in the Case of the Universe Versus War," in which the court was heaven, the presiding judge God, the prosecutor Euripides; the jury consisted of twelve angels empowered to reach a verdict on War, whose attorney was Julius Caesar.

The opportunity to have his work heard by a larger audience than just his professors drove him back to his original ambition, radio. The college owned its own station, the Antioch Broadcasting System, which eventually became Serling's personal toy; he became its manager and wrote, acted in, and directed dozens of productions. He was a natural, with an instinctive ear for dialogue and a voice that commanded attention. He didn't speak with the terse, chopped-off delivery he perfected during "The Twilight Zone" and "Night Gallery," but his voice had a seductive style and earned him many other jobs as an announcer. Reading his own work, in particular, gave him great pleasure.

As with his prose, many of these assignments seemed to be attempts at conveying the damage of war. In one particular short script, "Concerto," the plot is overshadowed by a passage in which the narrator describes the look of horror and anguish on the face of a mother who has just seen her little girl killed by an automobile; she sways from one foot to the other, then opens her mouth in a silent scream. They were the words of a man who had seen and felt such pain.

During his freshman year Serling met Carolyn Louise Kramer, an education major. She was pretty, bright, and articulate. Serling was undeniably smitten with this "shiksa goddess" (as one family friend put it) and did everything he could to get her attention and affection. He once tried to stand up on a motorcycle and turn circles below her dorm window. She held steady against his initial advances, not because she was uninterested but because she was aware of his reputation as a ladies' man.

"He struck me as being very intelligent, with a wonderful sense of humor. And there was something about him that fascinated me. I had never met anyone who was as self-assured before," she says. Serling credited her with saving his life. He felt he had been floundering without direction, and without hope, when they met.

Carolyn Kramer, born February 3, 1929, in Columbus, Ohio, was a child when her mother died and her father essentially abandoned her to the care of his wife's parents, Frank Caldwell and Louise Taft Orton Caldwell; the Taft stands for the Tafts of Ohio—William Howard Taft, the twenty-seventh president of the United States, and his son, Robert Taft, Senate Majority (Republican) Leader during Eisenhower's first term.

Louise Caldwell—affectionately known as Ann—was the daughter of Edward Orton, Ohio State University's first president. She became a mother to Carolyn Kramer, who was known as Carol, and raised her granddaughter to bear a patrician air of quiet and reserve—to be warmish, if not quite warm. Ann Goodman remembers Caldwell as being a "lovely, lovely lady," as did, apparently, most who knew her. Later, when Serling and Kramer were married, Esther Serling got on well with Caldwell, as did Serling, who called her, with affection and respect, "Grandmother."

Frank Caldwell, an impressive man by all accounts, headed the engineering department at Ohio State, in Columbus, from 1897 until he retired in 1939. Named the college's first-ever professor of engineering, he accepted the job at age twenty-four—four years before the department's expansion made him chairman over many older yet less accomplished men. Frank Caldwell was the man Sam Serling would have wanted to be—first an engineer, second a professor, third a successful inventor, and finally, a reasonably wealthy man. The bulk of his wealth derived from his most lucrative invention, a thermostat he patented and sold to RANCO, Inc., a major lighting manufacturer founded and then owned by Estelle Raney. Raney (who accented the first syllable of his first name to make it seem a male appellation) had apologized to Caldwell for having to pay him in company stock, not cash, for the invention. This inability, though, later turned to Caldwell's great advantage. The value of the stock increased steadily over the years, and the dividends alone created substantial income. A few years after Frank's death in 1953 from causes related to a fall and broken hip, Louise, then in poor health, told Raney that the stock enabled her to afford twenty-four-hour in-home nursing care. (After her death, the stock passed to Carol, as did the Caldwells' substantial land holdings near the College of Wooster.)

Serling and Carol represented the joining of two different cultures: he, the immigrant, Jewish middle-class, feisty, exuberant, and emotional; she, the WASPy, old-money blue blood, quiet, unassuming, and unemotional. Their relationship would have been unlikely before the war, which had the effect, in part because of the G.I. Bill, of redefining some of the traditional class distinctions and taboos. Yet a few of the stereotypes still fit. For most of their marriage, Serling always spent their money more frivolously, particularly on cars, and Carol had to rein in his spendthrift instincts. Old money just did not spend ostentatiously, as did the nouveau riche.

One can see how Serling could have fallen so hard for Carol. Her good looks aside, she represented a type of nobility, breeding, and stability that in the aftermath of the war seemed like an anchor to which he could attach himself. Serling was quite willing to remake the world and himself in that image. However, their difference in faiths evidently caused friction between them, not least because of their parents. Esther Serling, despite her liberalism and the fact that her boys had not been raised in a traditional Jewish home, was reportedly displeased at their plans to marry; she had always assumed that, religious or not, Rod and Bob would marry Jewish women. (A few years later, Bob too would disappoint her.) Carol's father, who surfaced from time to time during her life until his death in 1971, met Serling once and issued his estranged daughter a severe warning: "I absolutely forbid you to marry that black-haired little Jew."

According to friends, Serling volunteered, at Carol's urging (not necessarily to allay her father), to take on Unitarianism, a particularly liberal denomination that believes the deity resides in every individual and that stresses social activism. It was not Judaism, but neither was it Catholicism, and anyway Serling had never felt defined by his Jewish roots. The conversion was a symbolic act representing his desire and need for acceptance.

Serling could never "put up with the Jewish rituals, the reading of the Torah," says Ernest Pipes, pastor of the Unitarian church in Santa Monica to which the Serlings later belonged. Serling embraced Unitarianism the rest of his life and often sought Pipes' counsel and solace, particularly after catastrophic events, such as the assassinations of John Kennedy, Martin Luther King, Jr., and Robert Kennedy. Yet just as some childhood friends had been unaware of his Jewish blood, many adults never knew of his Unitarianism.

Rod Serling and Carol Kramer married on July 31, 1948. They honeymooned at Sheldrake, a cabin on Cayuga Lake in upstate New York that had been in the Caldwell family for more than one hundred years. (From then on, wherever they lived until Rod died, the Serlings missed only two summers at the lake house.) Before their junior year started in the fall, they moved into one of the small surplus trailers—trailer number ten—the school had bought to help house the enormous influx of married students; after the war, much of the student body, attending on the G.I. Bill, were older than the usual incoming students. Without running water or a private bath (there was, however, a hole in the roof to go with the old bed, four chairs, a couch, heater, and stove), this was quite a drop in accommodations for Carol Serling; yet the couple seemed happy and content.

For Serling especially, this was a good period. Except for

the insomnia that would plague him on and off the rest of his life, his postwar depression had, with Carol's help, mostly dissipated. Whatever forces had affected him and changed his disposition, they became part of the fabric of his life, invisible, submerged beneath the force of his cheerfulness and his need for attention. Just as at Binghamton Central High School, he was once again outgoing and popular, and the world of possibilities reopened to him. Those who knew him then remember his energy, which powered an offbeat sense of humor that sometimes ran to practical jokes.

One night Serling donned a rubber Frankenstein mask and prepared to scare the bejeezus out of his neighbor in the next trailer, a friend. Serling had always loved monster and horror films. He and his brother had seen *King Kong* easily a dozen times together, and *Frankenstein* and *Dracula* were almost as popular. (Throughout his life, whenever a television station played *King Kong*, he dropped all other plans in order to watch. In California his constant viewing companion became writer John Champion. Together, they saw the film at least twenty times over the years.) When these films came out within two years of each other in the early 1930s, they seemed revolutionary. Prominent talkies until then had been mostly parlor stories with a decided bent toward the stage, or historical dramas. Serling was at exactly the proper ages—seven for both *Frankenstein* and *Dracula*, nine for *King Kong*—to be willingly and completely terrified by the horror on the screen. He loved a good scare. And he loved to scare others.

Sneaking out of the trailer so Carol wouldn't see, the mask covering his face, Serling tiptoed stealthily across the grass. He hovered beneath his neighbor's kitchen window, where she stood washing dishes after dinner. Slowly he stood up, the mask illuminated from below by a flashlight emitting a red glow, and roared in a convincingly horrific voice.

"Rod," his neighbor said calmly. "How are you?"

Crestfallen, Serling turned abruptly and stormed back into his trailer. "Carol, goddamn you," he said. "You told her, you warned her."

During Serling's four years at Antioch, he held a variety of different intern positions at radio stations in New York and Ohio, some gained because of his writing skill and some because of his voice. In chronological order, he worked for: WNYC in New York City as a newsroom assistant and public service announcement writer (he also had one line in a play: asked by some state troopers what direction the bad guys were heading, Serling uttered "South"); WINR in Binghamton as an apprentice writer and announcer (he also had his own weekly show, "Six-Gun Serling's Western Jamboree"); WMRN in Marion, Ohio, as a music director, creative writing teacher, announcer, and writer (he wrote and announced everything from shorts aimed at young girls, who were supposed to shop for clothes at the show's sponsor, Sutton and Lightner, to scripts about the benefits of army life for army recruiting headquarters in Marion); the Antioch Broadcasting Station, in conjunction with WJEM in Springfield, Ohio, as station and program director, and he also wrote and directed an entire year's worth of long-form dramas performed by the Antioch Players Group, of which he was a member. All of these jobs, while supplying invaluable experience, paid him nothing, or at most a small stipend, for his internship.

Early in 1949 Serling submitted a script he had written for a popular radio anthology show called "Dr. Christian." Jean Hersholt starred as a kindly old country doctor. The show had debuted in 1937 as a spin-off of a Hersholt film, *The Country Doctor*, in which he portrayed real-life doctor Allen R. Dafoe, who enjoyed sudden celebrity the year before, after delivering the Dionne quintuplets. In 1941, on a whim, the producers of "Dr. Christian" turned to the audience for some scripts and offered cash prizes for the best writing. Within a few years, they mostly eliminated their professional writers; upwards of ten thousand scripts landed on the producers' desks every year in quest of the two thousand dollars first-prize money and second prizes of up to five hundred dollars. Sponsored by Chesebrough Manufacturing Company Consolidated, the show acquired an official nickname: "the Vaseline program—the only show in radio where the audience writes the scripts."

Serling's script, "To Live a Dream," told of a young fighter who discovers he has leukemia. Rather than simply resigning himself to dying, he courageously battles the disease while passing on what he knows to a younger fighter and steering him to the championship. It was maudlin, blatantly manipulative, and derivative—but good radio. "To Live a Dream" won one of three second-place prizes of five hundred dollars, and the producers provided Rod with a first-class, expenses-paid trip to New York, with his wife, for the awards presentation a full six months before the actual production. ("Serling Goes to Christian Reward," read the Antioch school newspaper headline.)

While his own words had been produced regularly for a few years now, Serling had never before been paid as a professional writer. "It was an incredible event," he said. "The most important thing about the first sale is, for the very first time in your life, something written has value, and *proven* value, because somebody has given you money for the words that you've written, and that's terribly important. It's a tremendous boon to the ego, to your sense of self-reliance, to your feeling about your own talent."

Serling was cocky about this success. He felt that he had gotten the break he needed and that his climb to the top was inevitable. While preparing to go to New York, he saw Tim Reynolds, a neighbor whose father was an anthropology professor at Antioch. Reynolds, fifteen years younger than Serling, had been the voice of a black child in one of Serling's productions, "The Passersby." Patting Reynolds on the head, Serling said, "Well, Tim, I just want you to know that when I make it big, there'll always be a place for you." (Fourteen years later, trying to support a wife and child—and his fledgling writing career—by passing out handbills in New Orleans, Reynolds wrote to Serling, then producer of "The Twilight Zone," looking for his "place." In a brief but pleasant reply, Serling apologetically explained that his production company was a small group and that everybody in it had a particular function; he had "no place to plug in anyone else.")

Standing in the CBS network studio in New York that easily dwarfed the relatively primitive facilities at Antioch, and even the other small stations upstate, Serling felt awestruck. Understandably nervous before the awards presentation, he somehow found the time and composure to gab. Hersholt, to whom he had introduced himself, apparently took a liking to this ingratiating, and obviously talented, young man. As they talked about the script and the business in general and how much Serling admired him, Hersholt spotted the president of Chesebrough. "Come on, I'll introduce you," he said. Serling was almost tongue-tied from fright.

"Mr. Richardson," said Hersholt, "I'd like you to meet one of our contest winners. This is Rod Serling." Richardson extended his hand.

"Rod," Hersholt continued, "this is Mr. Arthur Richardson, the president of Chesebrough Manufacturing Company."

"Oh, how do you do," said Serling, returning the shake. "I'm very glad to know you. I want you to know that I eat your product every night with beer."

"I wanted to die," he said later, after being delicately told that Chesebrough was not a dairy farm but the parent company of Vaseline. "I had no idea."

On stage for the presentation, Serling told Hersholt and the national audience that his and Carol's ambition was to "live in a large house, in the suburb of a large city, raise a family, a lot of dogs . . . and write." (One of the other second-place prizes was given to Earl Hamner, Jr., best known as the creator of the "The Waltons." He would also write several "Twilight Zone" episodes.)

Serling reveled in the first-class treatment in New York. The accommodations and restaurants convinced him, as if he had not yet acquired the desire, that wealth felt a lot better than poverty. If he could make five hundred dollars as an amateur, he could make thousands as a professional. He redoubled his efforts and reaffirmed his dedication to a writing career.

For a brief period he had moments of doubt: his competitors at "Dr. Christian" were, like himself, amateurs; how would he compete against real professionals? But the acceptance—and subsequent paycheck—of his unsolicited manuscript to "Grand Central Station," a midday Saturday CBS anthology that each week followed the life of a different character as he or she arrived at the famous New York terminal for work or play, dispelled most doubts. "A Little Guy Named Johnny O'Neil" seems to have been Serling's own fantasy-induced pronouncement that success would not change him or his desire for a large house in the suburbs with his family and dogs. Hero Johnny, who hails from a small town, is now a successful New York City architect engaged to Marcia, a bratty actress. Janie, his small-town girlfriend when they were teenagers, has come to New York for the first time and is wowed by it. She is a complete contrast to Marcia, whose cynicism and sarcasm surprise Janie, but not as much as Johnny's subservience to the actress. The conflict plays out when Johnny is forced to choose between a high rise that will make him a great deal of money and a community house for the disadvantaged that can be built only if Johnny agrees to do it for free. Marcia reminds him of his professional standing, and Janie urges him to remember his former idealism. When he chooses the high rise, Janie storms off, but not before surreptitiously maneuvering him into accepting the community house project. Rather than becoming angry when he discovers Janie's subterfuge, he tells Marcia to get lost and gets on the train with Janie back to their hometown, where they will marry. "You know, Janie," Johnny says, "I've made a lot of dough. I live in a fancy suite. I go to the best joints. But I've never been as happy, or as contented, as I was then—when people didn't know me except as that little guy Johnny O'Neil, the little guy with the big ideas."

So happy was Serling with the sale, which profoundly validated his ambitions, that he refused to cash the $150 check for three months, during which time he gleefully showed it to as many people as asked, "How are you, Rod?" A few months later he sold another script to the same show. Rod Serling, still a college student, was now a professional writer supplying some of those millions of words radio devoured. His income that year: $790. (Years later, when a young acquaintance of his sold her first television script, he poignantly told her to savor the moment, because nothing else in life was likely to feel that wonderful.)

Fatefully, radio would require many fewer hundreds of thousands of words each week in the coming years. And the end of radio drama would come more quickly than could have been anticipated—as quickly as the rise of television. Anyone planning a career as an anthology writer for radio suddenly had to make an adjustment.

When Serling and his parents had visited the 1939 New York World's Fair, they had seen billboards placed by the Du Mont Television Receivers Company, pronouncing, "Sooner than you think, television will play a vital part in the life of the average American." At the time no evidence existed to confirm that this was anything other than wishful thinking on the part of an organization that stood to benefit if only this primitive technology could catch on. After all, the cost of this curiosity was prohibitively expensive, and accordingly only a handful of television sets then operated—compared to forty-five million radios. The first regularly scheduled television programming had been broadcast eleven years before by the General Electric Company's fledgling Schenectady, New York, station, WGY. And it had been all but ignored. After the war ended, and with the country's pent-up demand for consumer products reaching a frenzied peak, still only five thousand sets had been sold nationwide.

Then came the paradigm shift that changed forever the way the world worked, lived, and played—indeed, even thought. Within three years an additional one million television sets were sold. As just one example of how quickly the public took to television viewing, Earl "Madman" Muntz, a Los Angeles used-car dealer, entered the burgeoning business after printing advertising on the backs of streetcar transfers. "Stop staring at your radio," was his slogan. Muntz alone would sell as many as five thousand sets in a single weekend.

All over the country, people began to be drawn to the cathode-ray tube, whose main attractions became the recognizable stars they had only heard before on radio. Still feeling its way in the programming darkness, television relied on the performers who had made radio so popular. In 1949 CBS premiered the first television situation comedy, "The Goldbergs," a simple, unadorned visual extension of the radio series starring Molly Berg, which had been playing since 1929. By the time "Amos 'n Andy," another show with radio origins, began later that year, nearly eight-million television sets had found homes in America. ("Captain Video," with its cardboard props and scenery, debuted in 1949 as television's first science-fiction show.)

Despite his three successful radio submissions, Serling must have felt somewhat unlucky: just when he had begun to write saleable products, the rules of the game experienced a startling revision. As radio production offices continued to shut down, some radio studios quickly converted to television facilities. The era when the entire family gathered around the living room radio to hear stirring drama had just about ended.

Fifteen thirty-minute anthologies originated from the West Coast, all filmed in a style understatedly described as amateurish. In New York, the six thirty-minute and three one-hour anthology shows broadcast live in the studio and at virtually no advantage over their filmed counterparts. On both coasts every aspect of the productions, from set design to camera direction, seemed to have been conceived by students, not professionals. In a sense, it was true. The most respected professionals in Hollywood worked in the legitimate business of making real films, and in New York they devoted themselves to the legitimate theater, not this crude infant form that many believed to be just a passing fancy.

Whatever else it may have been or had the potential to become, television was the most extraordinary advertising vehicle any Madison Avenue executive might envision. Viewers actually saw the product, as in newspaper ads, and heard its benefits described, as in radio. Television put a skilled salesman in every living room.

Just as they had on radio, sponsors underwrote the productions of television series in order to have those few minutes of each half hour or hour to push their products. The more viewers each show had, of course, the more inclined the sponsor felt to continue its patronage. Sometimes they based their sponsorship decisions on intangibles as much as ratings, because they felt that particular programs represented an image with which they wanted to be associated. "Ozzie and Harriet," for example, despite never receiving very high ratings, sold enough Kodak film every week to fill millions of cameras. (Conversely, in the early 1950s Philip Morris's sales of cigarettes are said to have fallen, despite sponsoring "I Love Lucy," television's highest-rated show.) And because they ostensibly owned the shows, sponsors also controlled the scripts. Chevrolet might not want a horse to "ford" a stream, while R. J. Reynolds Tobacco would insist that any reference to this country be to the United States, not America—because American was the name of a competing company.

No sponsor ever wanted its programs to reflect a controversial viewpoint. A program about the evils of McCarthyism, for example, might imply to viewers that the sponsor—whether it be Philco, Kraft, Campbell, U.S. Steel, or Armstrong—was soft on Communism and therefore un-American, a company whose products should be avoided. More shamefully, programs that might seek to illuminate any of the pressing social issues of the day could not be sponsored for fear that viewers would equate the sponsor with the controversial viewpoint and boycott the product.

In reality, these decisions about what was and was not acceptable were made by the advertising agencies, who held the real power over the programs and the program creators. The agencies literally bought the shows for their individual clients and tailored the products to fit the clients' needs. If Young and Rubicam liked the quality of a particular director's work, say, Franklin Schaffner, the creative director would hire Schaffner to work on several programs. The same held true with writers and actors. In this way, the agencies occupied the role taken today by the big networks. Rehearsals, and sometimes the shootings themselves, usually took place at the agencies.

The immense excitement in television revolved, of course, around the live dramas shot in New York. This was new and incredible ground being exploited, not like movies and Broadway, which had established standards and protocol. If someone in those two fields didn't understand or didn't know a particular how or where, there was always someone else to ask. In television no one had been around long enough to be an expert. The players wrote and rewrote the rules everyday as they went along. Everyone learned at the same time— and from all the same mistakes.

No bona fide stars emerged immediately. The actors, at least those in New York, usually arrived as out-of-work stage players. (Too often the Hollywood actors were unable to play television roles successfully; in film an actor rarely has to learn more than four lines at a time before the director yells "cut," giving him or her a chance to memorize the next few lines.) The directors, like John Frankenheimer, Schaffner, and Ralph Nelson—working for a quarter of what the actors got—were unknowns who may have just recently been cameramen or sometimes even still photographers. Until they mastered the technical kinks, they had to excel at logistics rather than nuance or mood. "No, no," they'd say to an actor, "you can't walk over there. The camera can't roll over this cable on the floor." The cameramen had been assistant cameramen who'd once taken a Polaroid snapshot. Lighting directors were guys who could screw bulbs in sockets. Stagehands were often hired right off the street.

The studios where the live shows were shot had been radio studios or motion picture theaters minus the seats. And because millions of people would instantly witness any flub, the biggest concern was avoiding catastrophe.

Jackie Cooper recalls a role he had in 1949, portraying clarinetist Mez Mezzrol, who died from alcoholism and general abuse. Realizing he has little time left, he picks up his clarinet and attempts to play a mournful solo, but fails because his lip is too swollen. Frustrated, frightened, and angry, Cooper's character was to throw the clarinet at the mirror into which he'd been looking, shattering the mirror and his image in it; the viewer would not know he'd been looking at the reflection until the mirror shattered. Simple, dramatic, symbolic. The screen would then go to black. But when Cooper threw the clarinet, the mirror didn't break. He picked up the clarinet off the floor and threw it again. Still, the mirror refused to break. A less experienced actor might have just walked away or started to laugh. But Cooper, who had himself begun to learn the craft of directing live television, knew Perry Lafferty, the director, would not go to commercial without a dramatic moment on which to fade out. Cooper grabbed the clarinet and repeatedly bashed it against the mirror. While a poor second to the scripted sequence, it seemed adequately dramatic. At the commercial, Lafferty hugged Cooper for his ingenuity.

Another time Cooper cut his leg on a stage brace that held the heavy pieces of equipment into the concrete floor. A large bolt protruding from one of the four wheels went deep into the side of his leg as he walked by, just before he was about to enter a scene. By the time he finished the scene, his blood had flowed into a large pool on the floor. In terrible pain, he ripped off his pants and wrapped a makeshift bandage around the enormous cut; the show had to go on. In the next scene his character was scripted to seduce the lead actress. Pain aside, that became problematic: the audience would have concentrated only on the still-bleeding injury, not the interplay between the lovers. At Cooper's suggestion, the camera shot him only from the waist up. Meanwhile, several stagehands knelt on the floor below him, mopping up the free-flowing blood with towels. (After the show Cooper was taken to a hospital and given a blood transfusion; a deep scar remains to this day.)

Occasionally, in the rush to satisfy the voracious hunger for more and more programming, the production crew lacked adequate time to work out every single flaw. For space reasons, set designers might build adjoining sets. In the place where the common wall would have stood had to be two cameras, each pointing into a different set. Unless the director had the cameras positioned properly, when a character exited one room and went directly into the next, it could—and sometimes did—look to the viewer as though the actor had just bumped into himself.

Everyone who labored through the birth and rearing of this era had a story to tell: directors unknowingly switching to cameras that had focused accidentally on another cameraman's rear end; actors who'd been "killed" getting up and walking away in the mistaken belief they were off camera; actors forgetting lines; live shots of stagehands moving equipment or crawling on the floor as the action above carried on; shots of empty sets when actors were unable to make speedy wardrobe changes; actresses who had had a major emotional catharsis in the previous scene still dabbing at their eyes in the next scene—when, according to the script, it took place two months later.

Had Rod Serling tried to break into the film or stage industries at the same time, he would most certainly have found the doors closed, if not locked. But television—that was another matter. Every producer in California and New York frantically sought out new material; whether it came in over the transom, under the door, or via postage-due mail mattered not. Their quandary: to find professional-quality scripts from mostly unprofessional writers. Even the out-of-work radio hacks had never written for a visual medium. Film writers and playwrights wouldn't be caught slumming.

By this time Serling had a role model for his writing. Whereas before he had admired Ernest Hemingway, he now had a genuine literary hero—Arthur Miller. In 1949, during his trip to New York City for "Dr. Christian," Serling went to the Morosco Theatre to see Lee J. Cobb play Willy Loman in *Death of a Salesman*. Although he had been to Broadway plays many times before with his parents, and even with his army buddies on three-day leaves from boot camp and paratroop training, no play had ever struck him with such searing force both emotionally and intellectually.

On the most immediate level, Willy Loman, an ordinary man with failed dreams, no doubt reminded him of his father—an ordinary man, a man whose name never got printed in the paper, a man who never made a lot of money, a man who didn't get the breaks and died too soon—but he also reminded him of himself: someone who talked too much, who joked too much, who cared too much about making a good impression on others. And in Biff he also saw himself, or at least the self he feared becoming. That night represented a crossroads in his life—the past, present, and future coming together—and here, on stage, was a terrifying depiction of a young man who had shown a world of promise in high school, who'd had the world at his feet but now lived only on past glories; what a horrible possibility to contemplate, that he might be Biff.

As he looked further, Serling understood that the dramatic spine of *Death of a Salesman* was not failed ambition or broken dreams, but morality—in this case, the futility of it in a society that does not necessarily reward the moral, the just, the upright, the ordinary. In the war he had seen with his own eyes that fate often paid no attention to good or evil, making each death all the more cruel. The lessons of his youth, taught to him by his father and illustrated by George F. Johnson's paternal benevolence, seemed to inhabit some other universe than the one he had entered. This was a godless world, one without reason.

Or was it? Serling looked still further. Hadn't Willy Loman been betrayed by his own values? Hadn't his life been one lie piled on another, and another on top of that, and on and on until the truth was buried so deeply he could never see it? Hadn't he been used because he believed it was all right to use other people? And finally, hadn't he died for these sins?

There, this was Miller's genius. The writing so miraculously created these flesh-and-blood characters, made them so credible, so real, that for the play's three hours—and long after—they lived inside him. Their suffering activated his suffering; their realizations, their sins, their failings became his. It showed him, painstakingly, the insidious, banal face of evil—the evil of selfishness and self-deception in everyone, and in himself. By God, it was a morality play. All without some narrator stepping from the wings to proclaim the moral for all to hear. Good and evil had clashed, and he had been shown the truth—no, had been allowed to discover it. And wasn't this the function of art—to entertain, to instruct, to change the beholder?

Equally stunned and envious (years later he paid other writers whose work he admired the ultimate compliment: "I wish I had written it myself"), Rod Serling resolved to move others as he had just been moved. Not surprisingly, Serling's most powerful dramas would hinge on character, the plots built on internal conflicts, not external circumstances. Although his characters and messages lacked the complexity of Miller's, his stories always intended to highlight morality, usually through illustrating its opposite. Those of his stories that were purely contrived plot, where twists and turns occurred apart from character, inevitably lacked drive, and they failed; he was not a good action writer.

In early 1950—the year "Superman" and "I Love Lucy" debuted—Rod Serling received $100 dollars from the Hollywood producers of the NBC television series "Stars Over Hollywood" for his script entitled "Grady Everett for the People," about a pro bono lawyer. It wasn't *Death of a Salesman*, but it was a beginning. A few months later he graduated from Antioch with a B-plus average and a bachelor's degree, neither of which opened any doors. Only decent writing could do that.

Artistry included, Rod Serling was nothing if not practical. Perhaps because he, like his father, had married into a family with more money than his, and because his father had suffered financial reversals the last years of his life, Serling decided to forego the starving-artist routine. Anyway, this was 1950 and husbands supported their wives, which he could not have done based on the rejection slips that began to pile up. So when WLW in Cincinnati said yes to his job application as a staff writer—paying him seventy-five dollars a week—he and Carol drove their station wagon full of belongings to the big city.

This was not the sort of writing he had expected, however. "The grind was murderous," he told interviewer William F. Nolan. "Everything from soap commercials to public service announcements to half-hour documentaries. I learned discipline, absorbed a time sense and a technique, but I was desperate to break away."

So desperate that, after a full day at WLW, he came home to their small Victoria Avenue apartment, ate dinner at the kitchen table, then continued to sit there until midnight, writing the thirty- and sixty-minute dramas that sprang quickly from his brain. In later years, after success granted him a secretary, he would dictate his work, leading him to become one of Hollywood's fastest writers. Even then, on his bulky typewriter, he was prolific enough to acquire nearly forty rejection slips in about a year's time. "These weren't bad scripts," Serling later wrote. "There was usually a kind of strength to them that showed in dialogue and a sense of character. But they were stamped with the lack of professional polish. They showed in many ways that they were done on a kitchen table during the eleventh and twelfth and thirteenth hours of a working day. They were always sharpened, but never to their finest points."

For a man who needed acceptance and validation as badly as Serling, each rejection slip felt like "a piece of your flesh cut to pieces." And every time an unsolicited manuscript came back with the standard terse apology, his job at WLW seemed progressively worse. If he couldn't sell any of his original material to producers, then at least he wanted his commercial writing to be as original as possible—much more original than was appropriate. In one instance, he turned in a script for a "documentary" that called for:

> a narrator and a 30-piece live orchestra, and contained the kind of prose that made GreenHills, Ohio, look like the Alamo!
>
> When I was called into the [program director's] office my script was lying face down on his desk, like a thumb in a Roman arena. He leaned back in his swivel chair and studied me pensively, as if searching for some velvet-glove language that could be utilized to castigate me without breaking my spirit.
>
> "Serling," he said, "it's this way. Your stuff's too stilted. You seem to be missing the common touch. We're looking for grass roots here. We want to be close to the people. We're obliged to use the 'folksy' approach. In short, we want our people to get their teeth into the soil."

As he was talking I knew exactly what he meant. The "folksy approach" did not include a 30-piece orchestra, or prose out of Norman Corwin's *On a Note of Triumph*. It needed only two elements: a hayseed M.C. who strummed a guitar and said, "Shucks, friends"; and a girl yodeler whose falsetto could break a beer mug at twenty paces. This was getting the teeth into the soil. And the little thought journeyed through my brain that what these guys wanted was not a writer but a plow!

In March 1951, after enough months on the job to know that he had to find another while waiting for his freelance career to take off, Serling applied to work for Voice of America, the radio network arm of the United States Information Agency, created three years before to act as, in essence, publicists for the United States in the post–World War II environment. "The Congress hereby declares," read the Congressional Record summary of the the law, "that the objectives of this Act are to enable the Government of the United States to promote a better understanding of the United States in other countries, and to increase mutual understanding between the people of the United States and the people of other countries."

According to the terms of the U.S. Information Act, no employee could be hired without first being subjected to a "loyalty check" conducted by the FBI. The bureau's background investigation took two months to determine that Serling had no foreign connections and that his mother and brother were not criminals or Communists (interestingly, no reference was made to his wife; in fact, Serling did not even list her on his USIA application in the column for "immediate relatives"). But shortly after that determination, he received the bad news that he had been rejected for the job based solely on qualifications.

VOA was, and is, essentially a news organization (although it is not licensed to broadcast within U.S. borders). Unlike many local news broadcasts, VOA does not employ "news readers." Its on-air personalities are also journalists who write their own copy. Serling had been a writer and a broadcaster, but he had not been a journalist reporting on news events in his own voice. The rejection naturally disappointed him, particularly in light of the job that awaited him every day. (Years later, he would work for USIA on his own terms.)

And his disappointment only magnified his existing pain over constant rejection. "I think there was a period of about eight months when *nothing* happened," he said. "Everything that I wrote crumpled up, and then it became a self-destructive thing, when you begin to doubt yourself, when doubt turns into—it's sort of like impotence. Once impotent, you're forever impotent. Because you're always worried about being impotent."

In the fall Serling made a minor breakthrough when he sold a number of thirty-minute scripts to WKRC-TV in Cincinnati. This confirmed his potency. No, the producers were not network luminaries like Fred Coe and Worthington Miner, but at least he had the satisfaction of reward, after toiling over his typewriter on the kitchen table. Not least of the rewards was financial; at $125 per script, which he seemingly could turn out in a couple of nights, it was also excellent compensation (according to the Consumer Price Index, one 1951 dollar bought slightly more than five 1989 dollars).

By January 1952 Serling had sold twenty-one scripts to WKRC. He now needed only a good excuse to quit the salt mines at WLW—and he soon found one. One afternoon he visited the taping of a program to which he had to contribute ideas. When the show's master of ceremonies—an "extent revivalist, a fat-faced slob I cordially detested on sight"—offered a lewd comment about one of the station's female employees as she exited their elevator, Serling suddenly found himself in no mood to tackle his next assignment: dreaming up "an audition show for a patent medicine currently the rage."

The "medicine" was Geritol, which contained

about twelve percent alcohol by volume and, if the testimonials were to be believed, could cure everything from arthritis to a fractured pelvis. I spent two minutes studying the agency's work sheet, which stated the general purpose of the program. I read as far as the second paragraph: "This will be a program for the people. We'd like to see a real grass-roots approach that is popular and close to the soil." The pattern of whatever future I had was very much in evidence. I was either going to write dramatic shows for television, even at the risk of economics and common sense, or I was going to succumb to the double-faced sanctimony of commercial radio, rotating words as if they were crops, and utilizing one of the approaches so characteristic to radio—writing and thinking downward at the lowest possible common denominator of an audience. That afternoon I quit the radio station.

In his continuing account, Serling appears to have taken some romantic liberties. "Freelance writing would now be our bread, our butter, and the now-or-never of our whole existence," he wrote, explaining that he and Carol, then three months pregnant, sat in a Howard Johnson's, where he tried to break the news to her. "She knew that it was a frustrating, insecure, bleeding business at best, and the guy she was married to could get his pride, his composure and his confidence eaten away with the acid of disappointment." Nonetheless, "All she did was to take my hand. Then she winked at me and picked up a menu and studied it."

The romanticism derives from what he omitted: not only had he sold WKRC those twenty-one scripts but he also was then about to sign, as both of them knew, a contract with the station for twenty-six additional half-hour scripts, each paying $125.

Perhaps just as important, the not-inconsiderable assets of Carol's grandparents behind them provided a financial safety net if the need arose. No matter how badly he might fall, they knew they were not likely to starve. Her income from RANCO, Inc. stock dividends, in addition to dividends from such other companies' stocks as AT&T, Great American Insurance, American Insurance Company, Providence-Washington Insurance, Eastman-Kodak, and Melrose Orchard Company—presented as gifts from her grandparents and Grace Chamberlin, an aunt, totaled several thousand dollars a year. With this kind of support, Serling was free most of the week, after polishing off his WKRC assignments, to churn out scenarios and send them off, unsolicited, through the mails.

One noteworthy proposal was sent to Walter Schwimmer, a radio syndicator in Chicago. Serling had enclosed a one-page synopsis describing the theme behind his proposed weekly anthology series, as well as a completed script and some plot outlines for future shows. Some of these stories—"Fifteen Minutes Before Midnight," "The Button Pushers," "Fate Is Electricity"—he had first worked on at Antioch.

Schwimmer, despite his success in the business, had failed in the past to recognize the talent and commercial potential of both Edgar Bergen and Danny Thomas. Add to that list the name Rod Serling.

"I didn't think what he sent me was any good," Schwimmer says.

The proposal was for a fantasy series called "The Twilight Zone."

4

SLAVE TO A
BITCH GODDESS

Prosperity's always just around the corner, isn't it, George? Just around the corner. And when you round it, and there's nothing there except more street, it's always the next corner, isn't it?"

Serling would soon give these words to the long-suffering wife who wishes her husband would finally stop chasing rainbows in "Face of Autumn." But after the despair of forty consecutive rejections, they may have been uttered first by Carol Serling.

In Serling's case prosperity *was* just around the corner. When "Armstrong Circle Theatre" aired "The Sergeant" (for which he had written only the story) the night of April 29, 1952, the logjam broke. Two months later, not only had he attracted the attention of Dick McDonagh, story editor of the "Lux Video Theatre" but also literary agent Blanche Gaines.

McDonagh was a sharp editor with an astute eye for talent, even if that talent arrived in a raw form, as in the case of Serling's "Welcome Home, Lefty," which came unsolicited through the mail. Lefty O'Bannion, a veteran baseball pitcher, has been released by his team of seventeen years. He bitterly refuses to accept reality gracefully and retire. A teenage boy, Jimmy, invites him to pitch in the annual game that pits a semipro team against the county's best high schoolers, for whom Jimmy plays outfield. Lefty refuses, contending that by game time he'll be back in the majors. When he sees a pro scout in the neighborhood, he assumes the man has come to sign him, but Jimmy's the one being scouted. Lefty decides to pitch.

Serling set up the conflict nicely: Lefty trying to prove himself—to himself—against kids; and the kids, especially Jimmy, trying to make their mark against a former pro pitcher. But because the show was allotted only thirty minutes to tell the story, the resolution seems forced. "It's a victory of youth over age," the game announcer tells us superfluously as Jimmy hits the game-winning home run in the bottom of the ninth, shortly before Lefty graciously accepts his forced retirement.

Just as the author would write consistently about the fine line between cowardice and conscience in war, and much later about compromising personal values for profit, the plot of "Welcome Home, Lefty" was one that Serling would work and rework in the coming years, culminating in late 1956 with "Requiem for a Heavyweight"; "The Face of Autumn" (boxing), "The Return of Socko Renard" (football), "The Twilight Rounds" (boxing), and "Old MacDonald Had a Curve" (baseball). All concerned sportsmen who had hung on too long, waiting for that one big break or to relive past glories.

In all, McDonagh would buy five Serling scripts that year and "Lux" aired four of them. To write, and write regularly, for "Lux" was an honor. The show "consistently aimed high," Serling said. "Its whole conception in terms of dialogue and production was adult, never hackneyed, and almost always honest." And it owed much of its success, at least in quality, to McDonagh.

Impressed with Serling, McDonagh worked overtime with him, not just to get each particular script in shape but also to counsel and point up the basics of professional drama: two words here, instead of ten; combine these characters into a single composite; have the emotional catharsis at the end of the act, not the beginning, and so on. Serling was a willing student and McDonagh a patient and capable teacher. (In New York McDonagh often invited Serling to stay at his home.)

Serling seemed somewhat intimidated by his good fortune. Flying or busing into New York as he often did for story conferences and rehearsals, "I had the strange and persistent feeling that I was wearing overalls and Li'l Abner shoes," he wrote.

During one meeting about his script "You Be the Bad Guy," McDonagh ushered him into the room at the J. Walter Thompson offices where the cast, including star McDonald Carey, had met for a read-through. Carey shook Serling's hand and told him he thought the script (a bitter story about a kindhearted police detective who has to kill his own younger brother, a small-time crook) was excellent. "Thank you very much," Serling said. He had nothing else to say. Looking at his watch, he excused himself on the pretext of having to catch a plane. Obviously ill at ease, he twirled and walked headlong into the wall. Embarrassed, he twirled again and backed out of the room, this time colliding with a secretary. His briefcase opened and onto the floor dropped some scripts, a few pairs of socks, and a couple pairs of underwear.

His face flushed, he hurriedly stuffed everything back into his briefcase. At that moment he might have preferred being back on Leyte to making an assumed fool of himself in front of these "important people." McDonagh grabbed him. "Look, little friend," he said by way of comfort. "These people don't give a good healthy damn what you carry in your briefcase, or how you leave a room. All they care about is what's in there." He pointed at Serling's head.

Soon after "Lux" broadcast "Lefty" on June 23, Blanche Gaines pitched herself to Serling—as he had pitched himself to her, unsuccessfully, in 1950. At that time, Gaines would not take on struggling writers without credits, especially one living in Cincinnati. But now, having noted his recent sales, she checked back on the possibility that he remained unrepresented. She apparently was the first agent to do so, and although she had a small office and lacked unlimited access to the top shows' story editors and producers, Serling committed himself to her for five years. Whatever he made, and for as many scripts as he sold, Gaines would take her 10 percent.

Flattered and honored that she, a reputable if small agent, wanted the job—which did not pay unless a script sold—he probably barely considered the terms of the contract at the time he signed. For a writer who had had so many rejections, Gaines represented a type of legitimacy. Her confidence bolstered him, and he felt indebted to her for all the efforts she made on his behalf.

The credits—on "Lux," "Hallmark Hall of Fame," and "The Doctor" (a show whose premise was to place its protagonists in "mentally disturbing situations")—and money amassed quickly. Despite Gaines's protestations, in September Serling signed a contract he had negotiated himself earlier in the year. At $550 dollars a week for twenty-six weeks, he would have the job of script editor for his former employer, WLW. As he later recounted to Gaines in a letter, the job "took very little in the way of work . . . helped pay off a mortgage, put us back on our feet, and in the long run was of little consequence in the forward motion of my career."

Gaines had insisted then that he move east, to New York, where the giant advertising agency J. Walter Thompson had begun producing a new sixty-minute anthology series, "Kraft Television Theatre." She wrote, "I have a very strong feeling that you should not sign the radio-Cincinnati offer, as an opportunity to write for this program and the other hour opportunities here in N.Y. are so much more important to your career, both for prestige and ultimate financial returns." She concluded, "New York or

Hollywood are really the two places where writers should live if they want to make a real living of writing for TV." (Serling, although he had negotiated the WLW contract himself before he signed with Gaines, gave her 5 percent of the take. She felt entitled to it, she reasoned, because he would not take her advice and move to New York where she could have made more sales for him; therefore she ought to receive some compensation. As he pointed out, she got paid for not working, rather than working.)

On Christmas, his twenty-eighth birthday, Serling sat in front of the tree, opening expensive presents with his wife and six-month-old baby girl, Jody. That night he watched his tenth show of 1952 broadcast on "Campbell Soundstage." Its title coincidentally reflected what had been the best year of his life: "The Happy Headline." He'd sired a daughter, acquired an agent, accumulated a back account, and established a career. Moreover, he knew he was finally recognized, his talent was confirmed, his highest hopes were closer to realization. Maybe he really would be another Arthur Miller.

Sadly, in those pioneer days of television broadcasting, the medium lacked both advanced technology and foresight. Without coast-to-coast cable linkups, videotape, and satellites, what the East Coast saw live had to be conveyed via a crude microwave system of relays to the nation's other time zones. Once the signal arrived, technicians would aim a movie camera at a television monitor and actually film the screen images. When the program ended, they rushed the film to a laboratory for developing and showed the completed kinescope at the appropriate time. (Thus began the practice of showing programs in the central time zone at the same time as the eastern zone, even though that meant they would begin an hour earlier; the one-hour delay would not have been adequate to make a kinescope. In some cases, kinescopes for the West Coast were delayed until the following week.)

By the mid-1950s, the networks had amassed thousands of hours of kinescopes and had no idea where to store them. Not surprisingly, considering how the prints and masters of some of the great films of all time are still badly treated by the studios, the vast majority of kinescopes were trashed to make room for the rest. Few people realized these years would soon come to be called the golden age of television. "If I'd known it was going to be an era, I would've paid closer attention," one actor quipped.

The remaining scripts and kinescopes offer a revealing glimpse into a writer who, if judged only on his themes, emerges as a humanitarian, if not an intellect; he created characters driven by emotions and principles. In "The Carlson Legend," the third of his produced scripts, John Carlson, Jr., has recently been elected to the (unnamed) state legislature. The son of deceased John Sr., himself a state senator but more a political legend—"a unique politician, a politician with a conscience and a hankering for the truth"—John Jr. still regards his father as just beneath a saint. Accordingly, on his first day in office, he plans to offer a resolution intended to clean up any corruption by making public all contracts drawn between the government and private enterprise. He soon discovers, though, that his resolution will, ironically, taint the late, great man's memory. "I know what I should do," he says. "I know what I ought to do. But I don't know if I can."

In the climactic scene, John delivers an impassioned sermon reminiscent of *Mr. Smith Goes to Washington* (as is, thematically, the entire script), and right triumphs over self-interest. John introduces the resolution, explaining, "My father, the late Senator Carlson, used to say, 'Clean up all dirt, even if it's on your own hands.'"

Serling displayed that same idealism, love of country, and fair play in "I Lift My Lamp," which aired in August. Anna has fled the totalitarian Communist regime in Czechoslovakia, where her father still remains imprisoned for speaking out. When her former lover, now a government operative, unexpectedly arrives to take her back home, Anna refuses. "What could be worse than chaos?" he asks her in defense of his decision to join the regime.

"Communism," she shouts in the shadow of the Statue of Liberty.

Besides vividly expressing Serling's patriotism, "I Lift My Lamp" was notable in that it marked one of the only times, outside of "The Twilight Zone," that Serling created a female protagonist.

These productions seem more like vaudeville blackout sketches than professional broadcasts. Glaring overhead lights illuminated actors who stood in front of black backdrops; only a few props adorned the stage. Consequently, the emphasis fell almost entirely on the acting and writing, both of which could be cheap and amateurish. While Serling's writing was often equal to the shows' production values, he intended to convey lofty messages: patriotism and righteousness. He had fought for his country and seen men die doing the same. He believed in America and what it could be.

Early in 1953 Serling climbed the next rung of the professional television writer's ladder when he sold two scripts to "Kraft Television Theatre," with Dick Mc-Donagh as story editor. "Kraft" and "Studio One," produced by Worthington Miner, were generally considered the most influential and prestigious anthology series of television's early days, until "Playhouse 90" debuted in late 1956. The regular writers of these shows became stars in their own right, similar to the way successful Broadway playwrights are the toast of the town. Serling, Reginald Rose, Paddy Chayefsky, Robert Alan Arthur, Gore Vidal, Tad Mosel, David Shaw, David Swift, and Horton Foote, among others, were in fact referred to as television playwrights. All of them presumably had aspirations to the legitimate stage but found only television hungry for their work. Most of them were literally paid to learn how to write. "It was a wonderful opportunity to earn as you learn," Rose says.

When national magazines like *Time* and *Newsweek* reviewed particular shows, they inevitably focused on the "playwright," usually photographed looking serious at his typewriter. This distinctly contrasted to radio, whose dramatists, with the exception of Norman Corwin (and possibly Arch Oboler, who wrote the very scary series, "Lights Out"), labored in anonymity. Television aligned the television writer with the stage writers in the public's consciousness.

Not since those days has the "television playwright" been accorded such fame: "The Hill," by Rod Serling; "Marty," by Paddy Chayefsky; "Thunder on Sycamore Street," by Reginald Rose. With the stage as a model (even the movies then gave short shrift to the screenwriter, listing his credit somewhere between the prop master and the make-up artist), the author's name was attached to the title; except in rare cases, that is no longer done. Writers may be much better paid today, but few of them are rewarded with equal recognition outside of the trade.

Ironically, unlike the stage playwright, who was protected from undesirable changes by the Dramatist's Guild rules, the television writer's words were less than sacrosanct. Virtually anyone from the script editor to the actors themselves felt qualified to make changes. "The most perishable item known to man," Chayefsky once said of the teleplay. (Even today, the writer of any work for the screen often has very little to say about the words used in the final product, and he or she is barely tolerated on the set—despite the zest producers show in pursuing a good, well-written story.) As poorly as Serling and the others may have felt they were treated, television established their reputations, and the careers they enjoyed on the big screen and the stage after they stopped writing for television would not likely have been as easily built were it not for the exposure and publicity that television granted.

Even after at least a dozen and a half sales, Serling still believed himself to be an impostor of sorts, undeserving of the company he kept. Martin Manulis, then the producer of the CBS anthology series "Suspense," recalls the first script of Serling's he ever read, about "mannequins

who come alive—and it was a very interesting script."
(This is reminiscent of "The After Hours" episode of
"Twilight Zone," in which Anne Francis portrays a department store mannequin who overstays her one-month adventure as a human being.) Manulis had unusual difficulty contacting Serling. The number on the script
reached a local New York answering service. By the time
Serling received the message and phoned Manulis back, a
day or so had passed.

"I didn't even suspect that he was young," Manulis says
of his first phone conversation with Serling. "He had a
beautiful voice, an interesting voice, and he spoke well,
which I think in the beginning fooled me, made me think
he was older."

Manulis asked Serling to meet with him to discuss the
script, unaware that Serling had phoned him long distance from Cincinnati. Sure, Serling said, he would love to
meet with him—tomorrow. Manulis was surprised. Every
other writer sending in unsolicited scripts would have
dropped everything. "We were working, as you did in live
television, on the button," Manulis says.

This charade went on for some months, on other scripts
as well, until Manulis, after telling Serling that his other
writers always arrived within a few hours of a request for
a story conference, asked why Serling could never do the
same. Serling confessed rather shyly that he lived in Cincinnati and was embarrassed, believing that Cincinnati
didn't sound like the home of a professional writer.

Judged by pure numbers, 1953 was the most prolific of
Serling's career until "Twilight Zone." He had at least
sixteen scripts produced that year, most of them entirely
forgettable. That in kinescope form they avoided longev-
ity probably comforted Serling in later years, when he
would have been embarrassed by their quality. Yet these
stories continued to display a genuine sense of caring for
people and their misery—in addition to revealing much
about Serling. In "Horace Mann's Miracle," a dramatization of how the great educator had saved Serling's alma
mater, Antioch, from financial ruin, Mann tells a graduat-

ing class shortly before he dies, "Be ashamed to die until you have won some victory for humanity."

In "Man Against Pain" Serling fictionalized the story of Dr. William Morton, who claimed to have discovered ether anesthesia. Useless as a history lesson, the script nonetheless provides some interesting information about the author. When Dr. Horace Wells, Morton's colleague who first—unsuccessfully—used nitrous oxide in dental treatment, abandons his experiments, he does so not because he can no longer tolerate his patients' terrible screams but because he cannot stand the laughter from other colleagues who believe his goal to be an impossibility. "It's the laughs," he tells Morton as he walks away. Since no historical proof suggests that Wells gave up his work from anything other than exasperation, or possibly his anguish over the pain his patients suffered, this scenario would have to be a clear projection of the author's feelings about himself and his work: he, Serling, could not bear the imagined laughs, the ridicule, the derision. It seems a strange set of priorities, indicative of a man harboring deep self-doubts and a compelling need to be accepted.

"A Long Time Till Dawn" aired on "Kraft" November 11, starring a nearly unknown James Dean as a troubled, persecuted young parolee who has the soul of a poet. He dreams of taking his wife to his hometown, where life undoubtedly will be better. "We're going to get a gas station, and we're going to both work in it," he declares hopefully, ignoring his wife's infidelities and dislike for small-town life.

Throughout his career, *hometown* was Serling's favorite metaphor for the land somewhere over the rainbow—a place without problems—and he would return to it often. "In the strangely brittle, terribly sensitive make-up of a human being, there is need for a place to hang a hat, or a kind of geographical womb to crawl back into, or maybe just a place that's familiar because that's where you grew up," he explained.

The hometown image almost always found its way into

a script when Serling was personally distressed about the present. His career developed well, but he undoubtedly felt internal pressures—impelled by his drive to be the best, to be noticed, to try to match or surpass the simple brilliance of one particular show he had seen that year: "Marty," a sixty-minute drama on "Goodyear Playhouse," written by Paddy Chayesfsky, whose talent he greatly admired. The story concerned a shy New York butcher, ill at ease with anyone but his pals, who eventually meets a lonely young woman. Starring Rod Steiger, "Marty" was poignant, moving, and insightful, and it became the high-water mark of television drama.

After "Marty" the television play gained more respect, and as such it competed with every other form of legitimate entertainment. Its great advantage, obviously, was that in a single evening it could play to an audience much larger than the total number of patrons who had ever seen, say, *Death of a Salesman* on Broadway.

Serling needed to have his "voice" heard by those potential millions. He wrote a minimum of twelve hours a day, turning out scripts one after the other, and when not writing he was traveling to New York for the business of selling or socializing with those who did the buying; Gaines insisted that he sell himself as well as his work. At home, of course, he had little or no time to be a parent to his toddler daughter or a husband to Carol. Still, Carol acted as his objective voice—his personal critic and story editor. She read all first drafts, if not each successive draft, and offered opinions that he generally trusted.

"My wife is a very solid dame; great taste, great judgment, very mature," he told William F. Nolan. For a long time, that quasi-professional contact comprised the majority of the time Serling spent with his wife, and when enormous success later obviated even that, Carol must have felt that she had been pushed out of his life. The struggle to achieve had been a type of glue between them, and as the struggle ended some intimacy was necessarily lost.

The scripts Serling submitted that year followed Hemingway's advice to "write what you know." "Twenty-Four Men in a Plane," "The Quiet Village," "Nightmare at Ground Zero," "Next of Kin," "The Inn of Eagles," and "A Time for Heroes" all played against the backdrop of war. But he began to tire of writing only what he knew, these same themes of cowardice, despair, and rejection.

What else, really, did he know? Certainly not much of the broader pageantry of life. He had lived a sheltered childhood in a sort of fairy-tale town barely affected by even the Great Depression. Yes, he knew very well both the terror and camaraderie of war; and he had been a college student and an aspiring writer. But he had not traveled extensively, not for traveling's sake, collecting stories, experiences, characters—as had all of his writing heroes, the great writers. Nor had he ever lived alone and faced solitude each night, having gone from his mother's control, to the army's, and soon thereafter to Carol's. This is likely why the protagonists in most of Serling's scripts have much in common with the author: he could write, convincingly and dramatically, about only himself.

So what attracted Rod Serling, the writer, to the world of the fantastic? Bob Serling says that his brother told him "The Twilight Zone" sprang from his frequent insomniac nights, when his active imagination—fed by his lifelong love of horror films, his war experiences, and the stories of such writers as Robert Heinlein, Ray Bradbury, and H. P. Lovecraft—contrived fantastical plots that somehow seemed plausible in the predawn. Carol Serling says that her husband "wanted to believe" in the unseen, but had no direct experiences himself.

Later, when he tired of battling network censors, Serling knew he could convey his feelings about racism without the censor's objections by having Martians mistreated on Venus—a concept he had seen both Heinlein and Bradbury employ. (Referring to "The Arena," a 1956 "Studio One" story about the United States Senate that the censors had butchered to avoid the appearance of political favoritism, he wrote, "In retrospect, I probably would have had a much more adult play had I made it science fiction, put it in the year 2057, and peopled the Senate with robots. This would probably have been more reasonable and no less dramatic." Even in Serling's imaginative universes, the stories were about people, not places, and bad guys always got their comeuppance in the end.) But Serling had created the "Twilight Zone" concept long before he ever had the pleasure of grappling with the networks' archaic sensibilities.

In the late summer of 1954, Florence Britton, the "Studio One" story editor, sent him a polite rejection letter: "NO NO NO NO NO NO NO NO NO NO. Never. My boys would have apoplexy. God knows what they want. But they certainly don't want that. I can see why it would intrigue you. It would intrigue me, too. But then I am not paying for this program. Fantasy in any form is out. And irony." Had those last two sentences really been true, Serling would have been left without a career.

It was a measure of his stature that Britton closed her letter, "We miss you and need you on the program. Don't sulk. Please come back with something else."

With stature came changes. Serling had been so involved in his career that he had let his acute social conscience go largely unspoken. He dared not risk the wrath of the House un-American Activities Committee or Senator Joseph McCarthy. While the entertainment industry was being ransacked in a witch-hunt for Communists— people lost their jobs, were blacklisted, or went to jail— Serling remained quiet. He had that luxury. As a generally unknown television writer creating innocuous television, no one had thought to ask him, "Have you now or have you ever been . . . ?"

But by the spring of 1954, with the country moving perceptibly away from the hysteria and McCarthy's madness, Serling allowed himself a public voice. In a March 21 letter to the *Cincinnati Enquirer*, he wrote to refute columnist Forrest Davis's defense of McCarthy's tactics:

"[Davis] gag[s] at the spectacle of shooting buckshot into a mob of a hundred innocents, and then blow[s] a triumphant bugle because a guilty one was among those knocked off."

It seems a small issue in retrospect, but Serling showed courage in publishing the letter. Although army lawyer Joseph Welch had recently put McCarthy in his place by issuing the famous quote, "Have you no decency, sir? At long last have you left no sense of decency?" and Edward R. Murrow, on his program "Person-to-Person," had allowed the Wisconsin senator's phoniness and evil to be exposed through his own words, those in the entertainment business still feared the blacklist. Significantly, Serling wrote that he shared with McCarthy and his supporters a "fear of Communist infiltrations both external and internal," a sentiment displayed in "I Lift My Lamp," when he calls communism worse than chaos. The Senator's tactics, not his quest, bothered Serling.

That Serling hadn't voiced his opinion beforehand likely reflected his business sense—the potential loss of livelihood; now he felt more comfortable. In the event he had been called to testify before the House un-American Activities Committee, he would either have had to name names he probably didn't have or defend himself against invective by pointing to his army record and such professional patriotism as "I Lift My Lamp." But to be forced to testify or take the Fifth Amendment would have made him either a stool pigeon or destroyed his career.

"If he'd tried, if he'd stuck his neck out as a big liberal, he might have had fewer assignments," conjectures William Dozier, the CBS programming executive who eventually said yes to "Twilight Zone" and was later the executive producer of Serling's "The Loner." "I don't think he'd let [speaking out against McCarthy] get in the way of his money-making machine."

The letter apparently represented the beginning—his coming out, as it were—of an unofficial career as an outspoken social critic, and from that point on his scripts became bolder and more courageous, even when the censors emasculated them. His tireless vendettas in the 1960s against any and all social evils he saw were conducted without fear of backlash or blacklisting, but by then, as Dozier says, "he was a little richer."

The Serlings spent the summer at the lake house and then moved to Westport, Connecticut, in the fall. They bought a house, on an acre of land, that cost 50 percent more than the twenty-three thousand dollars for which they had sold their Cincinnati home—bought when the work had come steadily. Doubts, insecurities, trepidations, and all, Serling could no longer abide the too-frequent traveling—and lost days that could have been spent working on new material. The area was beautiful, and living just across the river from New York meant he could attend conferences, rehearsals, and shootings and still be home on the late-night train. The move had not been made lightly or quickly. Blanche Gaines had pleaded constantly with the Serlings to move, if not to New York, at least in close proximity to the city, where, she claimed, she would better be able to serve his career needs.

It was in the new house that he completed the teleplay which would change his life.

The night the show aired the Serlings had gone out to dinner and a movie. They told the babysitter not to expect any calls, as they had only recently moved to town and had few friends. Although Serling was personally pleased with the script, he had no reason to believe this particular production would be received with any more ceremony than his thirty-plus previously produced scripts—that is, very little. He said, in fact, that his story of six months before, "The Strike," a war drama in which an officer must order an air strike in an area where he knows one of his own platoons is situated, "had more universality and more appeal."

Unlike Chayefsky's and Vidal's work, none of Serling's scripts had ever been reviewed in the *New York Times*, which then reviewed live television drama the way it reviewed stage dramas. Without ratings per se to tell the networks or creators how many people watched their programs, the focus of attention fell on the critical review, which usually came out in the following morning's paper. In modern television virtually the only factor guaranteeing a writer or producer success is ratings, but in the mid-1950s, excellent reviews built careers. Every time a show aired, it was opening night.

Richard Kiley, one of the show's stars, recalls an awareness among the actors in this production that something out of the ordinary was being created. "It was," he says, "a happy confluence of circumstances: script, casting, direction. I really felt it was a sensational script. I think most of the actors did."

Fielder Cook, the producer and director, had assembled the cast and crew shortly after the final dress rehearsal and announced gleefully, "This is the best goddamned show I've ever seen in my life."

Yet Kraft had not extravagantly publicized the show, which suggests that no one at the agency understood its out-of-the-ordinary greatness. In light of the full production treatment that the show received—making it by far the most elaborate television production to date—it is difficult to understand the company's reticence.

"Tonight," said the announcer, "we present the four hundred sixty-seventh play of this Wednesday evening series: 'Patterns,' by Rod Serling."

On January 12, 1955, the "Kraft Television Theatre" presented "Patterns." "One minute after the show went off the air my phone started to ring. It has been ringing ever since," Serling noted six years later.

Calls came from everywhere, to both Serling and NBC, expressing admiration. Florence Britton had been forced to reject the script in its original form, when Serling called it "The Pattern." Now she wrote that the show was "unquestionably one of the finest things I've ever seen on television. We all thought so. . . . I certainly hope that shows our boys what they missed. But I doubt it." More satisfying, his old mentor, Dick McDonagh, wrote that the show had been "one of the best television plays of all time."

Considering the immediate reaction, Serling must have been disappointed the next morning not to see a review of the show. Jack Gould, the *Times*'s noted television drama critic, did not even review "Patterns" until five days later, an indication he had not seen the show as it aired live but rather saw a kinescope later, when vocal audience reaction merited his viewing.

But what he lacked in timeliness he more than made up for in effusiveness. Serling read the column over and over and over again, then had Carol read it to him another few times, just to make sure. He had finally been praised by the venerable *New York Times*.

"Nothing in months has excited the television industry as much as 'Patterns,' an original play by Rod Serling," Gould wrote. "The enthusiasm is justified. In writing, acting and direction, 'Patterns' will stand as one of the high points in the TV medium's evolution."

A month later Robert Lewis Shayon wrote in *The Saturday Review of Literature*: "In the years I have been viewing television, I do not recall being so engaged by a drama, nor so stimulated to challenge the haunting conclusions of an hour's entertainment."

Never before had Serling experienced such fawning admiration. What television writer had?

"Patterns," Serling's seventy-second script, he claimed (he actually counted!), depicted a world of which he had no direct knowledge: the corporation. Ramsey (Everett Sloane), the president of his own firm, feels that Ramsey and Company must either continue to grow larger or fall behind its competitors. (Curiously, in the show itself the building directory lists the company as *Ramsie* yet all other references to it, including the published version, say *Ramsey*.) Andy Sloane (Ed Begley), Ramsey's third in command, is not nearly so ruthless as his boss and is in fact concerned about the toll of major company decisions on human lives, so Ramsey decides he must be replaced—but not cleanly, swiftly, humanely. He brings in an ambitious young man, Fred Staples (Richard Kiley), to replace him and sets about trying to force Sloane out of the company by involving him in a series of circumstances that will eventually, Ramsey knows, force Sloane to resign. "On our level, you don't get fired. You resign," Sloane notes. It is a classic confrontation of good against evil, with Staples, as anguished about the happenings as he is desirous of replacing Andy, representing the clashing of the two opposing forces.

What separated "Patterns" from being merely good, what elevated it to the level of sublime television for the times, was its climax. After Sloane too conveniently suffers a heart attack, and the story seems to have fallen into cliché—as well as appearing to skirt, *deus ex machina*, resolution of the central theme—it suddenly becomes fascinating.

Staples decides he will resign rather than appear to condone Ramsey's single-minded passion for success; whether or not humanity is betrayed remains, to Ramsey, entirely irrelevant. "You're a freak," Staples yells at him. (In the original text, Serling has Staples saying, "You're a washout," but Kiley, wonderfully in character, spontaneously yelled "freak" instead; it is a much more effective word in context.) "You're a genius, a production, organizational marvel with no compassion for human weakness."

But Ramsey, in a remarkable counterattack, compels Staples to stay by in essence defying his reasoning. He makes his own tactics seem moral and justifies them by explaining the manifest destiny of business. "Then what do you do [after you resign]?" he asks Staples. "You go work for a nickel-and-dime outfit run by 'nice people' who won't challenge you, beat your head in and make your talent reach a height you never dreamed of. A company where you won't have to fight for anything, because you're the best and there's no competition. Where everything is handed to you and there's nothing important to fight for."

More remarkably, Staples chooses to stay. Having faced his apocalypse by unleashing his fury on Ramsey—implicitly offering his resignation—he no longer fears Ramsey; he has nothing to lose. In fact, knowing that Ramsey wants him to remain—"I need help on my level, and you're the only one good person to function there," Ramsey tells him—Staples is free to confront the forces in himself that caused him to suffer the previous weeks while "a good man," Andy Sloane, was systematically destroyed to make room for him. Yes, goddammit, Staples wants these things, he craves what success and power provide. He knows that his wife is turned on by the sight of her powerful husband and is willing to suffer lonely nights to know that he stands at the top. It was she, in their own den, who manipulated the situation to his advantage (at a party she hosted, she brought Ramsey into the den and read the excellent report that her husband and Sloane had worked on together—but she led Ramsey to believe that her husband was the sole author); and no, Staples did nothing to correct the misunderstanding that has catapulted him to the top faster than his fantasies ever contrived.

Ramsey has known Staples's deep, dark secret even before Staples realizes it—in Ramsey's office—and tells him exactly what Staples wants to hear. Having confronted what he had always believed to be the worst in himself, Staples can now rationalize that it was not the worst at all and may in fact be the best. He no longer directs his anger at Ramsey but at himself, and it no longer seems a punishing anger but a liberating one. It may even possibly now be directed at Sloane, for his weakness. Alas, Staples is just like Ramsey. And, God help him, he loves it.

Ramsey wonders aloud at one point how the concepts of honesty and profit ever became incompatible in the public perception. Knowing Serling's aversion to Communism and his appreciation for George F. Johnson's paternal benevolence, it appears that much in Ramsey is derived directly from Serling's own philosophy. (The Ramsey character, Serling claimed, was based on an officer under whom he had served during the war.) And this is largely what makes "Patterns" so successful. Instead of stereotyping Ramsey as the greedy, evil capitalist, he paints him as ambiguously moral: his business presumably generates volume in the millions of dollars, and he puts thousands of people to work. At one point he angrily explains to Sloane, who fears that a temporary plant closing will devastate the surrounding community, that the money the company saves will be reinvested in the plant, allowing Ramsey and Company to compete more favorably in the marketplace, resulting in greater sales, which will in turn employ twice the number of workers.

In the end, the demarcation between good and evil has been all but obfuscated. "Patterns" can be considered a Darwinian study of the corporate jungle—like any jungle, one that obeys Nature's law. Deeming big business inherently ruthless, Richard Kiley observes, "is like saying the wolf is the enemy of the forest. Well, we killed off all the big bad wolves, and now we're inundated with the darling deer, who are starving to death." Serling admitted that the piece was not meant as an indictment of corporate America or of greed.

While there may have been much of Serling in Ramsey, he seems to have identified more directly with Staples—a young man tempted by the spoils of success. Like Serling, Staples hails from Cincinnati and has just rented a house in Westport. On his first day at Ramsey and Company his wife adjusts his new tie and tells him there is "not a trace of Cincinnati" in the way he looks. Staples's struggle to reconcile his conflicting generosity and selfishness, morality and ambition was exactly Serling's struggle—if not before, then certainly after the reaction to "Patterns," and for the rest of his life.

Serling said:

Patterns [is about] the price tag that hangs on success. If it professes actually to have a message, it is simply that every human being has a minimum set of ethics from which he operates. This minimum set of ethics often injects itself into a man's own journey upward against competition. When he refuses to compromise these ethics, his career must suffer; when he does compromise them, his conscience does the suffering.

"Patterns" was Serling's *Death of a Salesman*, and established a benchmark of the author's skill. ("We all thought he was going to be another Arthur Miller," Jackie Cooper reflects.) Serling's drama seems derived—almost certainly unintentionally—from the particularly heartbreaking scene in Miller's play when Willy Loman is fired from the company after more than thirty years, by the president, the thirty-five-year-old son of the founder. (In "Patterns," Ramsey is the son of the company's founder, and Sloane, like Willy Loman, had been hired and enjoyed his greatest success under the company's founder.) Useless now, he is discarded.

Before "Patterns" Serling had been a writer with talent, not necessarily an agenda. Nor had he established a reputation. He had been a writer of small stories simply trying to make a living. The one "big" story that he wanted to produce, about American POWs in the Korean War, had been rejected time and again. Now "Patterns" had suddenly thrust him into the limelight and made him a star of the young medium, one of its voices.

But because of some poor decisions, he would find maintaining that reputation more difficult than making it.

Within two weeks after the original broadcast of "Patterns" (four weeks after the initial airing, the show, in its entirety and with most of the same cast, was shown live again, the first time an encore performance had ever been granted; this time, with great fanfare), Serling received "twenty-three bids to write teleplays, several screenplay offers [he said yes, immediately, to two of them, including the adaptation of "Patterns"], fourteen requests for inter-

views [almost all of which he granted], two luncheon
invitations from Broadway producers, and two bids from
book publishers [E. P. Dutton asked him to write an original novel, while Harcourt Brace wanted him to novelize
"Patterns"]." What he often did not get were calls and
letters from old friends, who feared these gestures would
have been misinterpreted as a plea to climb aboard the
gravy train.

Later in the month, Serling signed with a second talent
agency, H. N. Swanson, just to handle the film offers that
continued to pour in. The week that "Patterns" rehearsed
its encore performance, Serling met in Hollywood with
independent producer Michael Myerberg to negotiate
rights for the big screen version. While there, he also
signed a contract with Twentieth Century–Fox for thirty-
five thousand dollars—an unheard-of figure at the time—
to adapt a book about convict soldiers, *The Day the
Century Ended*; the movie would be called *Between
Heaven and Hell*.

Yes, he had arrived. He was accepted. He was adored,
idolized, quoted, solicited. And he wanted more and more
and more of it. He had to have it now. The acclaim, the
recognition, the acceptance became like drugs, and he
grew rapidly addicted.

In that unimaginable headiness, Serling grabbed enough
rope to hang himself—and nearly did. Anxious to bask in
a continual glow of praise, he said yes to so many projects
that none received the time or attention each deserved.
Fearful that the flow of offers would suddenly dry up, he
could not say no. In fact, he never learned. While his
primary motivation remained to create art, he refused to
devote the time to craft each piece carefully. The money—
the next waiting offer—beckoned.

The Theatre Guild now willingly optioned "The Rack,"
after having turned it down months before. Serling, still
feeling the insidious effects of World War II, was fascinated by newspaper stories detailing the two hundred–some cases of American soldiers in the Korean War

breaking under torture and confessing to lies that their Chinese captors had invented. The captors then used these "confessions" for their propaganda, much as hostages today are shown on homemade videotapes renouncing their governments and sympathizing with their kidnappers' causes.

The story concerns Captain Edward Hall, who had been broken by the North Koreans. After the war he admits having signed surrender leaflets and propagandizing his fellow prisoners. His own attorney reasons that Hall has already paid his penalty, both by the physical punishment and the lingering guilt.

For his research, Serling spent time at the Pentagon (he refused to do this until the Theatre Guild commissioned him), talking to the officers in charge of "repatriating" POWs. He came away with a profound respect for the army's justice system and the men responsible for it. But he did not resolve his own feelings about guilt or innocence, despite the verdicts in the classified cases he had been offered to study. His ability to see both sides, coupled with his sympathy for these men, gave him a play populated by compelling characters—but no resolution, nor a coherent point of view. It was an admirable but misguided effort; compacting the story into sixty minutes only trivialized the complex subject.

"The Rack," which aired on the "U.S. Steel Hour" April 12, was ultimately more important for its insights into Serling. His personal involvement surfaces first through the character of the prosecuting officer, a survivor of the Bataan Death March, so-called because it was from there the United States–Filipino forces withdrew in early 1942. When they were later captured, the Japanese forced them into a long, cruel march to a prison camp near Cabanatuan, and en route many thousands died. "If you find Captain Hall innocent, three-thousand brave men who did not break are guilty of stupidity," the prosecutor argues.

The most compelling moment of the trial comes when the chaplain tells Hall what the chaplain in Luzon may have told Serling: "In the eyes of men you are guilty of weakness and must stand alone without honor. In the eyes of God, your weakness is the weakness of the race of men. And this guilt that shows itself in wars and prison camps and brutality, you can share with all of us." Serling, for one, never could.

Hall is found guilty, a reflection of Serling's complex feelings about his own war experiences.

While generally well received, the reviews hardly waxed enthusiastic, as they had uniformly for "Patterns." He had not written it "with the expert conciseness that distinguished 'Patterns,'" wrote *New York Times* reviewer J. P. Shanley.

Executives at MGM disliked the production qualities of "The Rack" but were intrigued by the subject, which they felt could come alive in Technicolor. Two days after the broadcast the studio optioned the screen rights, assigning the project to producer Arthur Loew, Jr. Meanwhile, Serling worked on the screenplays of both "Between Heaven and Hell" and "Patterns," as well as wrote the first chapters of the novelization of "Patterns" for Harcourt Brace. He worked as though in a frenzy, eager to finish each project in order to move on to the next. His discipline was remarkable, his patience nonexistent, his hunger for more and more relentless.

By June Serling had retained the services of a New York lawyer; hired an accountant to advise him on how to cope with the 80 percent tax bracket; hired a secretary, Kate Ford, who transcribed his Dictaphone belts onto which he now dictated his scripts, allowing him to give up the two manual typewriters that had absorbed the abuse of his punchlike typing; and bought a more expensive house, in the basement of which he built a pine-paneled office.

"Success is not always easy to cope with," Serling commented. "You wander, blinking, through the crazy, pink, whipped-cream world that it opens up, where everything's mink and mobile dollar signs—and life takes on a glittering, dreamlike quality."

What else do you have, television producers asked him?

Following what must have seemed to him like an aeon of anonymity, even their phony fawning—that they'd always known how talented he was—satisfied and gratified him.

"I suddenly found that I could sell practically everything I had in the trunk, and I had twenty of my scripts telecast that season," he remarked. Most of these scripts had been turned down, some of them five and six times, by the very producers who now hungered for them; he received two thousand and three thousand dollars for scripts that had been rejected at five hundred. "I still blush when I think of some of the bombs I unloaded that year, but I was the hungry kid left all alone in the candy store. Man, I just *grabbed*."

He grabbed eighty-three thousand dollars in 1955, much of it for work that should never have been taken from his trunk. In one week in November, three shows aired, each well below the standard set by "Patterns." "Incident in an Alley," the first of the three, had been written the previous year. He based it on a real-life incident in which a policeman shot and killed a young boy after the boy refused to obey his order to halt. Rather than confine himself to the fundamental story, Serling diluted the dramatic potential by making the policeman the son of a street cop who'd been gunned down, creating a jumbled mishmash of conflict without sufficient focus; the story was roundly panned. Before the show aired, he entered into a coproduction deal with Michael Myerberg again for a big screen version of "Incident," to be called *Line of Duty*. In his spare moments he spit out the screenplay version.

"Strength of Steel," which aired on "Star Tonight" the evening of June 16, concerned a young air force wife who, after her husband flies off on temporary assignment in Alaska, moves to Pittsburgh to live with her father-in-law, an old-country immigrant who has made a fortune in the steel industry. A bitter and crude man, he treats her poorly, even after they discover the husband/son is long overdue from a training flight. Predictably, when the two hear he has been killed, she informs her father-in-law that she is pregnant, then tells him off, then collapses into his arms, and they are bound forever to each other. "Anne Edwards, as the girl, and Frederic Tozere, portraying the father-in-law, were the principal players. They should be dealt with leniently. Mr. Serling is the real culprit in this case," wrote *New York Times* reviewer J. P. Shanley. "Rod Serling's Story of an Air Force Wife Is Let-Down After His Previous Hits" was the sub-headline on the review.

"To Wake at Midnight," on "Climax" seven days later, relied on a technique that would have been better reserved for "Twilight Zone." Wendell Corey portrayed a Wehrmacht lieutenant who comes to consciousness eleven years after suffering a head wound during the war. A prisoner held by the English, he escapes and returns to Germany to find that his father, Akim Tamiroff, has not renounced his Nazi past and is in fact indoctrinating his own son, to whom he is a stranger, into the Führer's ways. "The pieces of the plot were put together neatly, but the assembled product had no real style," said Shanley in the *Times*.

The fame and reputation he had established with "Patterns" and, to a much lesser degree, "The Rack" had become a double-edged sword. Sure, the money was remarkable, but with it came a set of expectations—what he expected of himself and what others expected of him. Neither side was satisfied. "So much of what I put on after ["Patterns"] was dictated by economic considerations, too. I had to live," he commented. Not so parenthetically, his second daughter, Nan, had just been born, but Serling could barely pull himself away from his self-imposed murderous schedule to help nurture her.

"I took assignments right and left, because they were waiting for me in a way they never had been, and also because I'm the kind of guy who depends on impetus, or I'll swear my brain's going to atrophy," he noted.

If this taking, grabbing, and hoarding of assignments had been confined to just this heady period after his initial success, it could be easily dismissed. But Serling's need for acceptance drove him to make such similarly poor choices the rest of his life. He viewed selling a script as an acceptance of him personally—an expression of affection. Likewise, rejections sent him into a downward spiral of self-questioning and doubt.

"I've seen him read, let's say, twenty-five rave reviews," Bob Serling recalls. "But if the twenty-sixth was a pan, Rod would mope, worry, be depressed."

Each time one of Serling's plays aired, he agonized, waiting for the reaction. And each time the reaction came back negative his insecurity grew. "I felt I was not a good writer," he admitted. But because he was both so prolific and had sold a large backlog of scripts after "Patterns," more of his work appeared on television in 1955 and 1956 than that of any other writer; consequently, he had more garbage broadcast than any other writer.

Buddy Adler, the Fox production chief who had assigned *Between Heaven and Hell* to Serling, had been patient with him, had reassured him that as talented as he was, he would have much to learn. In April Adler told H. N. Swanson, Serling's film agent, "If your boy comes through for me, I'll make him an offer on an assignment he chooses, to be done when he likes, and I'll match whatever the town will pay him and possibly give him a piece of my own percentage."

But Serling failed the test, turning in a pathetically poor draft that ran almost five hundred pointless pages. "I didn't know what I was doing," he admitted to William F. Nolan. When Adler saw his rambling work, he waved it away and told David Brown, the story editor, "Don't send us any more of your New York television writers."

While UA was not unhappy with *Patterns*, executives noted that Serling showed little understanding of the differences between television and the cinema. Simply adding exterior shots of the Ramsey and Company build-

ing or street scenes with taxis whizzing by did not necessarily justify the translation. Nonetheless, the studio
went ahead with its plans and released the film in the
fall—to nearly empty movie houses.

Meanwhile, MGM decided that his first drafts of the
screen version of "The Rack" lacked a cinematic quality
and turned over the project (which would later star Paul
Newman) to another writer, Stewart Stern (purported to
be a relative of producer Arthur Lowe). Harcourt Brace
viewed the first chapter of his "Patterns" novelization and,
as quickly as they had made him an offer, withdrew their
interest. At the same time the company decided not to
publish a collection of his teleplays.

Myerberg, Serling's partner in the screen development of
"Line of Duty," suggested that he "begin to restrict his
output and settle down to the intensive development of a
few properties each year," rather than sign to do so many
projects that none of them could be done carefully. But
Serling dismissed that notion and eventually dismissed
Myerberg, blaming him for their failure to make a firm
deal on the film. Instead, he signed a new contract with
MGM, which would pay him thirty-five thousand dollars
per script. Ensconced for three months in an office at the
studio in Culver City, he immediately set to work adapting a book, *The Red Car*, into *52 Miles to Terror*.

While Serling might have been capable of writing good
television very quickly, he never stopped to relearn the
screenplay format—to give it the time and care it takes to
develop a worthwhile film. "It's an indolent, quite-relaxing
writing form which demands little in the way of either
concentration or undue brain searching," he wrote to
Nolan Miller from his MGM office, indicating his own
ignorance and an arrogance born of impatience.

When he suggested that Serling cut back, Michael
Myerberg did not understand that the writer had begun to
wonder whether he would ever again have another success. Despite an astonishing output, he had not heard the
sweet music of applause since January. Rather than devote

himself completely to a few projects, taking his time to construct carefully, he aimed for quantity: while the getting was still good—before they all found him out—he planned to grab as much as he could.

He asked himself whether "Patterns"—the project that had enabled all of this—had in fact been a fluke. It was a good question. His original script had been significantly different from the final draft, which owed much of its intrigue to Arthur Singer, the script editor, and Fielder Cook, the producer and director. Serling originally placed the emphasis on Staples's wife as the motivating force controlling her husband, not the almost Greek chorus that she represented in the produced draft. Further, the business atmosphere Serling described in his script lacked "authenticity"—not surprising since Serling had never worked for a large corporation and had researched business life in the library—and it was left to Cook to authenticate the story by, in essence, simulating the J. Walter Thompson environment. Finally, the climactic confrontation between Ramsey and Staples that elevated the story had lacked *cojones* (Serling had wanted to have Staples resign) until Arthur Singer stepped in to punch it up.

Serling fought all of these changes, but late in 1954 he lacked the track record to challenge them too decisively. He could either give in or have the script discarded by Kraft. Later, after the program made him a star, he had the bravery and courtesy to express publicly both his mistake and debt. Nonetheless, he was the one who took the solo bow in the spotlight.

In Serling's mind, that bow did not belong completely to him; maybe not even legitimately to him. Maybe he really was not a good writer. Maybe none of this was real. Maybe this success had been only an illusion, a cruelly fleeting taste of caviar and champagne that would be snatched away later—and having tasted it, its absence would be far worse than never tasting it at all. He began to believe he was only as good as his next script and that he had better come up with a good one soon.

In September he signed a contract with CBS (beginning an association that would last ten years) similar to the one Reginald Rose had signed the year before, making him the first television writer contracted exclusively to a network. By 1955 the networks had seen that only a relatively few writers, out of the thousands that aspired, could turn out acceptable scripts, and each network wanted to hoard the riches. The first year of the three-year contract guaranteed Serling fifteen thousand dollars, rising to eighteen thousand the second year, and twenty thousand the third. In exchange for that piece of security, he had to provide a maximum of twelve ideas, out of which he would produce nine full outlines and finally six full scripts. He would also be paid fifteen hundred dollars for each adaptation and offer CBS first crack at any series ideas. Any of his work that CBS declined could be peddled to either of the other two networks. For Serling it was the kind of temporary financial security he needed in order to get back on track—to polish his image—without having to worry about eating.

Serling had met Reg Rose in the "Studio One" offices about a year before, when Serling's "The Strike" was in preproduction. Both men were favorites of the show's first producer, Worthington Miner, so when Miner had an original idea for an anthology series whose shows would be connected thematically, he called Rose and Serling and pitched them on the idea of collaborating on the pilot. Both agreed, and they flew out to California and took a huge, octagonal-shaped double room together at the Bel-Air Hotel.

For three days Serling, Rose, and Miner sat around the pool, which they had almost to themselves, refined the concept, and came up with the first thirty-nine ideas (a series shot thirty-nine episodes, with thirteen repeats run during the summer). Despite being late in the fall, the weather was hot and miserable, and every few minutes they jumped into the pool to cool off.

"This is really very strange," Rose said on the first day,

with the work going badly. "Here we are, sitting around this pool, the three of us, working on an idea, and we're three men with the most improbable names in the world: Worthington, Rodman, and Reginald. Whatever happened to Jack, Craig, and Charlie?" All three broke up laughing, which seemed to improve both the mood and the quality of their work.

The next morning Serling and Rose awakened to room service wheeling in their breakfast. Just as the waiter appeared, Rose happened to glance up at the cathedral ceiling, whose unusual octagonal design rose to a sharp point at the apex. A huge spider had taken up residence above them, and Rose pointed it out to Serling.

"Jesus," said Serling, "a spider." He grabbed a knife from the cart and flung it at the spider, mashing him flat on the first try. Rose stared speechlessly at Serling, who nonchalantly picked up the knife and buttered his toast.

They intended each thirty-minute episode of "The Challenge" to tackle a controversial issue and present it from as objective a viewpoint as possible while explaining its ramifications in human terms—as it might affect a particular individual. The pilot, which Serling and Rose concocted, concerned an extremely controversial topic of the day: loyalty oaths—whether, in the post-McCarthy era, companies ought to be able to demand that their employees swear an oath of allegiance to America. The oaths raised serious Constitutional and ethical questions.

Neither writer had ever before worked with a collaborator, and neither wanted to start now. They agreed, after working out the story's key elements, that Serling would write the first act and Rose the second; then they would exchange acts and each rewrite the other's work, with the synthesis emerging as the final product. "I was very fast, a very fast writer," Rose recollects. "I wrote the 'Studio One' version of 'Twelve Angry Men' in five days. Rod could have written it in two." In point of fact, Serling never rewrote Rose's second act, and Rose rewrote both. The end product—which starred Jack Warden as a none-too-bright bus driver who refuses to take the loyalty oath his company demands and ultimately emerges as a hero to his young son—was shot, but CBS deemed the series too controversial and declined.

Even if the series had sold, Serling would have gracefully bowed out for greener pastures. At the time he had no interest in weekly television and participated only because Miner asked him—precisely the reason Serling always participated in a project. He would remember the time spent with Rose for a much more practical reason.

Over drinks one afternoon the two men began talking about their agents. Serling mentioned that the charges for long-distance phone calls Gaines made on his behalf seemed to pile up quickly, as did costs for mimeographing and other overhead expenses. "What do you mean?" Rose said, exclaiming that agents customarily provide those services gratis.

Serling looked as though he'd been kicked, and asked the name of Rose's agents. Rose wrote down Ashley-Steiner, and the firm's Fifth Avenue address. Serling called on Ted Ashley and Ira Steiner, as he did Sam Weissbord at William Morris. Both agencies wanted him and wooed him. Although still under contract to Blanche Gaines, Serling signed with Ashley-Steiner on the condition that, until his agreement with her expired in 1957, Gaines would still represent him solely on television projects; on films, the two agents would split the commission evenly. He then fired H. N. Swanson and wrote Weissbord a pleasant note explaining that he looked forward to working with him some day, but now he needed the intimacy of a smaller agency.

By the end of the year Serling desperately needed a success. He even sought psychiatric assistance—not so much for a drought of creativity as for the burden of having to live up to a reputation that he felt may not have been deserved. He knew only a substantial hit in the near future could save him from again being thought of as an ordinary hack writer who had accidentally constructed a single remarkable script.

Evidently, this was not an uncommon occupational hazard. "I can tell exactly what stage of their analysis they're in by the scripts they submit," "Studio One" story editor Florence Britton noted.

"The Strike" had been a favorite of Serling's, and he thought it would benefit from enlargement for the big screen. One night at MGM he showed a kinescope to Harry Essex, a staff writer, and John Champion, a writer/producer. The three men had met the year before, when Serling wrote *52 Miles to Terror* at MGM. A secretary walking past his open door noticed the pot of coffee that perpetually occupied a spot on his desk. She asked to borrow some sugar for the coffee klatch Champion and Essex held daily.

"This sugar comes to you courtesy of New York television," he wrote on a note attached to the plate of cubes.

"Harry and I just cracked up at this," Champion recalls. The following day they repaid his loan: one cube, bearing a skull and crossbones, accompanied by a note: "TV writer—go home." Thus began a long friendship between Serling and Champion.

Champion and Essex loved the kinescope and played it for studio head Dore Schary in the hope of getting MGM to finance their production. Schary didn't share their excitement. Undeterred, they pooled their own resources and paid Serling seventy-five hundred dollars for the rights to codevelop the script with him.

In the meantime Serling needed an immediate fix, something to bring him the acclaim he sorely missed. It would have to be a big story, with a powerful message. But "The Arena," a "Studio One" drama about the U.S. Senate, suffered a painful castration when the sponsors would not permit his senators to speak of anything that might be construed as advocating a point of view to either the right or the left. The result was an incoherent mishmash, a cryptographic jumble of sentences that unintentionally made a mockery of political speech making.

Next came "Noon on Doomsday," written about a true-life event that had particularly stunned and outraged Serling the year before. Emmett Till, a fourteen-year-old black boy from Chicago visiting Mississippi, had made the mistake of whistling innocently at a white woman. Two local rednecks, provoked by "this nigger's" insolence, kidnapped and killed him and were later acquitted of the crimes by an all-white jury. Lawrence Langner, the president and founder of the Theatre Guild, which produced for "U.S. Steel," loved the idea of dramatizing the events but told Serling that the conflict could not be depicted as black against white.

In the first draft Serling made the victim an elderly Jewish pawnbroker who "dies at the hands of a neurotic malcontent who is in turn tried and released by his own neighbors," he said. "The story of a town protecting its own on a 'he's a bastard, but he's our bastard' kind of basis. Thus, the town itself was the real killer." His message, he thought, had been couched well enough to appease, while allowing a large minority of the viewing audience to comprehend the message and ramifications of the real tragedy: the need of human beings to find a scapegoat for their own deficiencies.

New York entertainment reporters, alerted by press releases from the networks and sponsors, regularly carried small stories about television scripts in rehearsal, and when otherwise innocent stories about "the story of the Till case" drifted to the South, the local citizenry, particularly the White Citizens Councils, became outraged. U.S. Steel, faced with a Southern boycott (Serling asked whether buildings would now be built with aluminum; it was explained that the company feared the industrial clients, including the automobile industry), forced Serling to make the pawnbroker "an unidentifiable foreigner" and the murderer "a decent kid momentarily gone wrong." They even removed a Coca-Cola sign from the set of a diner, deeming it to have a too-Southern connotation. The word *lynch* had to be omitted, also because of its implications, the letter *g* was added to all participles and gerunds, and the setting was moved to a small, identifiably New England town—precisely to show that this was not the South.

Serling later joked that the agency would have chosen the North Pole as the site of the show were it not for the problem of the resident Eskimos—another minority.

Predictably, the end result, on April 25, was horrendously absurd—and rightfully panned. (A coincidence, perhaps, but "Doomsday" became the last teleplay Serling wrote for "U.S. Steel Hour," which had aired both "The Rack" and "Incident in an Alley.")

Yet the disappointment had been mitigated by the Emmy Serling clutched in his hand. Five weeks before, on St. Patrick's Day night, he won the award for best teleplay of 1955, "Patterns."

Ed Sullivan, then the president of the National Academy of Television Arts and Sciences (a New Yorker, he was the Academy's first national president, having instigated the coalition of East Coast and West Coast chapters after jealously noting that the Emmys had been presented from Hollywood for the first eight years of their existence), intended to present Serling with the bronze statuette, but there had been a mix-up. When Serling took his bows, he realized he was alone; Sullivan had gone backstage. "So there I stood, lonelier than I shall ever again be the rest of my life," he recalled. Finally, as both the laughter and his embarrassment swelled, a representative from Price-Waterhouse strode out and presented Serling with his Emmy by shoving it into his stomach as though it were his army-issue fatigues on the first day of boot camp.

Presentation points aside, winning the Emmy was the most exuberant professional moment of his career—the greatest validation in a long series. This one came from his peers. Actress Sally Field's remarks, three decades later, on winning her second Oscar might also have been appropriate to Serling and may even have crossed his mind: "You like me. You really like me."

The timing of the Emmy Awards, telecast nationally for the first time (although, much to his consternation, the television audience had signed off by the time his award was presented; further proof, he noted, of the low esteem in which writers were held), could not have been better for Serling. A full fourteen months after his great success, the win generated further publicity, reminded producers and the public of his potential, and reinvigorated his reputation.

Serling received a call from Martin Manulis, recently assigned by CBS to produce its new fall anthology series, "Playhouse 90," which the network intended from the outset to be the preeminent show of its kind. Assembling the creative talent for a weekly ninety-minute live dramatic show was an awesome task—possibly one reason it had never been attempted. Rumors circulated that "90" was the brainchild of CBS chairman William Paley, who wanted a series that would grant him bragging rights among his elite, educated circle of friends; whether it made money was beside the point—as long as it didn't lose *too* much. (The show evidently had been conceived by vice president Hubbell Robinson.) Ironically, "Playhouse 90" began at a time when anthology series seemed to be dying quickly.

Six months ahead of the debut, Manulis wanted to collect excellent scripts. Between his producing chores on "Suspense" and then "Climax," Manulis had used four of Serling's scripts and knew the writer well. He offered him an adaptation of a novel, *Forbidden Area*, by Pat Frank, and asked if he had any other stories that might benefit by the ninety-minute format.

This, Serling thought, was a gift from the heavens—an astonishing opportunity to showcase his talent and climb back to the top of the heap. Like all the writers eventually involved with "Playhouse 90," Serling thrilled to the prospect of developing full-length scripts—seventy-two minutes' worth with commercials, a third longer than they had been used to. But what did he have to offer?

Men chasing dreams in sports—has-beens, never-weres, or hopeful romantics—appealed to him; he believed sports and playing fields were a metaphor for the real world. At least half a dozen of his produced scripts to this point had centered on that broad theme. These characters struck him as both pathetic and noble, embodying the best and the worst of humanity. A former boxer himself, Serling felt particularly close to the boxers, who train their whole lives for destruction, age too quickly, and are turned out into a society that disowns them unless they've been champions. Three of his previous scripts, most notably "The Twilight Rounds," had focused on that sad fact of life.

Whether or not Serling had read Budd Schulberg's 1946 novel *The Harder They Fall*, a retelling of the tragic life of boxer Primo Carnera who was used and abused by managers and promoters capitalizing on his enormous size—or had seen the filmed version that had just been released when Manulis called him, certain similarities between Schulberg's work and Serling's "Requiem for a Heavyweight" are apparent.

"Old fighters will always get me," Schulberg wrote early in the book. "There is nothing duller than an old ball player or an old tennis star, but an old fighter who's been punched around, spilled his blood freely for the fans' amusement only to wind up broke, battered and forgotten has got the stuff of tragedy for me."

Serling, in 1957, wrote in his commentary on the play in his book *Patterns*: "When your career is finished, the profession discards you. In terms of society it discards a freak, a man able only to live by his fists and his instincts, and too often a battered hulk covered with the unhealing scars that are the legacy of his trade."

Manulis says he had not seen *The Harder They Fall*, which starred Humphrey Bogart in his last film role, when Serling turned in "Requiem"; nor did anyone point out to him the similarities. While the plots are not wholly congruous, it seems entirely possible that Serling derived inspiration from Schulberg. Both evoke the same sensibilities—pity and pathos. And both show the seamy, sordid side of the fight game. One particular scene in the film (adapted by another writer from the book) shows a network sports reporter interviewing an old, used-up boxer, a man who earned a small fortune in his life but now has only an addled brain to show for his work. "Requiem" appears to focus on that boxer, one of thousands just like him, telling the same pathetic story more from his viewpoint than the handlers'.

The perceived appropriation of material was a problem that haunted Serling throughout much of his career. After the broadcast of "Patterns," several reviewers innocently noted the thematic similarities between Serling's play and a film then in release, *Executive Suite*, though all observed that Serling's work far surpassed the film (Jack Gould of the *New York Times* said that *Executive Suite*, by comparison, was "'Babes in Toyland' without a score"; Robert Chandler in *Variety* called the film a "pale cliché"; and *Time* compared the two and said that *Executive Suite* was more like *Little Women*). The catalyst for the final confrontation between Sloane and Ramsey, in "Patterns," revolves around the issue of authorship of a report. As Sloane notes, "The bigger the job, the more desperate you are to keep it." Coincidentally, the subject of Serling's very next script following "Requiem" was an adaptation of Ernest Lehman's novella *The Comedian*, about a writer who is driven to plagiarize in order to save his career (Serling won another Emmy for this).

Schulberg says that after "Requiem" aired, a great many people asked if he had watched the program, specifically because of the similarities to his work. He had indeed noted them and felt he had an actionable cause. A few months after the airing, he saw Serling at a party. "You're not sore at me, are you, Budd?" Serling asked, a question Schulberg believes to have been an acknowledgment of the debt. Schulberg feels Serling had not "intentionally stolen" his work but "unconsciously" did so. Significantly, six years later, Serling told *Newsweek* that "Requiem" originated as a short story in college—the same year Schulberg's novel appeared.

Further, both Ray Bradbury and Charles Beaumont later accused Serling of taking their material, with neither permission nor compensation, for "Twilight Zone," while writer Sy Gomberg claimed that Serling's 1970 "Storm in Summer" (which won an Emmy as best dramatic show of the season) and an acclaimed episode of "Night Gallery," "The Messiah on Mott Street," were both based on stories he had told Serling some years earlier. In a 1956 letter to two friends in Cincinnati, Serling encouraged them to have their son send him his beginning literary efforts for critiquing, adding parenthetically that he might just as well steal from the boy as anyone else. This is almost certainly a joke, of course, but judged against the other circumstantial evidence it can also be seen as a sardonic admission.

"Playhouse 90" was produced in California, at CBS's studios in Hollywood, a clear confirmation of the television industry's intention to move west. Producers in Los Angeles had both the luxury of employing well-known Hollywood actors and using brand-new, state-of-the-art facilities built solely for television production. "Lux Video Theatre" had taken Horace Greeley's advice two years before, and "Studio One" soon followed. The invention of the coaxial cable allowed transmitters to be farther distances apart—if not yet all the way across the country—to be joined live, making the resultant microwave signals somewhat clearer. If the program aired Thursday nights at 9:30—as "Playhouse 90" did—the production began in Los Angeles at 6:30 and was beamed live, via the coax and microwave, to the eastern and central time zones. Then the hot kines—the term for the just made kinescope—would be rebroadcast for the rest of the country. (Martin Manulis once summed up the process of producing "90": "You rehearse a show for three weeks, you put it on live for the East Coast, you go home and watch the hot kine feed for the West Coast, you cut your throat and go to bed.")

The move west, some said, sounded the death knell for live television. Soon, they feared, all productions would be done on film. They turned out to be right.

"Hollywood is a nice place to live, if you're a grapefruit," Serling would say, parroting Fred Allen's famous quip. He also referred to Los Angeles as Bubbleland, Disneyland, and the Land of the Mink Swimming Pools; this was then, as it has always been, the fashion. But he would too often announce his determination "not to go Hollywood" for one not to think that he protested too much. The movies were the older, respected brother, while television and its creators were still largely thought of as the ugly stepsister. Serling certainly would have wanted to be accepted. He also enjoyed the weather in California, as well as the area's preoccupation with automobiles—the bigger and fancier, the better. It was an infatuation he shared, as evidenced later by his buying at least one new car every year; the bigger and fancier, the better. (In a letter to his brother, written from Hollywood, Serling noted that while he missed his Connecticut home, his Connecticut friends, and the burgeoning New England spring, he most of all missed his new Lincoln Continental.)

Buzz Kulik, the director, who had moved to Los Angeles with "Lux" two years before, recalls seeing Serling at Dick McDonagh's house in Beverly Hills. "He walked in wearing a green T-shirt, showing off his muscles—always with the cigarettes. He was this young, vibrant man. Small, but built like a rock. He exuded great joy. It was difficult to be around Rod and not be caught up in this dynamic quality he had. Attractive, charismatic, intelligent, quick, bright, clever—he was all those things." He told Kulik too that he would not "go Hollywood."

Serling spent five weeks in Los Angeles, working with Manulis to polish the script about a used-up fighter whose new fight is for dignity in a world that no longer has a place for him. "Rod always had a tendency toward heavy-handedness," Manulis notes. "His characters would say things like, 'I felt it in the gut.' He had all these 'gut' lines. I'd say, 'This is just a little too much for the fuckin' gut,' and he would just laugh. He knew exactly; he'd get the joke. If he trusted you, he'd make the change. It was very easy working with him, I found. Most of that has to do with mutual respect and enjoying each other."

"Requiem for a Heavyweight" begins at the end of Mountain McClintock's last of 111 fights over fourteen years. Waking up in the locker room, McClintock says to Maish, his manager, whom the doctor has just told his boxer will fight no more: "I'm coming around now. Oh, Lordy, I caught it to tonight, Maish. I really did. What did I do wrong?"

"You aged," Maish tells him. "That was the big trouble. You aged."

Sadly, McClintock finds that used-up boxers have no skills demanded by the outside world. They've not been trained for anything but combat, and their cauliflower ears and dim-witted speech from being hit too many times qualify them for exactly nothing except the grotesque.

Maish, in fear of some hoods from whom he borrowed money to bet against McClintock's surviving the fifth round (Serling used this same device in "The Twilight Rounds," in which the fighter's girlfriend takes his own money to bet against his lasting), wants McClintock to become a wrestler dressed like Davy Crockett—a show-business gimmick trading on his mediocre career and moderate fame. (This also happens to Primo Carnera.)

In another creator's hands Maish might have lacked the sympathetic side Serling gave him; the added dimension gives the play a soul. "That's this precious business of ours," Maish notes bitterly. "[McClintock] gives them a million dollars' worth of fighting for fourteen years, and then they're not interested in paying for the dump truck to cart 'im away." As in "Patterns," Serling attributes the evil that men do to innate human failings.

To Manulis, the original ending seemed, if not too hopeless and despairing, too ambiguous. Serling had wanted the proud fighter, after refusing to don the wrestler's outfit and climb into the ring, simply to go to the train station and board a train for wherever, his future left to our imaginations. In the final draft the show ends with McClintock on a train, where he happily begins to teach a young boy to box. Serling never liked it; he'd preferred to maintain the thread of agony that had infected McClintock.

A parable of failed ambitions and unrealized dreams, "Requiem" is a sad, poignant, extremely well-written tale. The characters are sharply drawn, the dialogue terse and expressive. The author had clearly reached an artistic pinnacle.

"Playhouse 90," even before its debut, had attained considerable prestige. Anxious to justify the expectations with reality, Manulis wanted "Requiem" to open the series, on October 4, 1956. "I won't say that I knew 'Requiem' was going to bring the house down," he admits, "but I thought it had the chance to be a real hit." However, a high-ranking CBS executive thought it too risky as the premiere of the the first original ninety-minute program ever written for television. "He had read it and didn't like it. 'Forbidden Area' was a perfectly good show, but it was an adaptation, which I really didn't want to open with, because I thought the big thing was to do originals. Anyway, I had to give in."

The delay equally disappointed director John Frankenheimer. Promised the debut of the series, he thought "Requiem" would be his. As a compromise, Manulis offered him the choice of either opening with "Forbidden Area" or doing "Requiem" the following week. One could not have both; with a three-week rehearsal period for each show, the productions necessarily overlapped. When Manulis refused to delay "Requiem" until the fourth show, Frankenheimer chose the debut, and "Requiem" was given to Ralph Nelson.

First, Manulis suddenly had to conquer another major problem—one that applied to all six of the finished scripts, including "Forbidden Area." When he had first begun collecting scripts early in the summer, he told the writers simply to write a three-act play, figuring to place the commercials naturally after each act break. Since no three-act plays had ever been produced on television, the precedent for his instructions was the legitimate theater. In retrospect, Manulis should be excused from this naivete. Having originally come from a stage background, he believed the purpose of the artistic media was to entertain. He could not have anticipated the lack of respect about to be exhibited for the material—certain proof that the principle motivation of television was to sell products, not to entertain or instruct.

With the rise of filmed series and the anthologies' subsequent loss of luster, the ad agencies preferred to sell their clients sponsorship of episodic shows in which likable characters said and did funny things every week. No controversy, no threat of boycotts, no hassles. To counter this trend and sell their grand new anthology show, the CBS salesmen emphasized all-star casting (including "stars" who had never done television because they'd never before liked the parts well enough), scripting, and directing and first-class production values—in short, prestige.

According to Manulis, during rehearsals for "Forbidden Area"—a story about the political and moral consequences that ensue when several Soviet politburo members resign after ordering a surprise attack on United States targets—CBS head of programming Hubbell Robinson told Manulis to insert nine commercial breaks instead of three; each of the three half hours would be split the way an ordinary half-hour program is split—in half.

Manulis feared the reaction of his writers and directors, and he got what he feared. Frankenheimer screamed and ranted. "You can't do that," he said. "You can't. You just can't do that. It can't be done." Not without breaking the continuity and compromising the emotional impact of the story.

Manulis took a late-night flight to New York, where he met with the sponsors' representatives, the agencies, and CBS executives. "I made a really big pitch. They knew how important it was, because I was flying home the same day," he says.

When he arrived back in Los Angeles early the next morning, Manulis received a call almost immediately from Robinson. "Well," he said, "you gave it the old college try. I knew they wouldn't go for it."

"It just can't be done," Manulis said.

"Someone'll do it," Robinson told him.

"So we started to adjust," Manulis recalls. "Luckily, I had Rod."

Faced with the prospect of either compromising or having nothing but money to show for his work—and with no other outlet for the two ninety-minute scripts he'd completed—Serling set to the task at hand; perhaps not happily or enthusiastically, but skillfully. "Surprisingly, it didn't take as much adjustment as we thought," Manulis remembers.

Into each scene an artificial emotional "curtain" had to be inserted where none had originally been intended, this to act as the inducement for the viewer to sit patiently for the resumption of action after the commercial. Serling believed that the net effect of these additional high points was to weaken the climactic emotional wallop.

By the time Serling had made his appropriate changes, all of the other writers had a prototype for their forced curtains.

Although "Forbidden Area" rehearsed well, the show received a general panning. Jack Gould, claiming that "Playhouse 90" "did not have a very auspicious debut," underlined the show's failure to be all the more disappointing because CBS had not been "stingy with its production budget" or cast—Charlton Heston, Tab Hunter, Victor Jory, Vincent Price, and Charles Bickford.

The production crew took no time to cry over the reviews. Rehearsals for "Requiem" had been going horribly. Manulis cast Jack Palance in the role of Mountain McClintock—an excellent choice in that Palance, built like a real fighter, convincingly conveyed the quiet despair called for in the role. Keenan Wynn played his cruel and pitiless manager. And in the crucial role of McClintock's second, an older man who is neither naïve nor without ambition yet whose humanity remains at the fore, Manulis cast Keenan's father, Ed Wynn, though he had never before played a straight dramatic role.

"As a producer, you do try to give what you can in showmanship," Manulis explains. Measured in those terms alone, the baggy-pants comedian, "the Perfect Fool," had been wowing them since vaudeville. Keenan Wynn had been a close friend of Manulis, and through their friendship Manulis had met the old man. Only Keenan had at first liked the idea of his father playing a role that lacked a single laugh. If Ed Wynn reverted for even a single moment into his shtick that had been refined over fifty years, the play would have failed immediately, its just-so tone of pathos, sentiment, and realism dissolved by laughter.

After ten days of readings, Ralph Nelson had commenced rehearsals. No matter how often he read the part, and despite repeated run-throughs, Ed Wynn could not remember his lines. With just six days to go before the Thursday night airtime, Wynn had not improved a whit. Nelson brought Manulis down to rehearsals to prove to him that Wynn must be replaced. "The worst part," Nelson told him, "is that the moment he gets the least bit insecure, he reverts to the Perfect Fool, giggles and all." Even Keenan finally pleaded with the producer to pull him.

Yet Manulis held firm. "I just decided to gamble on Ed's big-star training. Those people are set apart from the rest of us. No matter what it is they do, they just have something inside that they turn on as soon as it is for real.

After the run-through, I went straight to Ed and told him that he was going to be wonderful in the part." (A year later, Manulis recalls, the great actor Paul Muni also could not remember his lines as a courtroom lawyer. Finally, when Manulis refused to fire him, too, the director, George Roy Hill, equipped Muni with a one-way walkie-talkie, into which he fed him the lines; Muni won an Emmy.)

Both Serling and Nelson demanded that their names be erased from the credits if Wynn continued in the part. Keenan became increasingly insistent. In live television, ninety minutes' worth, the opportunity to make an authentic perfect fool out of Wynn loomed large. "He's my father, and I love him, but I just can't do it," Keenan said to Manulis. "I'm afraid he'll disgrace himself before twenty million people." Still, Manulis remained firmly committed to Wynn.

"I'm not usually that adamant," he says.

He did, however, compromise and agreed to hire another actor, veteran Ned Glass, to learn the part, provided Wynn not know about it. Glass hid under the bar, behind the locker—any set apparatus from where he would be prepared to step out and assume the role. It would have been a shock to the audience to see a change in the portrayal, but that was preferable to a complete collapse. And anyway, Wynn might still pull it off.

Watching the show head right into the toilet—and with it, his career—Serling could no longer stand the anxiety. He flew home to Connecticut a few days before the broadcast, just in time to read a short interview with Ed Wynn in the *New York Times*. "The first thing I had to do was to un-learn everything I've done for half a century," Wynn said. "I've a scene in which I cry emotionally. I went home and practiced in front of a mirror. I was so funny. I got hysterical. Try as I might, I unconsciously tended to make it comic." No doubt these admissions did nothing to calm Serling's fears.

The night of the show, he sat in his living room with

Carol, his new best friend, Dick Berg, and Berg's wife, Barbara. The four had met the year before. Hearing that the author of "Patterns" now resided in Westport, Berg had arranged through a mutual friend to meet Serling. "Nothing ever knocked me out in my life as a television viewer the way 'Patterns' did," Berg remembers. "It took my breath away. Not in watching television or movies was I that taken aback by what the typewriter could do to my psyche. I've never been as excited, never as challenged, never as grateful to a storyteller as I was to Rod Serling, whom I did not know then." At the time, Berg, an aspiring writer, ran a retail art gallery in town.

"We met, the four of us, one night," he recounts. "And we were best friends until the day he died." Berg credits Serling for having "emboldened" him to follow his heart. Serling gave him scripts to read in order to learn the teleplay form and encouraged his taking a risk, as he had done himself. Despite having a wife and two children to support, Berg sold the gallery and endured a "treacherous, angst-ridden" year before selling his first script and beginning what would be a long and generally successful career as a writer and then producer of film and television.

Berg had read "Requiem" some months before the broadcast and had not been overly impressed by the material— feelings not significantly changed by the production either. Of course, watching it while the author paced continually back and forth—"smoking at least two cigarettes at a time"—was not the optimum method for viewing. Each time Wynn reached for a word or looked as though he might revert to his shtick, Berg says, Serling died a little—"and I was dying for him."

Serling's contagious anxiety and insecurity made an objective opinion impossible. Berg, particularly, retained his doubts, and Serling saw that. "As competitive as all writers are, I really did want to be proved wrong, though," Berg says.

A few minutes after the production, the phone rang in the control booth at the CBS studios in Hollywood. Over the loudspeaker, a voice called for Manulis: "Marty, it's for you. Long distance. Mr. Paley is on the phone."

Walking to the phone, Manulis was naturally apprehensive about hearing from William Paley, the founder and chairman of the board of CBS. A rare occurrence, it usually meant displeasure. He thought the show had gone very well and felt pleased. "But sitting in the control room, with the nerves and the sweat, you really never know. You never know what you had," he remembers.

Paley had watched at home, with his family. "Marty," he began, "you put television strides ahead with this show. Congratulations."

Wynn came through as Manulis had predicted and in fact would be nominated for an Emmy as best supporting actor. The show itself would win for best single performance of the year; Jack Palance gave the best single performance by an actor; Ralph Nelson won for best direction, one hour or more; Albert Heschong won for best art direction, one hour or more; and Serling won for best teleplay writing, one hour or more—the second of what would be three consecutive times Serling took home an Emmy.

That night at the Serlings', though, no one had any real idea whether the show had been a critical success. Serling called Hollywood to talk to Manulis and Nelson and heard about Paley's congratulatory call. But the sense of anguish remained until the reviews came in. Cruelly, the early edition of the *Times* did not carry a review of the production. Finally, in the late morning edition, Jack Gould praised the show profusely. It was, he wrote, "a play of overwhelming force and tenderness. . . . Mr. Serling wrote a searing, inspired indictment of the worst side of the prize-fight game."

"Rod Serling's Drama Scores a Knockout," said the subheadline.

"When he got through reading Gould," Berg says, "he realized how much he loved it."

Ironically, only Keenan Wynn received poor marks for his performance. Even "Slapsie" Maxie Rosenbloom, an ex-boxer making his acting debut, earned praise, while Ed Wynn was said to be "very good."

Having lived the story behind that "very good," Serling laughed at the apparent off-handedness of the statement. Then, self-satisfied, he laughed very hard—and shouted out loud. He screamed a scream of joy. At last. He had been a success; he had lived up to his potential; he had lived down all the bad reviews; he had surpassed "Patterns." And joy of joys, there was talk of producing "Requiem" on Broadway.

"The money's in the bank, the name's established, and the future is reasonably secure," he five weeks later told the *New York Times*, coming to interview the most famous—and successful—television writer in all the land. "The order in which I name these things is the order in which they hit me. They represent the things I lacked in the beginning. I'll probably write less from now on, unless I can't help it."

Like the "very good" assessment of Ed Wynn's performance, Serling's casual words mocked the richness of the drama behind the whole story. He had learned, and would continue to learn, that of all the artistic media, only television judges its creators on their failures, not their successes. But for the time being, he remained the heavyweight champion of the television world.

5

A Thousand Dollars a Week

R equiem for a Heavyweight" ignited an explosion. In March Serling won his second consecutive Emmy, followed in April by a George Foster Peabody award—the first time in its seventeen-year history that a Peabody had been presented to a writer for his "distinguished achievement." No writer in any field was more sought after than Rod Serling. Television, movies, Broadway, book publishing, they all wanted some Serling—and he intended to satisfy their cravings. But with his passion for saying yes, for accepting virtually every offer coming his way, he had neither the time nor interest to develop a long-term career strategy. Another ten years would pass before he could look back and reflect how far he had come in so short a time.

Martin Manulis immediately assigned him the adaptation of Ernest Lehman's story *The Comedian* for "Playhouse 90" and asked for any other material Serling might have. "Requiem" itself was optioned as a stage play, by Panama and Frank. His script "The Strike" was included in an anthology of television's best scripts, edited by Gore Vidal.

Film offers poured in, despite his terrible track record on the big screen. *Patterns* closed its run almost as soon as it opened, possibly because it had already aired on free television twice and nothing new had been developed in the big-screen version to recommend it. *The Rack*, of course, had to be rewritten by Stewart Stern but still lacked sufficient material to justify translation, and even Paul Newman could not save it from terminal claustrophobia. The film version of "The Strike," which he had wanted to coproduce with John Champion and Harry Essex, was abandoned when it became clear that no studio would release a war story about less-than-heroic heroes. (Essex wanted Serling to repay a large portion of the seventy-five hundred dollars in option money, but Champion refused to go along, resulting in a break-up of their partnership. Champion soon joined with producer Hall Barlett.) Meanwhile, the release of *52 Miles to Terror*, shot by MGM in Jerusalem, had been permanently delayed.

Nonetheless, producer Armand Deutsch asked Serling to write his western, *Three Guns*, to star Robert Taylor and newcomer John Cassavetes in a story about a range war. The title would later be changed to *Saddle the Wind*.

Perhaps the greatest measure of Serling's celebrity—and certainly his most profound professional validation—was the invitation by Simon and Schuster to publish a collection of four of his teleplays. *Patterns* included the title play, as well as "Requiem," "Old MacDonald Had a Curve," and "The Rack," each followed by some candid observations about the writing and production qualities they either, in his opinion, enjoyed or suffered. More significantly, the book began with a long, revealing discourse of autobiography and comment entitled "About Writing for Television." In it he detailed his thoughts, reflections, and frustrations about the medium that had made him so wealthy and famous. He used much of the space to bite that generous hand, blasting the sponsors for their timorousness and oversensitivity. "At their very worst, their interference is an often stultifying, often destructive and inexcusable by-product of our mass-media system," he wrote. "I think it is a basic truth that no dramatic art form should be dictated and controlled by men whose training, interest and instincts are cut of entirely different cloth. The fact remains that these gentlemen sell consumer goods, not an art form."

Now one of the few writers whose fame made him relatively impervious to fears of unofficial blacklisting by sponsors for unkind remarks, Serling began an unofficial second career with the book's publication as television's white knight—the man who attacked squalid programming, network and sponsor censorship, and lack of government-mandated quality standards for the airwaves. Along with his desire to delineate for audiences the differences between right and wrong and good and evil, this outspokenness would earn him calls from every newspaper and magazine writer doing a feature story on the sorry state of the medium; a reputation as a Don Quixote tilting at windmills, a man unwilling to compromise his values; and, in three years, a trip to Washington to testify before the Federal Communications Commission.

Serling enjoyed life in the eye of the hurricane. It kept him in the public perception and allowed him a constant forum for his views. He believed that maybe, if the sponsors or networks wanted to get too heavily involved in the editorial process, the resultant publicity would dissuade them. (He was wrong.) But most important, the reputation as an angry young man with a typewriter created expectations that each of his scripts would "say something." They did. If the stories were not "big," like "The Dark Side of the Earth," a dramatization of the 1956 anti-Communist revolt in Hungary, then they were painfully revealing about human foibles, like "The Velvet Alley"—his story about the flip side of success.

Without question, the next three years became Serling's personal golden age; he would never again write as well or as convincingly. Just as he began to find a voice that really may have placed him artistically alongside Arthur

Miller—writing with clarity and self-awareness—he soon found himself in a perpetual state of limbo, the victim of such forces beyond his control as videotape and film, which together killed live television; and he also found himself victim of his own insecurities.

"The Comedian" aired on February 14, 1957. Serling had scripted a brilliant, biting comment on the loathsome bowels of show business. (After the show's first reading late in January, Serling wrote to Dick Berg that he was "convinced this will set the medium back at least twenty years . . . seventy minutes of unrelieved horseshit and the comedian evolves as the most single-level monster ever conceived in a lab.")

Edmond O'Brien portrayed the head comedy writer to Mickey Rooney's comedian, as cruel and uncompromising off camera as he is funny and charismatic on camera. (Serling's own comedy attempts—"Mr. Finchley vs. The Bomb," "Old MacDonald Had a Curve," and "O'Toole from Moscow" had been cute at best. He would later tell Bob Schiller, the great comedy writer of such shows as "Maude" and "All in the Family," that he aspired someday to write comedy.) O'Brien's character has hit a dry spell, when the gags just won't come, and he knows his job is only as secure as his last laugh-riot script. After agonizing with his conscience and wondering what other kind of writer he might have become had he not been seduced by television's money, he finally stoops to stealing material from a writer he'd known and admired long ago, a man now dead whose scripts had been considered the stuff of genius. This theme, a man (always a man) compromising his morals in order to save his career, recurs in many of Serling's scripts.

Thanks in large measure to Serling, "Playhouse 90" quickly became the most prestigious show on television, and at ten thousand dollars a script, Serling, when he wrote for television, wrote exclusively for "90." Each time he worked on an assignment for "90," he sojourned to Hollywood for a three- to five-week stint—four times in 1957 alone. His screen assignments, three of them that year, also kept him away from Westport for similar periods.

Most of the time Serling traveled alone. Success had produced an absentee father and husband. Taking on so many assignments that "when I bend down to pick up a pencil, I'm five days behind," Serling could no longer use Carol as his first-line editor. She had been his sounding board—an educated woman with sharp tastes and intelligence. Now there were professionals to do that; he no longer needed her input. "I just don't have the time to sit around in the evenings and talk over the script like I used to with her," he told William F. Nolan. "And she's saddened by it. . . . She lived in a time of development when she was important to me; in this sense, she no longer is."

In many ways, Serling's little girls grew up as strangers to him, particularly Nan, born in 1955, the year he had begun to travel as often as he stayed at home. And when he stayed home, his parenting seemed more an obligation than a joy. In an early 1959 letter to Henry Blankfort, the public relations director for Revel, whose model airplanes Serling assembled in whatever spare time he managed— he offhandedly indicated some annoyance at the demands on his time made by his daughters.

When he knew he would have to be in Hollywood the first several months of 1957 to write *Saddle the Wind* (Deutsch insisted on daily story conferences), he and Carol and the two girls moved into a rented home on North Cañon Drive in Beverly Hills.

Saddle the Wind was to be directed by Robert Parrish, with whom Serling began a lifelong friendship while working together on the script. Though the film, for which Deutsch had miscast Serling as the writer, was rightfully bombed by the critics and ignored by moviegoers when it came out early in 1958, both men would always look back fondly at the working relationship they had together under gentleman "Artie" Deutsch.

"There was not *one* redeeming feature in that script," Serling said. "My only defense is that they handed me a story line that had stuff in it like, 'You're mighty pretty, ma'am, you must be the new schoolmarm,' and 'I've shot men for less than that.' And by the time I'd rewritten it eleven times . . . the most articulate performer was a horse." He nicknamed the film *Stop that Fart*.

A more appropriate vehicle—one seemingly ordained for him—paid him thirty-five thousand dollars: *Company of Cowards*. A novella by Jack Schaeffer set against the backdrop of the Civil War, *Company* was "so exciting I couldn't turn it down," Serling wrote to Nolan Miller in early May.

Serling's first-draft treatment may be considered an emotional autobiography. Captain Jack Heath, after refusing to lead his men into an obvious suicide mission (the colonel ordering it, a sadistic, unfeeling man, may have been drawn from the World War II officer on whom Serling claimed to base the character of Ramsey in "Patterns"), is arrested and convicted of cowardice. His men, including a young lieutenant who before the battle, his first, walked "the line between boyish excitement and stomach-crawling fear"—most likely a description of Serling himself at Leyte—spit on Heath as he lies broken on the ground. "Heath starts to sob as only a broken man can sob," Serling wrote. "God makes his human beings so fabulously strong in the midst of their weakness."

A ranking officer soon orders Heath to assemble a company of other presumed cowards and rehabilitate them into a fighting unit. Their reputation precedes them—"a company of cowards"—and when a banker from a small Western town begins to disparage them, Heath tells him that "unless you've slipped on blood or winced at the sound of screams or felt strangled in the throat because of the nightmare you're living through—ask yourself about your own behavior and keep in mind the possibility of your own cowardice."

Company of Cowards eventually underwent four drafts and had two other writers before being abandoned by the studio; it remained one of Serling's great disappointments, in no small measure because of his relationship to the material.

The previous year, moved by the unsuccessful Hungarian uprising against the Soviets, Serling had quickly assembled a brief precis of a story that he called "The Dark Side of the Earth" and tried to sell it to MGM. When refused, he pitched it to Martin Manulis for airing on "Playhouse 90." Manulis immediately liked the story, which Serling scripted during the summer at the same time as another topical story, "A Town Has Turned to Dust," his second reworking of the Emmett Till case. (Ironically, for all his complaints about censorship in the television medium, Serling could never have sold a "topical" story to film executives; only television was willing, albeit reluctantly, to tackle such themes.)

Directed by Arthur Penn and starring Van Heflin (who had taken Richard Kiley's role as Staples in the film version of "Patterns"), Dean Jagger, and Earl Holliman, "Dark Side" opened the second season of "Playhouse 90." It was a big story, spread against a broad canvas—perhaps too big and too broad for a live television drama; with tanks in the streets, it seemed more stagy than real. But the sentiment, acting, and writing saved it from what could have been an ambitious disaster. (During the first read-through, always attended by the agency men looking out for their client's interest, Serling watched them as they watched the actors. For the first time in his memory, they sat without jotting down notes about what could not be said. Finally, Serling thought, they're actually enjoying the story, not waiting to tear it apart. When the read-through ended, they had a single comment. From the one R. J. Reynolds representative came the proviso: "Make sure the Russian officers don't smoke so many cigarettes.")

After nineteen films, this was Holliman's first live television role. He expected the famous writer to strut the set like a king peacock, so Serling's affability and unpretentiousness surprised him. Holliman approached Serling about his character, a young, stern Russian army officer;

in his opinion, the officer had not yet been fully fleshed out. "Rod," he said, "this guy needs another scene. I'd like him to say something like, 'I know what you did in Stalingrad, and I know what you did in Leningrad.'" Serling looked at him without saying a word, then began writing quickly on a pad of paper. The speech he provided Holliman nearly recreated the words Holliman had used.

Holliman was lucky. If Serling hadn't liked the actor's suggestions, as he often did not, he would have smiled sardonically, a twinkle creeping into his eye, and said in measured tones: "Let me put it this way: you're wrong."

By the time "The Dark Side of the Earth" aired on September 19, the Serlings had put their Westport house up for sale, hoping to finalize the transaction and finish packing before the planned New Year's move. Serling had decided he could no longer shuttle between his home and the place his career demanded he be. With fewer and fewer live shows on the evening schedules, television's future clearly headed toward filmed shows. New York would soon play a minor role. And to write movies, one had to be in Hollywood. The writer made his contacts there, had lunch at the commissary, met producers and directors, wrote and rewrote the scripts. Books and Broadway plays could be written anywhere—or so went the rationale. At least, the Serlings reasoned, they would always have the summer cottage on Cayuga Lake.

That fall Blanche Gaines sold her final script for Rod Serling: "Panic Button," to "Playhouse 90." After five years of a relationship in which she played the role of nursemaid almost as much as agent, Gaines could not provide the services Serling now required. He now belonged entirely to Ashley-Steiner.

Serling felt some ambivalence and guilt, however misguided, over leaving Gaines; like Fred Staples in "Patterns," the price tag for continued success would be a kind of betrayal of his small-town sense of loyalty. Although she knew that she would likely be cut out, even for television sales, when her contract expired, Gaines reacted

Rod Serling in 1956, soon after signing his trend-setting exclusive contract with CBS.

Portrait of the man as a serious young artist, circa 1958, shortly before deciding to undertake "The Twilight Zone."

Rod and Carol Serling at the Emmy Awards for the 1959 season. Serling was surprised to win his fourth Emmy that evening, for episodes of "The Twilight Zone."

The Serlings enjoying the awards dinner following Rod's winning his fourth Emmy, May 1960.

Reginald Rose, left, and Rod Serling in the "Playhouse 90" production offices, 1959.

Serling on "The Twilight Zone" set.

Serling holding aloft his fifth Emmy, May 1961.

Rod and Carol Serling at the Emmy Awards banquet for the 1960 television season. That evening Serling won his fifth Emmy for "The Twilight Zone."

The Serlings at home in the Pacific Palisades soon after moving to California. From left: Jody, Carol, Rod, and Nan.

Serling introducing the airing of the French short film *Occurrence at Owl Creek Bridge,* which "The Twilight Zone" licensed to air in its final season.

Serling at the party held for cast and crew following the cancellation of "The Twilight Zone" in 1964.

Serling in his role as host of "The Liar's Club," 1969.

Serling during the "Night Gallery" days, circa 1971.

Robert J. Serling, 1981.

James Burrows, left, and Serling during rehearsals for the San Diego stage production of Serling's *Storm in Summer*, which Burrows directed.

A few months before his death, Serling's face seemed to suddenly show the effects of his devotion to the sun; his forehead, eyes, and cheeks developed lines much deeper than a man should have at age fifty.

badly. A year later she intimated that he'd behaved ungratefully, and she (paraphrasing William James) accused him of having become "a slave to that bitch goddess success." Serling understatedly pointed out her shortcomings in negotiating and contract analysis.

He later romanticized the story of their breakup in "The Velvet Alley." In it, the writer, a forty-two-year-old overnight sensation, Ernie Pandish, has no good reason to leave his agent, Max Salter, a kind, considerate, thoughtful man. This does not reflect the reality of Serling's circumstances, only his emotional misgivings. Pandish, who had been nurtured by Max, becomes a slimy, selfish worm who eventually drives away even his wife.

At a Hollywood party one night, the camera finds Pandish (Art Carney) surrounded by several glad-handers from the Chambers Agency. Loyal to Max until this night, Pandish listens to agent Freddie making a pitch for him: "We covered the area of career planning, our whole approach with our writers—our important writers, that is.... You're being forced to make decisions your representatives should make for you. In this town you're either a giant or a midget. You're neither. You're in limbo. You should be making a million dollars a year."

Pandish signs on the dotted line, only to be chastised by his wife: "You didn't get represented tonight, Ernie. You got raped."

The real-life pitch to Serling from the agents at Ashley-Steiner had been very close to the script's dialogue. "He left Blanche because he needed a full-service shop—more than a mom and pop agency. That was the bullshit we gave him," recalls Alden Schwimmer, the agent assigned to him after Ted Ashley and Ira Steiner pitched him. "But if ever there was a case when the *spiel* was for real, it was Rod's case, because it wasn't long after he came to us that we put together 'The Twilight Zone.' I'm afraid that little lady in New York didn't know how to do that, to package television shows and sell them and operate them after they're on."

The quality of the agency's clientele spoke volumes about them, Serling thought, and the list confirmed his judgment. Other clients included Neil Simon, Larry Gelbart, Sidney Lumet, John Frankenheimer, and Ralph Nelson. Schwimmer had been a comedy writer under contract to NBC ten years before. A writer by night, he worked daytime as a messenger for the William Morris Agency, which also represented him. For a time, until the New York office chief forced him to decide between the two careers, Schwimmer's commissions earned more for the agency than it paid out in his weekly salary of twenty-eight dollars.

As an agent, Schwimmer attacked his job, reading every unsolicited manuscript that landed on his desk, certain that every script he picked up would be the next "Marty" or "Patterns." The vast majority of the time, of course, they were garbage. Yet Schwimmer maintained his enthusiasm and quickly built a reputation as a tough, smart businessman. Serling liked Schwimmer a great deal, particularly his sense of humor.

During one visit to the office shortly after the birth of Schwimmer's son, Serling offered congratulations and asked to see a picture of the newborn. Schwimmer showed him a small photograph of a baby chimpanzee he had long ago cut out from a magazine and placed in his wallet, for no other reason than it had become a running gag between him and his wife. Serling looked at it wordlessly. He suspected a joke but couldn't afford the chance—just in case. "What a nice smile," he finally managed.

The move to Ashley-Steiner paid immediate rewards. Serling signed a new three-year contract with MGM that would pay him $250,000 to write three films. Ecstatic, certain that his financial future had been solidified, he nonetheless continued to say yes to virtually every deal offered. He found it so pleasurable to be in demand that he now required daily affirmation, as if to reassure himself that the dream had not ended sometime in the night—when, no doubt, his insomnia had kept him up inventing stories.

As Carol packed up the house, on which they so far had received only a very few inadequate offers, Serling spent the late fall in Hollywood, rewriting *Company of Cowards* for MGM, polishing his first draft of the Broadway version of "Requiem," and making some necessary changes in "Panic Button" for "Playhouse 90."

Fortunately, by then he dictated all his scripts for a secretary to transcribe; he could not have typed if he had wanted to. An uncomfortable tingling numbness had crept into his right index finger. At first he thought it was a mysterious injury, but when the symptoms worsened, he flew back to his physician in Westport for an examination. The blood tests revealed he had an elevated cell count. As he admitted to the doctor, he had upped his smoking, which approached four packs a days now, to cope with the stress of—well, success. "Please limit the number of cigarettes to a pack a day or less," the doctor advised in an accompanying letter.

Serling ignored the advice. He was considering an incredible offer from CBS: to enter a joint production agreement with the network for a weekly anthology series whose stories would be joined in concept only by their relationship to imagination—"The Twilight Zone."

Serling had once mentioned to his agents an idea for a radio anthology series he could never sell. Little discussion followed, so he was surprised both that they found it appealing and that CBS had been tempted enough, after the agents had floated some trial balloons, to talk; other scripts with science-fiction or fantastical plots had been met with cold rejections.

Ambivalence clouded his thoughts about writing a weekly series, as though a series, despite whatever benefits it delivered, fell beneath him, was a degradation of his artistic ambitions. As the agents pointed out, though, working for ten thousand dollars a television script or twenty-five thousand dollars per film is all well and good, but even doing six "Playhouse 90"s a year and two or three film scripts paled against the kind of major money being made by the creators of the shows and films, whether or not they wrote them. His talent deserved more, they argued. (The agency, of course, stood to earn sizable packaging fees—a percentage of the production budget, over and above the budget, payable directly to them if they sold a series—so they had little to lose and much to gain.)

Serling still believed "Requiem" would be produced as a play in the fall of 1958, even though the rewrites—the second, third, and fourth—lacked the professional playwright's touch. "Where is it written that a writer can't have both a series and a play?" the agents asked. He had made nearly $100,000 dollars in 1957. With a hit television show on his hands, he would make at least five times that much. And, they assured him, he could still write films, books, Broadway plays. At worst, the network would say no and Serling would continue with his career zigzagging in the direction it was already headed. At best, everyone would make a small fortune. Their logic sounded impeccable.

Serling met one day with William Dozier, the network's chief of West Coast programming, to pitch his idea. Dozier had been introduced to Serling before, and the executive liked the writer immediately, finding him amiable and charming. He remembers also being struck by Serling's too obvious elevator shoes. "Rod was very conscious of his shortness," Dozier points out. "He would stand at his full height all the time."

In his usual style, Serling paced the room, using furniture and drapery for props, as he animatedly and enthusiastically tried to sell his series idea. Executives who didn't know Serling could have been excused for forgetting that this was a writer, not an auditioning actor. But that had become his style; he entertained. The stories, Serling said, would be science fiction, but not really science fiction; fantasy, but not really fantasy. Imaginative fiction.

"Wait a minute, wait a minute," Dozier said. "I can't make any sense out of it this way. Why don't you just write a script, a pilot script, and we'll pay you for it whether we use it or not."

One of Serling's recurring fantasies after the war, when plagued by combat nightmares and resultant amnesia, was a scenario in which he rescues Pearl Harbor from devastation. How, he wanted to know—fascinated by the (apocryphal?) stories of the Americans soldiers' lack of preparedness, their complacency, and even outright stupidity—could such a catastrophe have occurred? Several times he imagined himself going back in time, changing the historic events, issuing the brass at Pearl Harbor a stern warning. In fact, one of his short scripts at WLW in Cincinnati explored that idea.

In their easy rapport during the preproduction of *Saddle the Wind*, Serling and Robert Parrish had talked of working together again but on a project both of them found appealing. Serling trusted Parrish's instincts and admired his intelligence; he judged Parrish to be a writer's director. Parrish liked Serling's time-traveler idea, and the two of them worked out the particulars of the story line.

Serling presented Dozier with a sixty-minute script, "The Time Element," about a small-time bookie who walks into a psychiatrist's office one morning to tell him about a persistently recurring dream in which he wakes up, hung over, astounded to find himself in a Honolulu hotel in early December 1941. (Serling had in common with the character, Pete Jenson, the nightmares, visits to a psychiatrist, and a father who's a butcher; Jenson also hailed from Scranton, which is south of Binghamton, about fifty miles from the New York/Pennsylvania border.) His first thoughts, of course, after satisfying himself that he has indeed gone back in time, are of betting: the money to be made on football and baseball games, championship boxing matches, Olympic events, and so on—the outcomes of which he already knew.

The scenes shift back and forth from the psychiatrist's office to the retelling of events in Hawaii, where Jenson is unable to convince anyone that the Japanese plan to attack. The military brass are seen as wooden, unyielding buffoons—as though they should have believed a semihysterical man who claims to be from the future. Eventually, Jenson, who always awakens before the Japanese attack, wakes to the sounds of Japanese bombers and is killed. The script cuts to the psychiatrist, in his office, alone, uncertain why he is even there—as though he himself has just awakened from a dream that recedes slowly from memory. Somewhat shaken, he goes to a nearby bar and orders a drink. He sees on the wall a picture of a man he believes he recognizes yet doesn't know. He asks the bartender about the photograph. Pete Jenson, the man says, was a former bartender there; he was killed at Pearl Harbor, December 7, 1941.

Although Dozier liked the script, he could not commit CBS to an hour of what was generically called science fiction. The network might go for a weekly half hour, he explained, but didn't Serling know that anthology shows were dying, that the audience wanted to see the same characters week after week? It was going to be a tough sell to the network, let alone the sponsors, even at a half hour. But an hour a week? Impossible. Give me a half-hour script, Dozier said.

Serling argued persuasively. Years and lifetimes had passed since he last wrote thirty-minute scripts. He, Rod Serling, playwright, author, screenwriter, creator of at least two of television's finest moments writing simple half-hour episodes—the thought appalled him. Dozier agreed with his thinking, but his logic had been built in a vacuum: the network would not budge, that much Dozier knew.

Downcast by the news that he would have to write thirty-minute scripts like any other hack, but determined to mine a fortune in imaginative fiction, Serling feverishly set to work on a thirty-minute pilot called "The Happy Place," a dark parable about a place and time in which no one is allowed to live past the age of sixty. On their sixtieth birthdays, people are led into an elevator that takes them to the "happy place"—euphemistically, death. The plot centers on three generations of the Harris family—the grandfather, a fifty-eight-year-old doctor, old enough to remember when society cherished old people; Steven, his son, the leader of one of the old people's camps where the executions take place; and Paul, Steven's son, who has never known any other way of life and has been completely indoctrinated into the state's methods. Dr. Harris, a vocal opponent of the state, is made to pay for his outspokenness by having two years officially added to his age, meaning he will be put to death now—in the camp run by Steven, who refuses to stand up for his father. In the end, it is discovered that the grandfather has been betrayed by Paul, who dutifully informs his father that the execution age ought to be lowered to fifty—not at all that far away for Steven.

Dozier liked the script. The pilot would be shot, and if the sponsors agreed to buy time, Rod Serling's own production company (to be formed later) and CBS would each own 50 percent of "The Twilight Zone," with the network picking up the production costs. (For packaging the show, Ashley-Steiner would receive 9 percent of the production budget for each show, in essence making the final budget 109 percent of the stated budget.) Dozier added that the network would like to have additional scripts as a backup for the advertising agencies, after showing them the pilot.

"It's really a pretty equitable arrangement," Serling excitedly told his brother. "CBS hands out the money and I supply the blood. I'll drown myself in my unpaid-for pool if something happens and it doesn't go." In February, he incorporated Rod Serling Productions, an entity without any employees and whose officers were he and Carol.

Serling returned to his home in Westport for the last time—a happy man but burdened by a remarkable work schedule. In addition to the new "Twilight Zone" episodes, he had the films for MGM and more drafts of the play. He wrote *No Blade of Grass*, his first script under the new deal with MGM, hurriedly, over a few weeks in November. And it showed. The ludicrous science-fiction parable begins with an enormous seismic quake: the Chinese have dropped atomic bombs on both Peking and Shanghai as a method of reducing their population by millions (incredibly, despite the seismic readings, the newspapers carry no news of this event, and the rest of the world continues in its ignorant bliss); the "Cheng-li virus" has destroyed virtually the entire country's wheat crop, and rather than have a billion people rioting for what little wheat remains, the Chinese leaders kill millions to save millions.

Back in England, where the plot is played out, the powers that be consider the same course of action. Isotope 717, which the Americans have sent over—in short supply, it is available only to America's best friends—is discovered to be only a momentary remedy to the virus destroying the world's food supply. Scientists race to find a real cure before the country's leaders drop the big one on their own people.

MGM executives passed the script around by hand. If they hadn't spent more than eighty thousand dollars on it, they would have laughed heartily. They wanted their money's worth and demanded a rewrite.

Serling had already begun to lose some interest in "Requiem" as a production for the stage. Although it would still be his greatest source of joy, the project became an albatross—constant writing and rewriting; how often could he continue to reconceptualize the same story? Each time he thought he had developed a workable script, the producers declined, making the original fall production date impossible. His always brittle patience had been sorely tested.

Ironically, the week he arrived at home, Serling had an article published in the *New York Times Magazine* that contrasted live television with filmed series; he praised the former and mostly lambasted the latter. "It can be said safely that the vast majority of film shows need never be accused of letting facts interfere with drama," he wrote.

In his sanctimonious defense of live dramas, he either unwittingly or very cleverly argued in compelling fashion in favor of filmed series. As he pointed out, a show that can be seen only once before being discarded cannot possibly turn a profit—not unless sponsors buy commercials every five or six minutes—anathema to the story itself. Economics, after all, had been the driving force behind television's move west. Lucky to recoup their production costs the first time around, producers and the networks needed reruns to make their shows profitable.

Still, the overall tone of the piece provided the impression that Serling expected the networks to operate at a perpetual loss—as CBS did with "Playhouse 90"—for the sake of dramatics. It only enhanced his reputation as a forlorn swordsman tilting at windmills.

Serling's life now imitated Serling's art. Removed from the deal-making atmosphere in Hollywood, he wondered with no little trepidation whether his move to California would enable him to retain his ethics and self-respect. He had pondered the same question once before, when moving to Westport. And both times, he, like Fred Staples, could not say for sure whether he survived with both interior gauges intact. Arthur Miller had not faced this dilemma. Or maybe he had. But Miller likely did not aspire to write television the way Serling aspired to be a playwright. Serling did not want to have to learn, from scratch, a new art form—not when he was so well paid for doing what he had already learned.

Serling's quandary would work its way into his next several television scripts in only slightly varying forms. He based "Panic Button," which aired soon after he arrived back in Westport, on a hypothetical predicament imagined by his brother. Bob, UPI's aviation editor, had been doing research for his first book, *Probable Cause*, a behind-the-scenes look at the factors contributing to several plane crashes. A lifelong aficionado of airplanes and aviators, Bob found himself wondering how many surviving pilots of commercial airplane crashes had lied to the Civil Aeronautics Board investigators in order to save their careers. "I always suspected," he says, "that it happened more than once."

Bob voiced that fantasy to his brother, providing a feasible scenario in which a copilot at the controls of a plane makes a critical error, causing the DC-3 to crash, killing the pilot. The copilot, who miraculously survives after his mistake, then tells the suspicious CAB investigator that the pilot had been operating the controls when the plane crashed. (In the production, Robert Stack played the copilot and Lee J. Cobb the investigator. During one exchange, Stack's character says to Cobb, "You think I'm a lousy pilot," to which the investigator says, "No, but I think you're a liar." During the final dress rehearsal, Stack said his line as written; Cobb replied, "No, but I think you're a lousy actor.")

Serling ran with the story idea, finding it a perfect vehicle to explore the sacrifices in self-respect one makes to save the achievements of a life: the more someone has, the more desperately he wants to retain it, and the rationales that he constructs to support those betrayals of idealism become increasingly convoluted. This theme had supplanted over-the-hill athletes and cowardice in wars as his favorite topic.

Carol's grandmother, now a widow, and Serling's mother arrived for a final Christmas visit to Westport just two weeks before the move west. Both women helped them pack up the few remaining belongings, and on January 5, 1958, the writer, his wife, and their two children boarded an airplane in New York for the twelve-hour flight to their new home in California. In the morning, under blue skies and seventy-degree temperatures, Jody ran outside their rented Amalfi Drive home, owned by actress Virginia Bruce, in her pajamas and proclaimed that, by flying across country, they had changed seasons; it was now spring.

One of the first social outings the Serlings made as new residents of California was to a dinner with Mr. and Mrs. John Champion. Serling had grown to like Champion a great deal since their first encounter over the sugar cubes at MGM. He knew Champion to be a man of his word and found him intelligent, friendly, and warm—not the kind of man he expected to find in Bubbleland. The two men became close friends. They and their wives would often spend evenings and even weekends together in Palm Springs. When Champion formed a partnership with producer Hall Bartlett to make films for Paramount, Serling tentatively agreed to write a war picture for them, but the deal fell through when Champion was struck by a misdiagnosed case of bleeding ulcers.

The talk on this particular night soon turned to business—not surprising considering Serling's schedule; he had little time to do anything else, and it was usually the only thing on his mind. CBS wanted additional scripts to go with his "Twilight Zone" pilot, he said, and could John think of any? John couldn't, but Madelon Champion could. What if, she proposed, some astronauts (a very topical group, considering the recent proclamation of the space race) landed on what they assumed to be an uncharted, arid asteroid? After fighting and killing each other for the precious remaining drops of water, the survivor of the three discovers that they have landed in the desert near Las Vegas.

Serling loved the idea and asked Madelon to write it up just as she had told it to him. She protested she wasn't a writer, had never written anything in her life. He assured her it didn't have to be perfect. Just retell it. A week later Serling bought her story and in a day or so had adapted "I Shot an Arrow into the Air" and turned it into Dozier's office.

Weeks later Serling received word from Florida that his mother had had a severe stroke. For a few years she had suffered from high blood pressure and periodic bouts of depression. He flew to Mercy Hospital in Miami, where she had moved five years before with her sister Betty and brother-in-law Ed, but Esther did not regain consciousness during his stay. Tests showed she suffered massive brain damage. Tubes protruded from almost every orifice. The doctors conjectured she could die at any time or linger indefinitely. Her heart remained strong. Sadly, he returned home to his busy schedule and spent the next three weeks calling Florida at least once a day. He was relieved to hear that she remained alive yet was tortured by her vegetative condition.

On March 5, Esther Serling suffered another stroke and died.

Serling flew to Syracuse, where the Rosenthals had shipped the body for the funeral. He stayed only a few days before leaving again, consumed by his busy schedule, while Bob, now the manager of the UPI Washington, D.C., radio news bureau, flew to Miami to organize her personal effects. In an April 15 letter to his brother, Bob wrote that Esther's room "was a literal shrine to both of us." Esther had saved newspaper clippings, both by Bob and about Rod, as well as their letters to her over the years. One of these bore a note on the back: "When I am gone, please give this letter to Rod. It is one of the letters I treasured so much."

Bob, as executor of the estate, decided that the Rosenthals, Betty and Ed, who had been so kind to Esther and her children over the years, ought to get more than the five hundred dollars Esther bequeathed in her will. Out of the brothers' own proceeds, Bob doubled the amount and then bought them an expensive refrigerator. "I hope you agree with me," Bob wrote, "that we owe [Betty and Ed] far more than we could ever pay out, in the loving care, affection and understanding they gave Mother in the years when both of us were busy with our own careers." Serling agreed.

Perhaps because he was too busy to be able to allow himself to grieve properly, Serling did not appear overly shaken by his mother's death, despite her relatively young age—middle sixties—and sudden demise. Letters written within a few days of her death are cheerful and focused on work and make no mention of the event. Nor was he obviously sentimental, anxious to hold on to something that she had held dear in her life. When Bob sent Esther's ruby watch to Carol, Serling told him that he planned to sell it, but he also expressed some quiet remorse over what he felt was his failure to be a good enough son.

March was a strange month for Serling, one filled with contradiction, irony, exultation, and devastation—a month right out of "The Twilight Zone." He signed to write and produce his own television show. His mother died. He won his third Emmy in a row, for "The Comedians," but when getting out of his car on the way to the awards ceremony he closed the door on his leg and ruptured a vein, leaving him with a noticeable limp as he climbed the stairs to collect the statuette, as well as a lingering painful injury that took until well into the summer to heal properly. *Saddle the Wind* was released and, like the wind, disappeared after the critics spoke. He bought a beautiful new house—its swimming pool measured forty-five feet by twenty-two feet, with a surrounding grove of various citrus trees, a separate outdoor studio and an adjoining office for his secretary—which the Serlings would move into late in June after some extensive renovations. His second and third drafts of *No Blade of Grass* were in "shambles," he said. And his finger, because of his smoking, grew increasingly painful—so painful that many days he could barely use it.

That same month interviewer and journalist Martin Agronsky set up his NBC cameras in Serling's home for an in-depth interview. The director of Agronsky's "Look Here" was John Bloch, who had met Serling a few years before while in Fred Coe's office in New York. (Bloch once overhead someone say to Serling, "You write about the little man," to which Serling took instant and severe offense; he had taken the statement literally and thought it was a jab at his height.) In doing the prep work for the interview Bloch spent a fair amount of time talking to Serling, who had impressed him in New York with his intensity, intelligence, and good humor—the same qualities he now exhibited in California.

But now there was more: an ironic subtext. "He was getting cynical," Bloch remembers. "He felt he was being sucked into projects that were not personal, that he didn't care that much about—or not worthy of his beliefs. Most of Rod's early stuff came out of very strong statements he wanted to make. That was the turning point. He was having the world offered to him financially—but not to make his statements; to write entertainment."

That characteristic Bloch observed was given a voice during the interview. "There comes a time when caviar becomes a necessity," Serling coolly observed. In those days, as had been true since the 1930s, any apparently "serious" writer, which Serling was now considered, not writing books or stage plays was automatically deemed by the literati to be selling out. East Coast wits like Robert Benchley and S. J. Perlman, even Hemingway and Fitzgerald, had suffered the same jealous gibes when they wrote screenplays. Serling's critical mistake was to listen to their taunts, yet he sought and needed their acceptance. He went to great lengths to justify his decision to move west and write for the mass media. His prison, he explained, could be compared to a "velvet alley." He was pleading guilty—with an explanation.

Bloch is convinced that both phrases were uttered in absolute spontaneity: honest, thoughtful answers to an intelligent interviewer's questions. Less than a year later, he was amazed and delighted to view Serling's "Velvet Alley" on "Playhouse 90." "You know how they do it, Ernie," says Eddie Kirkley, the alcoholic producer, himself a victim of the velvet alley.

They give you a thousand dollars a week. And they keep on giving you a thousand dollars a week until that's what you need to live on. And then everyday you live after that, you're afraid they'll take it away from you. It's all very scientific. It's based on the psychological fact that a man is a grubbing, hungry little sleaze. . . . In twenty-four hours you can develop a taste for caviar. In forty-eight hours fish eggs are no longer a luxury; they're a necessity.

In 1959, when both "Velvet Alley" (in January) and "The Rank and File" (May) aired, Serling continued to rework this central theme of men whose ambition and passion for the sweet life, to which they have grown accustomed, cause them to compromise their morals and become human monsters.

While "Velvet Alley" was in so many ways purely autobiographical—the story of a fallen man, and intentionally so—in "Rank and File" Serling intended to tell the story of labor rackets corruption. He even asked his brother to locate transcripts of the recent labor hearings from the UPI offices. But the story mutated into a reflection of his own unease and became Serling's *mea culpa*, as revealing as "Velvet Alley."

Van Heflin, as Bill Kilcoyne, a former rummie tolerated only out of pity, begins his rise as a labor leader by an accident of fortune, then climbs through the ranks because of his guts and idealism. Along the way he finds himself feeling more pleasure out of his success than the causes for which he was supposed to be fighting. Ambitious and shrewd, he becomes almost completely corrupted, able to order the murder of his once best friend—a man who, unlike Kilcoyne, refused to be corrupted, refused to share in the spoils; a man who represented what remained of Kilcoyne's decaying conscience.

Reflecting on what he has become, Kilcoyne might easily have used the same words as Kirkley, the producer in "Velvet Alley." A resigned tone to his voice, he notes, "There was a time when I was like everybody else. I could drive a Tin Lizzy and live and die on the front porch in some grubby, little, dirty factory town, and I didn't want anything better. It was good enough. Saturday night in a bar. Sunday, sleep all day. Who could want anything more than that? But they fixed it and they fixed it so I can't go that route anymore. They fixed it so I can't go back to the way it was."

The tone in both monologues is virtually identical—sad, poignant, and resigned. They share a fictitious "they"—the they who fix it so Kilcoyne can't "go back to the way it was" and the they who might take away the thousand dollars a week from Eddie Kirkley. Serling seems not only to be admitting his own anguish over "selling out" but also contending that all humanity is made of the same weak fiber.

These are the portraits of a man who knows he has been seduced, sucked into a perpetual cycle of desire, despair, then rationalization, and more desire. He can see the top and sides of the world closing in around him. He can glance at the "little" people on the street and know he's no longer one of them—and not entirely dislike it either. As Ernie Pandish says to Max when presenting him with a fine watch, "It was a very nice feeling giving a guy ten dollars to get a job of engraving done in three hours. A very nice feeling. And now that I got it, I don't want to lose it."

Now that Serling began finally to achieve what he had worked so hard for, he found that he was miserable.

His finger continued to worsen. A Los Angeles physician prescribed medicine and soaking, but the painful symptoms remained. The digit was sore, swollen, cold to the touch, and had a yellowish tinge. But the biggest pain, for a man of such lofty ambitions, would come from elsewhere.

Serling was notified by Panama and Frank, the producers planning "Requiem" for Broadway, that his last draft still failed. Nor were negotiations with Anthony Quinn for the part of Mountain McClintock proceeding well. With no trace of irony, Serling told his old Antioch mentor, Nolan Miller, that such high-priced actors as Anthony Quinn work only after they're satisfied every possible cent has been wrung from the deal. And as though he himself were immune from such considerations, he explained that these actors want to act only in the movies— where the "fat money" is—and not on Broadway. All things considered, it was impossible to plan realistically for the coming fall season. The option continued for another twelve months, with the production put on the boards— tentatively, of course—for the fall 1959 season.

At least there was still the series.

As the preparations to shoot the pilot, "The Happy Place," continued, William Dozier hired William Self, the network's director of program development, as executive in charge of production. He gave Self the script to read, and Self and Serling met for the first time shortly thereafter, on the late April day when Serling walked into Self's office at CBS to hear the bad news: "While it's a very good script, Rod, it'll never sell the series."

Serling angrily demanded an explanation.

"Because," Self said, "it deals with euthanasia, killing old people, putting them on elevators and sending them to this so-called 'happy place,' which really means executing them. I think it smacks of Nazi Germany, and I think no advertiser is going to want to put his name on it."

Serling said that yes, of course, it smacked of Nazi Germany; it was a parable. It said something. It made a point.

True enough, Self agreed. "I told him it was a good script, a very good script," he remembers. But no advertiser could afford to be misinterpreted as endorsing that sort of thing. When dealing with the public one had to be painstakingly cautious in maintaining a corporate image that offended as few people as possible.

It was only one show, Serling said. Did "Requiem for a Heavyweight" imply that "Playhouse 90" did stories about boxers every week?

"This was the first episode," Self said. "In my judgment that means it is the *kind* of show we are going to deliver every week."

Rebuffed again, this time by a man he had never before met and knew nothing about, Serling stormed out, apparently anxious to go over Self's head and take up the matter with Dozier.

Self soon received a call from Dozier, who had just entertained one very angry and prideful Rod Serling. "What the hell happened with you and Serling?" Dozier asked.

"I told him the truth," Self replied.

"Well he's very upset, and he's making noises like you shouldn't be executive on the show. Let me see if I can put this all together. Just sit tight."

Dozier wanted to appease Serling, the network's star writer, who argued for the concept of the show, not necessarily this particular script. Tactfully, Dozier pointed out that Self had made a good point. With the agencies, a network and a creator had really only one chance to sell a series. If the agency did not like the pilot, they would not buy time for their clients no matter how much they liked the concept of the show.

Serling threatened to take his case to New York, but Dozier told him that Hubbell Robinson shared Self's opinion; in fact, Robinson hadn't liked the script at all. The news quelled Serling's visible anger, and Dozier suggested that he simply write another pilot. Serling offered "I Shot an Arrow," but both men quickly agreed it lacked a strong enough story to typify the series. When Serling walked out, Dozier was not certain what the writer would do.

Serling had to feel that, for as well as things were going, they weren't going very well. Disappointments heaped on top of successes. No series. No play. And his brother had just hit forty, which gave Serling great pause. All his adult life Serling feared getting older. "Forty's not much older than thirty-nine," he told Bob. "But I'm getting to be thirty-nine myself (he was thirty-four), and I sure as hell don't want to be forty."

"Rod had a premonition he would die early," his brother says.

At least there was still the Cayuga Lake house.

The Serlings planned to leave for the summer home about two weeks after finally moving into their huge, new Monaco Drive house—the same day as "A Town Has Turned to Dust" aired on "Playhouse 90."

It was very likely the distasteful experience on "Town" that convinced him to write another "Twilight Zone" pilot.

There are indications that Serling, feeling he should not write beneath his status and sell out to a "filmed series," had abandoned "The Twilight Zone" after Self's dismissal of his script. Never one for patience anyway, he had grown tired of the endless problems. First "The Time Element" had been too long. Then when he gave them a thirty-minute story, they'd had the temerity to contend that, while good, it could never sell the sponsors.

The previous year Martin Manulis had asked Serling to reattempt a dramatization of the Emmett Till kidnapping and murder that wary sponsors butchered so badly in 1956 on "U.S. Steel Hour." Manulis promised he would get the script through the gauntlet thrown down by the agencies and sponsors every time a controversial subject arose. Serling was wary, sick of sponsors and the problems they caused. But his social conscience likely overcame his skepticism. A rising number of hatred crimes were being committed in the South as the civil rights movement gathered momentum. Bombings and beatings, often committed by Ku Klux Klan members, occurred almost every week. In one particularly gruesome crime, Klansmen forced a black truck driver in Alabama, whom they'd accused some weeks before of speaking to a white woman, to jump to his death from a bridge into the Alabama River; it was the truck driver's first day on the job, so he could not have been the man the Klansmen wanted—a fact that only underlined their cruelty.

Serling wished with all his heart that this phenomenon of hatred would simply disappear. "I happen to think that singularly the worst aspect of our time is prejudice," he would later say. "It is from this evil that all other evils grow and multiply. In almost everything I've written, there is a thread of this—man's seemingly palpable need to dislike someone other than himself."

Unfortunately, Manulis had been overly optimistic. When "A Town Has Turned to Dust" finally aired June 19, at least seven different sponsors—including Bristol-Myers, R. J. Reynolds, and Kimberly-Clark—had "chopped it up like a roomful of butchers at work on a steer".... "They ganged up on us; we never had a chance."

In a May 1 directive from CBS executive Guy della-

Cioppa, the network demanded several changes that Serling considered all too ludicrous:

1) In Act 1 completely eliminate fact earlier killing was colored man. He will have name like "Diego" without specifically labelling him Mexican.

2) Modify reason why attack occurred to eliminate whistling at girl connotation. Use simple explanatory line indicating boy had gotten out of line and didn't know his place rather than making a pass at a woman of a different class.

3) Entire script to be carefully examined to soften implication Anna and Mexican kid enjoy jumping in the hay together.

As *Time* noted, "Emmett Till became a romantic Mexican youth who loved the storekeeper's wife, but only 'with his eyes.'" And to lose as little Mexican purchasing power of their products as possible, the sponsors omitted any potentially offensive epithets: "Mex," "enchilada-eater," "bean-eater," and "greasy." The phrase "twenty men in hoods" was remade into "twenty men in homemade masks" (although Rod Steiger, who had rehearsed the phrase with *hoods* many times before the live show, mistakenly said it anyway).

"My sheriff couldn't commit suicide because one of our sponsors was an insurance firm [Allstate] and they claimed that suicide often leads to complications in settling policy claims," Serling said. "The lynch victim was called Clemson, but we couldn't use this because South Carolina had an all-white college by that name. The setting was moved to the Southwest in the 1870s."

(Dozier remembers another remarkable instance of network censorship, instigated by della-Cioppa. The script had been approved ahead of time, as usual, by the program's sponsor, American Gas Companies. When della-Cioppa read it, he called the sponsor's agency and asked whether they'd read the script. Told it had passed muster, he asked whether anyone had noticed the line about "Hitler's ovens." "Doesn't that bother you?" he said. Says Dozier, "All of a sudden they said, 'Oh, yeah. We don't want that aspersion cast at our gas company.'" The line had to be bleeped.)

Serling wondered how much more of this pettiness he could take. He felt that a series—one in which he not only had complete creative control but also could use that control to make his points metaphorically; use Martians, for example, instead of Klansmen—demeaned his talents less than this relentless stupidity that ensued each time he wanted to say something, to make a point. To him, illuminating absolute, not relative, wrongs could not be construed as controversial. Controversy arose when both sides had debatable merit. Calling a murderer a murderer was not controversial.

He knew now without doubt that William Self had been correct: no agency would dare buy time for a series in which a supposedly representative script revolved around killing old people—and white old people at that.

What else could he do besides the series? Broadway beckoned, although much less enticingly than before, and even then he questioned his abilities to write for the legitimate stage. He had in his file six unworthy drafts of "Requiem." Perhaps, he thought, he didn't understand the rules of this game.

He also questioned his ability to write screenplays. MGM was increasingly disenchanted with his work, and he with them. He finished the last draft of *No Blade of Grass*, which producer Joe Pasternak disliked as much as other production executives had disliked *Company of Cowards*.

Mulling over these developments, Serling took his family to the lake house, intending to enjoy a relaxing two-month vacation. Instead, it grew nightmarish. His finger became acutely painful, and after a team of doctors studied test results, they determined he had Berger's disease—a vascular condition caused primarily by smoking; nicotine, a vasoconstrictor, reduces the blood flow to the extremities. For a four-pack-a-day man, like Serling, Berger's disease was not too uncommon. The prescription: quit smoking—or amputate.

As nervous and addicted as he was, Serling could not cut out tobacco entirely, not even with the threat of amputation hanging over his hand. Years later, in the hospital after his first heart attack, he would bribe orderlies and nurses to bring him cigarettes. Smoking felt as natural a part of his existence as breathing—it was often, in fact, through cigarettes that he took his air. His secretary, Marjorie Langsford, says that Serling would "attack" his cigarettes, drawing on them so deeply he could finish one in just a few drags. Langsford, who also smoked, recalls that sometimes the smoke in his office got so thick she could not see him as he dictated to her; they would have to go outside.

By late July, on a ration of a few cigarettes a day, the finger had improved considerably. With the pain subsiding, Serling found that he would miss the attention paid to him by his family. He wrote to Dick Berg that he planned to have a "sympathectomy" performed by a surgeon. (Berg had by now moved his family to Los Angeles for his career's sake.)

Somewhat of a hypochondriac, Serling once dragged his brother with him to the doctor in Beverly Hills, certain he had "cancer of the heart." It turned out to be gas. He acted miserably while his finger hurt, unconcerned that his sour disposition over a condition that he had caused himself obtruded on others. In midsummer, while driving one day with the Serlings near the lake, Carol's grandmother suddenly suffered a stroke and was rendered speechless and oblivious. She improved quickly though, and her courage after such a traumatic and frightening affliction caused Serling to compare his own whiny reaction over his bad finger to her composure after the stroke. Where she acted bravely and with resolve—the embodiment of a paratrooper—he seemed like a whining child. (In a letter to his brother in which he both praised her and maligned himself, he urged Bob, his old horror film companion, not to miss *The Fly*.) By early fall he had returned to smoking as much as ever, apparently resigned to his addiction—and, if necessary, the cutting consequences.

Serling still had not decided whether or not to rewrite "The Twilight Zone" pilot, although he clearly leaned in that direction; he wanted no more "A Town Has Turned to Dust" experiences ("a script has turned to dust," he told William F. Nolan). However, some indecision remained.

Through a mutual friend, actor Everett Sloan, Serling arranged a meeting with Saul David, then the head of Bantam Books (later he would produce such films as *Our Man Flynt* and *Fantastic Voyage*). "He wanted to know how to write short stories," David recalls. "I remember that very clearly. He said he didn't know how and said he'd never written one." (Apart from his college assignments, he had not.)

David, who had had "a memorable encounter" with Otto Preminger in the recent past and knew other Hollywood personalities in that same egotistical vein, remembers being struck by Serling's "extraordinary humility. It was really quite unexpected. I was not thinking in terms of humble Hollywoodniks. He very evidently wanted to be liked. He really wanted everybody to like him. Rod wagged his tail the whole time you talked to him."

David agreed to help Serling learn the rudiments of short-fiction writing, and the two became friends. A man who could write "Patterns" and "Requiem for a Heavyweight," and a man who could tell jokes as well as Serling, should have no trouble learning the art form. "He was a superb raconteur," David recalls. "He did dialects, he understood the pauses, he really gave you a show. And he really loved to hear them himself. He was really infectious about that. He laughed hard, had a wonderful time."

It seemed clear to David in helping Serling (the stories they worked on together were in fact the prose stylizations of the first "The Twilight Zone" scripts Serling had assembled) that the writer doubted his own talents and abilities. "He had come to Hollywood earlier that year, expecting to build on his successes, but nothing worked," David observes. "All of a sudden it occurred to him that maybe he was mistaken."

Fatefully, Serling received word from Hollywood that would postpone, at least temporarily, his drive to be a serious fiction writer. Bert Granet, the producer of "Desilu Playhouse," had just purchased "The Time Element" for shooting in the fall. Not least of the good news: Robert Parrish planned to direct.

Granet had met Serling through Parrish earlier in the year, during his quest to find quality writers who might provide decent enough scripts to attract the kind of actors he wanted in his shows. Granet believed that viewers like or dislike shows based on the character—that is, the appeal of the actor playing the part; the better and more ingratiating the actor, the more firmly rooted to the story will be the viewer. "Desilu Playhouse," which presented anthology dramas, had never landed the quality talent Granet, a former film producer, demanded; "Playhouse 90," which employed all the "quality" writers at CBS, got the fine actors he coveted. His anthologies, he knew, were in truth filler for the three weeks out of every month when Lucy and Desi did not present their variety specials with big-name stars like Red Skelton and Milton Berle. The agencies bought time on the weekly show only in order to be in line when Lucy and Desi performed—and the ratings shot up. Granet wanted to change all that, to make the dramas as popular as the song-and-dance-and-laugh shows.

Serling told him at the time of their meeting that he had no scripts for him, that everything he once stored away had already been bought. However, he remembered, there was this one particular science-fictionish story that CBS had bought and put aside, about a man who dreams he tries to save Pearl Harbor.

Unbeknownst to Serling, Granet used his wiles to locate the script and bought it from Dozier for ten thousand dollars. By the time he notified Serling, Granet had already fought and beat the advertising agencies, who violently opposed any sort of speculative fiction stories. Granet had to vow solemnly to them that he would never again air a science-fiction story. "At the time, no one wanted unfinished stories," Granet explains. "They wanted a bow on everything."

If Serling had known that that had been the agencies' position, he might never have begun work on the new pilot to "The Twilight Zone," a series in which none of the stories was finished, nor wrapped with a bow. (Aaron Spelling once asked Serling, "How can you write so many 'Twilight Zone' scripts?" "Easy," Serling replied. "I don't have to write a third act. The third act is, 'That's the way it is in "The Twilight Zone."'")

Late in the summer he returned from Cayuga Lake to make changes that the agencies had mandated in "The Time Element" script. They would not allow the main character to try to convince the military of the impending Japanese attack, so Serling had him approach an unsympathetic newspaper publisher. (Serling was disappointed when Robert Parrish backed out of the show because of a film commitment, *The Wonderful Country*, starring Robert Mitchum.)

Serling walked into William Self's office and laid another script on his desk, "Where Is Everybody," about a man who appears to be the only inhabitant of a city, yet everywhere he sees signs of having just missed others; a still-burning cigarette figures prominently. The longer he goes without finding other living beings, the more panic-stricken the man becomes. The events build to an emotional climax, and we finally learn he is in fact an astronaut undergoing isolation experimentation. The entire story has been a construct of his contact-starved imagination.

Why Serling chose this particular subject is not too

difficult to ascertain. The year before, the Soviet Union had launched two Sputnik satellites, starting a race for space that would come to be seen as representative of America's superiority. Immediately, America began an astronaut training program that would capture the public's attention and make the whole country aviation- and space-crazy. That year the first American earth satellite was launched, the Navy flew an X-15 jet at Mach 6, and American-made jets flew transatlantic and transcontinental routes. At the same time, according to Serling's own explanation of the story's origin, finding himself wandering alone on a film lot among its sets of cities one night induced a severe sense of isolation.

Self loved the story and agreed that it hit a tenor appropriate to sell a series of speculative fiction. It was not science fiction per se, nor was it even impossible on any level. He did not foresee a problem, assuming its production qualities were adequate. This was as effusive as Self ever got. (Years later, in a script conference between the two men, Serling would animatedly tell his story, acting out all the parts, while Self sat quietly. "That's good," Self said flatly. Serling was incredulous at the reaction. "Good? It's good? That's all you have to say? Remind me to never again tell you a story.") His lack of unequivocal enthusiasm did not provide Serling with much comfort. As a safety, he signed out in early November to write a war picture for the Mirisch Corporation, *33rd Squadron*. Technically, he had to be loaned out by MGM, but at that point the studio seemed only too glad to let him go.

"The Time Element" aired November 24 and received more telegrams, phones calls, and, eventually, mail than any other drama CBS ever aired. Not surprisingly then, the network made "The Twilight Zone" top priority and ordered a pilot on which preproduction work began in a rush.

Serling left a meeting with Self and Dozier to find Earl Holliman, whom he remembered well from "The Dark Side of the Earth" the year before, walking to his car.

Holliman had been rehearsing a "Playhouse 90," "The Return of Ansel Gibbs," about a crusading journalist. The actor had not been overly impressed with the role and felt uncomfortable in it. He expressed those insecurities to Serling in the parking lot.

"Well, we're putting together a science-fiction series," Serling told him.

Holliman immediately recalled the only science-fiction film he had acted in, the classic *Forbidden Planet*, playing the role of the cook, Cookie, whose every scene is with Robbie the Robot. "I thought, 'Oh boy, another space show with a space ship and thirty guys on board talking to robots,'" Holliman says.

Serling explained that negotiation for Tony Curtis to act the lead role had broken off over the actor's firm, and prohibitive, fee (as a profit participant and executive producer now, he suddenly became concerned with such matters). "How would you like to do it?" he asked Holliman.

Visualizing his previous experience on *Forbidden Planet*—"I remember standing in front of the camera wishing the floor would open up and swallow me"—Holliman did not exactly leap at the opportunity.

"I'll send you the script," Serling said.

Holliman drove home thinking he would be playing one of the thirty spacemen. The next night, while eating dinner, he read the script for "Where Is Everybody?" that Serling had sent to the "Playhouse 90" set.

"I thought I would just kind of peruse it, but I couldn't stop turning the pages," Holliman remembers. "It was fascinating. The goose pimples stood up on my flesh. First of all, there was nobody in it but me, plus I was fascinated with this guy who went from place to place and constantly just missed somebody who must be there—but there was never anybody there. I was so pleased with the script. Just delighted. I called him the next morning and said, 'Yes, yes, yes.'"

Dozier and Serling hired Robert Stevens, a friend of

Dozier, to direct. A somewhat offbeat man, Stevens had done some very interesting work on "Web" and "Suspense" and had an excellent reputation. At the sole read-through, only Serling, Stevens, and Holliman were present. The very next day production began on the back lot at Universal, where most of the sets they would need already existed.

It was a cold and dreary December day. Holliman still felt he did not have the role down pat. But each time he approached Stevens during a break in filming, Stevens avoided him, usually by picking up a telephone. Stevens either did not want to discuss the role with him, or he was helping to induce the isolation and panic Holliman needed to make his character credible.

At twilight, after many hours of very hard work, while the crew lined up the second-to-last shot of the day, the assistant cameraman muttered, "Uh-oh." Instinctively, everyone knew what he meant: the camera had malfunctioned the entire day, leaving them without a single frame to show for their efforts.

Everything went smoothly the next six days, and the entire crew felt that they had contributed to a very fine product that would sell a series and possibly guarantee them at least a season of steady work.

(Holliman, perhaps remembering his previous victory with Serling during "The Dark Side of the Earth," suggested to the writer during filming that his character, at one point apparently trapped in a phone booth, should tear out a page of the directory and stuff it in his pocket; later, when the audience discovers that this has been the imaginary odyssey of an astronaut in an isolation booth, he wanted the page to fall from his pocket. "Let me put it this way," Serling said with a smile. "You're wrong." But, subsequently, in Serling's first collection of short stories, called *From The Twilight Zone*, which he had begun a year earlier with Saul David's help, the character in *Where Is Everybody?* finds in his pocket at the end of the story a ticket stub that he had placed there after going into an empty theater.)

Serling busied himself now with rewriting "Velvet Alley." Exactly a week before it aired, January 22, Serling repaid the one-thousand-dollar advance Panama and Frank had given him for the Broadway option to "Requiem." It seems in retrospect a particularly symbolic act that only serves to underline the bitterness written into "Velvet Alley"—a bitter story about bitter people written, apparently, by a very bitter man. The show ends with writer Ernie Pandish sitting on the stoop of his former residence in New York, the snow falling, sobbing as he tries desperately to brag to the little neighbor boy (played by Mickey Bradock, later Mickey Dolenz of The Monkees) about his huge swimming pool and the orange trees that grow all around it.

Ernie Pandish presented a pathetic picture of the internal conflicts that Serling himself could not justify in 1959. Serling could never be satisfied with what he had attained and felt as unworthy of his successes as he was anxious for them. "If I were to write a next chapter for 'Velvet Alley,' Ernie would be jacking out scripts for some TV film factory," Serling told the *Los Angeles Times*. "But I've decided that's not for me."

The response to "Velvet Alley" was strong and sharply divided. Dan Jenkins, Hollywood bureau chief for *TV Guide* and an acquaintance of Serling, had one of the more interesting reactions. A native of Los Angeles, Jenkins took Serling to task for implying that Hollywood had been the corrupting influence on Pandish, that the writer would never have turned bad had he returned to New York to continue writing. Serling replied with one of his standard comebacks, mentioned many times over the years: "Criticizing it this way is sort of like taking *Death of a Salesman* to task because all salesmen don't commit suicide."

Serling also revealed to Jenkins the depth of his own insecurities by explaining Pandish's reasons for staying in Hollywood after Eddie Kirkley has given his "thousand dollars a week" monologue. Pandish remained, Serling explained, not because of the message of the speech but because this man, Eddie Kirkley, a man with power in an industry he had wanted to be part of all his life, actually needed him—and he needed to be needed.

(Blanche Gaines, noting that Ernie Pandish's leaving his agent, Max, had precipitated Max's heart attack and death, wrote Serling to say that this was "Freudian.")

By mid-February Serling had written several "Twilight Zone"s and abandoned the Mirisch war film, 633 *Squadron* (like many of his film scripts, it was rewritten by another writer and finally released four years later). He wrote "The Lonely," about a prisoner on an asteroid who falls in love with a female robot; "Escape Clause," about a man who makes a pact with the devil for immortality only to be sentenced to life in prison for the death of his wife; and "Walking Distance," in which an executive returns to his childhood. He took extra care with each of them, aware that a line here or there might mean the difference between a sold series—one that he now cared deeply about—and a denial. Completing "Rank and File" for "Playhouse 90" demanded all of his minuscule spare time. (When the show finally went to rehearsal in May, he told his brother that the show would be either a "bombshell or a bomb." He praised Van Heflin but reviled Luther Adler. "He thinks, and when you get actors who think, you're in real trouble. He's a little Jewish fag"; the epithet *fag* became one of Serling's favorites in the coming years.)

In March Serling flew to New York with the pilot and a short filmed introduction in which he starred. His audiences were the agency men and their clients, who would decide whether "The Twilight Zone" saw the light of day. After so many years of fighting these people over minutiae, he was now attempting to become, in essence, their partner. "How do you do," began the filmed introduction in which Serling stands alone on a sound stage. "You gentlemen, of course, know how to push a product. That essentially is your job. My presence here on this set is for much the same purpose—simply to push a product. . . . This is a series for the storyteller because it's our thinking that a mass audience will always sit still and listen and watch a well-told story."

Later in the introduction Serling walked over to a table on which sat a bottle of sand, a cogwheel, a legal document, a handgun, and a vial of liquid. He talked about them as props, as they pertained to each of the other scripts he had so far written but which had not yet been shot—and would not be unless the sponsors bought the show. He concluded his talk: "We fully expect they'll go to the stores on the following day and buy your products. We think it's that kind of a show. So gentlemen, sit back and take your first trip into . . . 'The Twilight Zone.'"

The show was sold that trip, as quickly as they could have hoped. Both General Foods and Kimberly-Clark agreed to buy all the commercial time on the first twenty-six episodes. After thirteen shows they would evaluate the ratings, demographics, and trend and then decide whether to renew their sponsorships for the final thirteen shows. Much of their enthusiasm for the series derived from the fact that it was Serling in charge. The renowned writer had promised them, in exchange for a complete lack of interference, a show without controversy. Over celebratory drinks and dinner with the sponsors and their respective agency contacts—Foote, Cone & Belding for General Foods and Young & Rubicam for Kimberly-Clark—Serling realized again that "Where Is Everybody?" had been the only show that could have sold them; these were not the type of men to commit to a season of anthology based on a script like "The Happy Place."

Next task: setting up a production entity. Rod Serling Productions became Cayuga Productions (after the lake house, which had come to symbolize for him peace and serenity). Serling asked Bill Self to produce, but Self preferred to stay at the network, where he had greater job stability; no one knew whether the series would be a hit (within a year, though, Self would leave CBS for Screen Gems). Serling then decided that his old friend John Champion should produce "The Twilight Zone." They had an easy rapport, and Serling respected Champion's taste and judgment.

Champion had never produced a foot of film or tape for television. Prior to 1959 his film credits included *Zero Hour*, *The Last Hunt*, and *Shotgun*. He was skeptical about trying his skills on television. Serling, though, convinced him it would be worthwhile.

Serling drove Champion over to CBS to introduce William Dozier and William Self to the new line producer of the series. Driving with the top down on a pleasant, early spring day, Champion and Serling were in high spirits. "With his gorgeous tan and jet black hair, no one ever looked better in a white Continental," Champion says.

The meeting in Dozier's office went well, and after shaking hands, apparently consummating the deal, Serling took Champion into the basement to show him the pilot. Twenty minutes later Dozier came in to tell them he could not accept Champion as series producer.

"Why?" Serling asked, clearly perturbed. "This man has been in the film business for fifteen years."

"Because he's never done television," Dozier said. "We can't entrust a show like this to someone who hasn't done television. I know he's talented, but I'm sorry." He turned to leave.

"Oh, shit," Serling said. "I don't know what to say, John. I'm embarrassed as hell, but that's the way it goes. There's nothing I can do."

(Five months later, Lew Wasserman at Universal signed Champion to cocreate and produce "Laramie"; four years after that, he created "McHale's Navy.")

CBS believed Serling had acted irresponsibly in choosing Champion. If this were typical of the decisions he would make as executive producer of a series in which they were investing hundreds of thousands, if not millions, of dollars, then they needed a strong producer to rein him in. Self suggested Buck Houghton, whom he had known at "Schlitz Playhouse." Houghton, who got his start in films in the Office of War Information during World

War II, had been at RKO and Paramount before working on the first one-hour television series, "Wire Service."

The executives felt uneasy about Serling's possible reaction to Houghton, a man he had never met and might assume to be a network spy. But he allayed their fears almost immediately. Serling walked into the room where Dozier, Self, and Houghton were already chatting. Houghton stood to shake hands, rising to his full six-foot, three-inch height. Taking his hand, Serling surveyed him from top to bottom, then turned to Dozier and Self. "Don't you have any short producers?" he asked.

"I think we're going to get along fine," Houghton said.

Thus began a fruitful working relationship. Serling and Houghton each respected the other's talents and capabilities. "My attitude as a producer," Houghton recalls, "was that I am a creative administrator. I can't write, I can't compose music, I can't act. I can't do one goddamned thing—except that I know how to pick people who can."

Because his contract called for him to write almost the entire first season of a hoped-for thirty-nine shows, Serling worked feverishly. Reruns never ran in the middle of the season, so in order to guarantee on-schedule production of each show, the approved scripts had to be mostly completed before the series debut in October. (Production on the first show, "The Lonely," began the first week in June.) Once he found the germ of a story, the rest happened quickly. Composing the plot mentally, exuberantly acting out parts as he dictated the dialogue and camera directions into his Dictaphone, and polishing the draft took less than a week; he finished some scripts, as deadlines demanded, in as little as a day. When his fertile brain seemed to run dry of ideas, Ashley-Steiner helped him locate the rights to short stories he had once read and thought might be adaptable. (During the first season, "And When the Sky Was Opened" was adapted from a short story, "Disappearing Act", by Richard Matheson, who became a frequent freelance contributor to the series; "The Hitch-Hiker" was adapted from a radio play by Lucille Fletcher; and "Time Enough at Last" from a short story by Lynn Venable. Serling wrote almost as many adapted scripts as original ideas.)

That summer he spent only a week at the lake house in New York. He left Carol and the girls and returned home to work in his newly completed study by the pool, a pine-paneled room with a huge stone fireplace and walls of shelves that held both books and bound copies of his scripts. He woke early in the morning, dictated for several hours, broke for lunch, then drove to the Cayuga Productions offices at MGM, the studio he had chosen for its facilities. After attending to the business affairs, consulting with Houghton and, if necessary, other writers and CBS, he returned home and often worked till late at night.

The problem of finding a narrator had not been solved. The network demanded at least some sort of continuing character in this otherwise anthology series and wanted an authoritarian man's voice to narrate brief introductions and epilogues. (The idea of having a narrator on camera had not yet evolved.) The actor originally hired to do the pilot, Westbrook Van Voorhis, had a rich, stentorian voice that everyone agreed had been the only incompatible element of "Where Is Everybody?" A search ensued. Orson Welles's name remained at the top of the list, but his exorbitant price disqualified him. For a time the actor Marvin Miller had the inside track. When that deal fell through, Serling suggested himself for the role.

Although he later claimed to dislike performing, Serling eagerly approached the job. No one knew of his extensive experiences behind a microphone more than fifteen years earlier, but when the executives and ad men heard the tape, on which Serling exaggeratedly chopped words for dramatic effect, they knew they'd found their narrator. ("I could never get him to say *zone,*" Bill Dozier remembers. "He always said, 'Twilight *Zun.*' I'd say, 'Rod, say *phone,*' and he'd say *phone.* I'd say, 'Say *loan,*' and he'd say *loan.* I'd say, 'Say *tone,*' and he'd say *tone.* Then I'd say, 'Say *zone,*' and he'd say *zun*. He had a block about it. He wanted to, but it would just not come out that way.")

In the fall of 1959 Serling left on a whirlwind tour through the East and Midwest to promote "The Twilight Zone" by currying favor with critics and local network affiliates; he personally previewed completed episodes. Plagued by a cold and an ear infection, and averaging four hours' sleep a night, this became a miserable odyssey. He began to second-guess his decision to enter series television. He felt in some senses he had joined the enemy. ("The advertising men are a much maligned group," he told *Daily Variety* with no intended irony. "Of course, I take issue with much of their timorousness when it seems needless, but I understand their concern now and look for a compromise, hoping to find some middle ground.") Television critics, the sponsors, and the agency men suddenly had control over his life. Before, if one or the other disliked something he wrote, the next project always awaited. This time, on this project, the all-or-nothing principle applied.

Fittingly, the last stop on the tour before returning home was an appearance on "The Mike Wallace Interviews," a thirty-minute weekly network series in which the famous broadcast journalist conducted an in-depth discussion with notable celebrities and newsmakers (the show itself debuted the night "Requiem for a Heavyweight" aired, nearly three years before).

Wallace of course hit hard on the subject of Serling's appearing to abandon "writing anything important for television." This provided Serling with an opportunity to state publicly what he had been rationalizing internally these previous months.

"If, by important," Serling responded, "you mean that I'm not going to try to delve into current social problems dramatically, you're quite right, I'm not." No apologies. He explained that he had grown tired of fighting the sponsors and that on "The Twilight Zone" he called the content shots. He noted that in the eighteen scripts so far completed, only one change had been mandated: General Foods, the maker of Sanka instant coffee, had taken umbrage at a line in which a sailor on a British ship sits down and orders tea.

When Wallace asked him why he did not get out of television entirely to write the accepted "serious" works—legitimate theater and novels, like Paddy Chayefsky and Gore Vidal—Serling said, "I stay in television because I think it's very possible to perform a function of providing adult, meaningful, exciting, challenging drama without dealing in controversy necessarily."

Wallace, as though reading Serling's heart and mind, asked whether he thought the writer "could make it outside of television."

"I'm not sure I could," Serling said. "And I suppose this is an admission of a kind of weakness, or at least a sense of insecurity on my part. I've never had a Broadway play produced, and what few motion pictures I've written have been somewhat less than spectacular. . . . This is the medium I understand."

The talk turned to money, and Wallace implied that Serling had chosen television just for the money, as though it were a crime. This was the corrupting-influence-of-Hollywood-big-money theory, and Serling acknowledged it. He explained: When someone experiences the kind of relative overnight success he did, with all its trappings, one often succumbs to "a preoccupation with the symbols of status: the heated swimming pool, the big car, the concern about billing—all these things. In a sense, rather minute things in context, but they become disproportionately large in a guy's mind."

And what becomes small? Wallace asked.

There were, Serling admitted, fewer hours to spend with his family.

Rod Serling had come very far very fast since telling a national radio audience on "Dr. Christian" that he wanted to "live in a large house, in the suburb of a large city, raise a family, a lot of dogs, and write."

On October 2, 1959, at 9:30 P.M., CBS broadcast the premiere of a new show. Eerie theme music (composed by Bernard Hermann), soon to be recognizable to millions, played over the screen's tableau of surreal images. Then the chopped, teeth-clenching voice, destined to become as famous as the music, spoke these words: "There is a fifth dimension, beyond that which is known to man. It is a dimension as vast as space and as timeless as infinity. It is the middle ground between light and shadow, between science and superstition, and it lies between the pit of man's fear and the summit of his knowledge. This is the dimension of imagination. It is an area which we call The Twilight Zone."

Over the following years this dimension would evolve into a prison from which its creator, narrator, and soon-to-be on-camera host could never completely escape—just as if he himself were a character in one of the 156 plots to come.

6

ANOTHER DIMENSION

The Twilight Zone" became a true phenomenon. Three decades after its premiere, it arguably remains the most recognizable and evocative series from television's childhood and actually seems to have marked an evolutionary leap—almost revolutionary for the way it broke out of a mold—in the medium's messages.

The 1950s of "Father Knows Best," "I Love Lucy," and "Leave It to Beaver" reflected an obsession with normality. These fictional characters who embedded themselves deepest in the masses' consciousness had lives with narrow problems, all of which could be resolved in a logical scene or two. At the end of the half hour, their minor faults or foibles just made them more endearing to us.

"The Twilight Zone" felt different from the beginning, and not just because it lacked a single continuing character: this reality was hardly claustrophobic. "The Twilight Zone" defied laws of convention and made the fantastical possible to an audience who willingly suspended disbelief. Characters, while not identifiable from week to week, were always recognizable, protypes of Everyman playing a

186

game with more liberal rules; ordinary people in extraordinary circumstances: a man who longs, like many daydreaming people, to return to a simpler time in memory—and then does so; a young boy, like most young boys, wishing over and over for something special to happen—and then it does. For the shows' signature twist endings, Serling gained a reputation as O. Henry in outer space. (One of Serling's better radio scripts in college was an adaptation of O. Henry's "Gift of the Magi.")

"All the scripts were about average people with a common problem," Buck Houghton observes. "A problem where people can say, 'I never wanted to fly, but I can imagine it.' These were common problems with common people. We never told a story about a king."

Serling trusted the audience and targeted intelligent adults. What surprised him, and everyone connected with the show, was its appeal to young people. "If you do write back a letter to me, while you're at it, I wish you'd tell me what fairyland is like," wrote one young teenager. "I know that a man like you would have visited 'Fairyland' sometime or another. And if you haven't, nobody should."

The greatest impact of "Twilight Zone," then, was made as one of the first shows to be aimed at the baby boomers—or so it seemed to them—the oldest of whom were in their early teens when it premiered. Houghton remembers that much of the earliest mail came from parents asking them to put the show on at an earlier hour, so that their younger children would not plead to stay up late.

While young and old watched together, the young felt possessive of the show. Until "Twilight Zone," they had not found a reason to be home at ten o'clock on a Friday night. Each installment was awaited with great anticipation, its arrival an event. Come Monday morning, students all over America asked each other, "Did you see it?" The "it" didn't have to be defined. As a cultural icon, "it" became part of the same historical wave that swept John Kennedy to win the presidency and the Beatles to alter music history. (Reginald Rose, then writing and producing

"The Defenders" on CBS, asked his soon-to-be ten-year-old son what entertainment he would like at his birthday party. "'Twilight Zone,'" the boy said. Rose showed three of them.)

At the time, Houghton admits, "we didn't think by any means, we were doing anything notable." But in fact a good case can be made for "The Twilight Zone" having contributed significantly to the youthful idealism of the 1960s. Unlike science fiction, which often takes imaginative joyrides just for the pure pleasure of going, "The Twilight Zone" traveled to worlds in which honesty and ethics and principles were as indigenous as gravity. "It takes a strong sense of irony," Houghton says, "to write a story about a set of bank thieves who get away with a lot of gold. Then after they're sequestered for a long time, they discover gold is worth only a dollar a pound."

Assembled together, the various stories comprise the breadth of Rod Serling's rules for righteous conduct: punished are the vain (a man who discovers that he towers over a race of people intends to become their god, until the true giants appear and crush him), the greedy (on the night a rich old man lies dying he forces his gold-digging heirs to wear gruesome Mardi Gras masks that will permanently disfigure their faces), and the wicked (after condemning as obsolete and sentencing to death a man who reads outlawed books and believes in an outlawed God, an official of a future totalitarian state is tricked into revealing his own deep-seated faith, and then he too is condemned as obsolete). Rewarded are the innocent (a man who has the power to tell what someone will need in the immediate future saves himself by telling his tormentor to wear a pair of slippery shoes), the kind (an elderly street vendor averts the death of a little girl by making one last pitch to Mr. Death), and the meek (a proverbial loser who tries to commit suicide is given a second chance at life and becomes a contented trumpeter named Gabriel).

At their most elemental, the majority of "Twilight

Zones" are morality plays. Week after week, Serling's devotion to fairness and justice seeped into a collective consciousness: in "The Twilight Zone," bad guys got their comeuppance and peace and love were noble goals. By the time the series' last original episode ran in the late spring of 1964, most of the entire emerging generation had received regular doses of subtle moralizing. And with the United States becoming increasingly involved in a jungle war ten thousand miles away for a cause that lacked immediate identification, many of this same generation would soon find themselves demanding explanations that fit, coincidentally or not, Serling's ethos.

For all its significance, if "The Twilight Zone" had debuted in 1989 instead of 1959, it would likely have lasted about six shows before being pulled for a replacement. CBS slotted the series against ABC's immensely popular "77 Sunset Strip," which not only began its new season the same night as "Where Is Everybody?" but also started half an hour earlier. Not many people turned the channel halfway through. Despite almost uniformly excellent reviews, some of which proclaimed "The Twilight Zone" as *the* new show of the year, the premiere got trounced in the ratings.

Ratings mattered much to the sponsors, General Foods and Kimberly-Clark, and Serling was nervous. He jokingly told many people he had composed a new song, "Kookie, Kookie, Lend Me Your Ratings," a takeoff on the novelty hit of the previous spring, "Kookie, Kookie, Lend Me Your Comb," by Edd Byrnes, whose character of Kookie on "77 Sunset Strip" became famous for combing his hair.

But the sponsors showed patience. James Andrews, the product manager for the Maxwell House division of General Foods, wrote to Serling immediately after the debut to assure him that the company had every intention of letting the series build, as they felt it should, by word of mouth. Serling thought it a "kind" gesture and thanked Andrews profusely. (He regularly corresponded with the sponsors, praising them constantly; if the renewal decisions had hinged at all on personal relations, then the scales would be tipped in his favor.) Meanwhile, the agency demanded that CBS increase the number of on-air promotions.

Kindness, courtesy, and assurances aside, Serling believed that "The Twilight Zone" needed to establish itself as quickly as possible. Although the contractual evaluation period would come in mid-January, realistically the decision might come as early as November. The series would have to show significant ratings or risk a sponsorship withdrawal.

He scheduled episodes that he thought balanced quality and accessibility. Following "Where Is Everybody?" were: "One for the Angels," Ed Wynn's star turn about the pitchman who saves a girl from death; "Mr. Denton on Doomsday," about a rummy gunslinger, Dan Duryea, who resorts to a magic potion; "The Sixteen-Millimeter Shrine," starring Ida Lupino as an aging actress who longs for her glory days and returns to them—and becomes her own screen image; "Walking Distance," in which Gig Young stumbles upon his own childhood; and "Escape Clause," about a hypochondriac who gives his soul to the devil in exchange for immortality, only to be sentenced to life in prison.

Serling was polishing the last of the twenty-six scripts to which the sponsors had committed when he heard that the top brass at Kimberly-Clark had been displeased with "The Sixteen-Millimeter Shrine" and "Walking Distance," the final two shows of October. Believing that this news presaged the falling axe, he disappointedly began to make alternate plans.

In an interview with syndicated Hollywood writer Hal Humphrey, Serling intimated that the sponsors felt uneasy about the show; some viewers, according to their letters, could not reconcile many of the show's twist endings with their own logic. Kimberly-Clark in particular had heard from a number of people who didn't quite understand where exactly Ida Lupino had disappeared to at the end of "The Sixteen-Millimeter Shrine." It's impossible, they said, for the woman to be transformed into a character in a movie, even if she is an actress. Serling suggested to Humphrey that anyone seriously interested in making sure that "The Twilight Zone" stayed on the air should write to the network. Within a week CBS had been deluged. Although the network forwarded the letters to the ad agencies, ratings still counted most.

Cancellation of "The Twilight Zone" would have been devastating to Serling, regardless of the probably minimal damage to his career in the long run. For as ambivalent as he claimed to be about "selling out" to weekly television, he had devotedly invested much of two years and not a little of his reputation. When *The Worker*, a far-left-leaning periodical accused Serling of driving off into the sunset in his bourgeois Continental, leaving the battle for political and social enlightenment on television to someone else, Serling wrote, "Old man Serling's son [is not] a quitter. . . . I'm trying to touch upon prejudice and bias— again to my knowledge the first time that this has been done in a half-hour anthology."

Long before "The Twilight Zone," Serling had been somewhat recognizable from his many appearances on television talk shows and the numerous magazine and newspaper articles about him. But after appearing at the end of every show to tease the following week's story, he became a household face. People stopped him when he walked down the street. Letters arrived, care of CBS, from old army buddies he hadn't seen since the war; they had seen his name before but were uncertain if *that* Rod Serling had been *their* Rod Serling. Neighbors in Cincinnati, from his lean years, wrote congratulatory letters. He reveled in the adulation and was unfailingly polite to autograph seekers, no matter when they stopped him. Carol and the girls may not have been too pleased with constant interruptions in their restaurant dinners, but Serling always put on his best happy face; he loved it. Fame could be fun, particularly for a practical joker.

At dinner one night in New York with Thomas Brennan, broadcasting director at Foote, Cone & Belding, the agency handling Kimberly-Clark, the restaurant's female entertainer, a zither player, spotted Serling and spent much of their meal playing to his table. By the time she finished her set, the men had had several drinks and were in a deviously playful mood. They invited her to sit down with them, and over more drinks she told of the grand career she planned in show business. They cruelly egged her on, praising her zither playing. Soon they convinced her that she deserved her own television show, and to that end they would call Kimberly-Clark and arrange a sponsorship—just like that. The woman believed them. Zither in hand, she walked outside with them to a phone booth where they staged a call to Neenah, Wisconsin, corporate home to the company. Brennan and Serling each got on the phone and testified to her remarkable skills which would, they said, be best displayed on a weekly series. The woman could not believe her good fortune. Even if this doesn't work, Serling assured her, I'll always have a place for you in "The Twilight Zone."

Having just polished the final draft of *Stories from the Twilight Zone*, he knew he could not sustain a career as a fiction writer; these few adaptations of scripts from the show's first year—stories he'd already written in another form—took him eight agonizing months, too long for both his customary impatience and accustomed earnings. (He had just ordered a brand-new, black, convertible Continental.) Further, the movie companies had stopped clamoring for him, at least for the time being, and the market for his true strength in writing, long-form television anthology, would soon vanish almost entirely with the demise of "Playhouse 90." While not planned that way, Serling's "In the Presence of Mine Enemies," a dramatization of imaginary events in the Warsaw Ghetto in 1939, would be the show's swan song.

On November 6, "Escape Clause" not only won its time

slot in the Nielsen ratings but also earned the largest Friday-night share, 35 percent of the entire viewing audience; if it stayed at that mark, renewal would be automatic. Before, when writing only single-shot shows, good Nielsens had always been an additional reward, not a requirement. His show's existence, Serling said, relied on "some weird never-never land of statistics."

As usual, he bore the anxiety well on the outside, hiding behind the practiced calm and happy facade. Inside he felt jumbled and began taking Miltown, a new tranquilizer that had become all the rage in the white-collar world of stress. He reacted poorly to the drug, though, and grew acutely depressed. After hours of examination and conversation, his doctor diagnosed physical exhaustion, a by-product of this remarkable twelve-month stretch in which he had written a book of short stories, twenty "Twilight Zone" scripts, and three "Playhouse 90"s; rewritten a Broadway play at least once; and supervised production on a weekly television series. The doctor prescribed a substantially lighter work schedule in addition to exercise. Serling began taking a nap in the afternoons and downing a sleeping pill every night to counter his insomnia.

In early January Serling testified before the Federal Communications Commission during its hearings on the state of broadcasting, to decide whether or not the government regulatory agency ought to be more involved in determining program content. He had been invited, based on his reputation for outspokenness and well-publicized fights with sponsors, by FCC chairman Newton Minnow—who would later refer to television as the "vast wasteland"—to offer input. Serling accepted gladly. Besides having a forum for his viewpoint, he could see his brother in Washington and then fly down to Aunt Betty and Uncle Ed's in Miami for a few days of sun and quiet.

Aware that he would be taking the devil's advocate position when the commissioners questioned him, Serling in his opening comments established a context for the criticisms, as though excusing television for its shortcomings:

> This is a medium unlike any other which, of necessity, has to not only supply several thousand hours of entertainment each month, but has as its implicit aim the satisfaction of the vast majority of the viewing audience. Contrast this to the standards of success which apply to either a novel or a legitimate play, in which a minute fraction of the population can be pleased, with a corollary guarantee of success. A successful television venture has to please thirty million people. Consequently, television programming must be developed with an eye toward what is a mass taste. With this as its basic nature, I think it is altogether understandable that we find low level programming and a low level approach as a standard operational procedure.

Serling concluded his introductory remarks by highlighting the double standard that judges television more harshly than other media. He noted that the *Los Angeles Examiner* had recently run a banner headline, "Flynn Love Letters Bared," with an accompanying article about an alleged relationship between a seventeen-year-old girl and Errol Flynn, while an incidental story on the bottom of the page told that General George Marshall had died.

> All right, gentlemen, I think we are discussing legitimacy now. We are discussing taste and morality. We are concerning ourselves with ethics. I think this particular front page is commentative on all of these areas. I heard not one whit of protest from the PTA, which uses a blunderbuss on us in television from week to week because of the violence we show. There was not one letter of protest from a religious organization who specifically decry our presentation of naked sex on television and accuse us almost hourly of presenting sensational, immoral sex relations or intimations of such relations on television. To the best of my

knowledge, no member of the United States Government ever made a statement as to what has been the responsibility of the daily press in connection with a similar responsibility that we in television are asked to exert.

That said, Serling then got his digs in at the interference of the agencies and sponsors. In the course of his long testimony, he cited his horror-story experience on "A Town Has Turned to Dust" (but he praised CBS for having had the "guts" even to consider putting on such a show). He also referred to censorship problems on "In the Presence of Mine Enemies," the final "Playhouse 90" show, which would not go on the air for another five months and which, at the time of his testimony, he believed would not be produced at all because of the usual sponsorship problems.

"Eight months ago," he said, "I submitted an outline to the network based on a historical study of the occurrences in the Warsaw Ghetto under the Nazis. The outline was passed, and I was given the go-ahead to write the script." Informed he had been granted the OK despite some great trepidation at the network, Serling had requested absolute assurance that the script would be produced; remembering previous experiences with controversial material, he did not want to undertake the research and writing without foreknowledge that his efforts would not be fruitless. The assurance was granted, the script written, a production date chosen, and a cast and director assigned. But Guy della-Cioppa soon told Serling that the sponsor had changed its mind, asserting that the subject matter was "too downbeat, too violent, and too dated."

The FCC commissioners were duly impressed by Serling's cogent analysis of the current state of affairs in broadcasting. As usual in such hearings into abstract solutions, his arguments disappeared into a bureaucratic black hole, never to be acted on.

When Serling arrived back in Hollywood, he believed that Kimberly-Clark planned to cancel sponsorship of

"The Twilight Zone." Mr. Kimberly, Thomas Brennan told him, had not been sufficiently pleased with the ratings trend. After rising well in October and early November, the numbers dropped again through December and early January. General Foods leaked hints that it too would not renew after the twenty-sixth show. Then Kimberly-Clark announced it had in fact decided to drop out. Pleasant letters were written back and forth between Serling and the agency men, and Serling and the sponsors' men, each thanking the other for jobs well done and friendships made. Not wanting to stand alone, General Foods also announced its withdrawal. More polite letters changed hands, and it appeared that "The Twilight Zone" had suffered an early demise. But by the end of February, while Serling examined his future without a series, both sponsors experienced a change of heart and renewed their options on the final thirteen shows. The series rushed back into production, although only ten new shows, instead of thirteen, would be shot.

Ratings began to rise again, steadily every week. Yet with the whole reevaluation routine due again in late spring for the fall season, he could not relax (throughout its five-year history, "The Twilight Zone" suffered the same on again–off again fate every season). Of the two sponsors, Kimberly-Clark had demonstrated somewhat less latitude, so Serling decided to schedule what he believed to be the strongest shows for the weeks the people in Neenah, Wisconsin, footed the bills. He told Al Weisman, a Foote, Cone & Belding account executive who oversaw the Kimberly-Clark account, that "Big Tall Wish," "A Stop at Willoughby," and "A Passage for Trumpet" were "the best we will have done or at least they shape up that way now."

All three shows were written by Serling, and, like "Requiem," "Patterns," "Velvet Alley," and the rest of his better work till now, they reveal some of the hidden Serling. In "Big Tall Wish," a young boy watching his mother's friend in a prizefight on television wishes so hard for his victory that the fighter suddenly finds himself the winner instead of lying flat on the canvas. But when the fighter then refuses to believe the boy's claim that wishing had turned the fight around, he just as quickly finds himself waking up after the knockout the boy's wish had saved him from. For Serling this was a statement of faith—and an acknowledgment of fear. He worked as hard as he did, accepting offers from everywhere, for fear that they would disappear overnight.

"A Stop at Willoughby" was similar to "Walking Distance," also written by Serling. Both are about advertising executives who can't tolerate the competitive strain of their jobs and long to return to a purer, gentler time. The protagonist in "Willoughby," chastened by his boss and demanding wife, boards a commuter train for home and is mysteriously transported eighty years back in time to an imaginary small town where everyone knows him and the pressures of ambition and competition do not exist. We discover at the end that he has been dreaming—prior to jumping from the train to his death. Written at a time of major uncertainty over whether the series would be renewed, and also in a probable state of exhaustion, "A Stop at Willoughby" reflects Serling's abiding nostalgia for his hometown and childhood—themes that recurred each time Serling felt hemmed in.

"A Passage for Trumpet" was his version of Frank Capra's *It's A Wonderful Life*. After committing suicide and finding himself in a sort of purgatory between life and death, a man realizes how much joy can be found in living and is given a second chance. Written after "Willoughby," it appears to be a re-thinking. All things considered, Serling felt reasonably happy—or as happy as he knew how to be. The series had been renewed, CBS had notified him that "In the Presence of Mine Enemies" had been installed on the schedule, the Bantam collection of his "Twilight Zone"-originated short stories had been released (he dedicated it to his brother, Bob), and another Broadway producer, Richard Halliday, had optioned "Requiem for a Heavyweight" and planned a September production.

Even at his happiest Serling retained a built-in compulsion to worry. Early in 1960 he wrote to writer Lee Pogostin that he felt somewhat guilty over the money he had been earning, and in March he wrote to Carol's grandmother that, despite "The Twilight Zone" renewal, he felt he should move on to other creative arenas, and more mature ones at that.

Yet at the same time he began to see Cayuga Productions as a potential ministudio as it turned out more than one series at a time for television. His contract with CBS obligated him to two pilots, both of which he would coproduce on the same co-ownership basis as "The Twilight Zone." His first pilot,-"Mr. Bevis," was about a ne'er-do-well, James Bevis, whose constant companion is a guardian angel; Burgess Meredith would star. But the network did not like it enough to shoot the pilot, and he adapted the script for "The Twilight Zone."

He then began shopping the concept of "The Loner," his post–Civil War western, as an hour-long "adult" drama that, unlike the average western, would not be dependent on action and gunplay. In the three-page series description, he asserted that emotional scenes between men and women can be as engrossing as shoot-outs at high noon. CBS didn't immediately warm to "The Loner" but wanted the pilot anyway. His contract allowed that if he had a second series on the air his commitment to write "Twilight Zone" scripts could be halved so long as he made up the total between the two series; his obligation was for twelve total scripts the first year, then ten the second, then eight, six, and six; CBS would even pay for a script editor and supervisor on "The Loner" to remove that obligation. But unable to find another editor or writer he trusted enough, Serling insisted on doing all the rewriting on what would be hour-long scripts. Ashley-Steiner suggested he not subject himself to such a tortuous schedule. Carol insisted he not. And "The Loner" was put aside for another year.

At 153 days—January 15 through June 15—the strike of 1960, over the issues of residuals for movies shown on television and the creation of a pension plan, was the longest in the history of the Writers Guild of America until 1988, when a work stoppage ran a single day longer. Any script that needed even a single word changed before production could not be produced during the strike; production had to be postponed or the script used as-is. Short of scripts to complete the year, the new producers of "Playhouse 90" (Martin Manulis had departed to produce films, the first of which was *The Days of Wine and Roses*) may have convinced CBS, and CBS the sponsors, that a controversial script was preferable to no script at all. The network reluctantly chose "In the Presence of Mine Enemies," despite its thematic difficulties, because it had been finished and polished before the writer's strike.

Striking, Serling told several people, cut to his core and ran contrary to his natural instincts. Also, as a producer, he struck against himself. For the owner of a vested interest in a weekly series, the potential income denied multiplied prodigiously. Should the series be renewed for the fall, no scripts would be ready—not even his own; severe sanctions would be taken against the offending writer if the Guild discovered he'd committed a single word of a script to paper before settlement. Until the strike ended, no writer would be allowed to write, procure, polish, or discuss any project for the screen. (James Clavell, author of numerous screenplays, including *The Fly*, and the rewriter of Serling's own *633 Squadron*, grew tired of inactivity during the strike and wrote the novel he had long threatened to write, *King Rat*, about his own experiences in a prisoner-of-war camp; thus began his amazing career as a novelist.)

At a New York strike meeting a few months into the stoppage, Serling loudly accused the Guild Council of improper negotiation. He wanted to approve the contract at the producers' last best offer and assumed that the rank and file felt the same. He was wrong and took some heat; among other faults, the offer gave the agencies the right to negotiate for the producers. Luci Ward, the outspoken California screenwriter—who had actually tutored Serling and gave him confidence to continue writing after receiving his first big screen assignments five years before—accused him of undermining writers and the union by not checking for a broader opinion. "All you had to do was pick up the phone and call us to find out what was really going on in the rank and file. But you didn't," Ward wrote him.

Controversy followed Serling, and he did not entirely dislike it—in fact, he seemed to want to attract it. As in his strike speech, he always spoke, at least publicly, with passion. He drove himself hard and gave off palpable energy and vibrancy, even when still. Sitting, he seemed a cobra ready to pounce. Of their many times together early in Serling's career, Hall Bartlett cannot remember Serling ever sitting back on the couch; he always hovered on the front edge, ready to rise. He had a charming arrogance and a committed point of view on virtually everything in his experience. Fierce and combative, he loved a good argument, usually over politics, but with few exceptions he separated the opinion from its owner; he could hate the opinion while tolerating the owner. He was either that fair-minded, or that fearful of being disliked himself. His feud with Leon Uris, the author and devout Zionist (*Exodus*), is a case in point.

After "In the Presence of Mine Enemies" aired May 18, Uris, in an open letter to CBS, complained it was "the most disgusting presentation in the history of American TV." He wrote:

> I cannot conceive how you would permit such an insult and defamation of the Jewish people by public mud-slinging on the graves of half a million Jews who were killed in the Warsaw Ghetto. The historical inaccuracies, the caricature of characterization and absolute false conflicts were a crying deception of the public. Joseph Goebbels himself could not have produced such a piece of Nazi apologetics. I

demand that CBS burn the negative of the film and publicly apologize for the scandal.

The story was about a small family locked up in the ghetto, which was about to be overrun by the Nazis. The daughter of a rabbi is in love with a young Nazi soldier, and he with her. Her brother, a ghetto freedom fighter, is vilified by their father for the hatred he displays toward the Nazis. Of the two Germans portrayed in the story, one was gentle and kind, full of misgivings about Hitler's goal; in a symbolic act, he saves the rabbi's daughter. The other was stereotypically despicable.

Serling, rather than take the debate public, wrote a detailed personal letter to Uris explaining his position: the young German sergeant was not a Nazi; he had never intended to provide a history lesson, only tell a human tale; that the rabbi's tolerance was also Talmudic. He concluded that he and Uris were both adults, capable of agreeing to disagree without a loss of respect between them.

Uris had a great deal of company in his disgust, including some survivors of the Holocaust, several militant groups, rabbis, and other assorted protestors (the Steuben Societies of the United States called Serling a "dirty, Jew-loving bastard"; another letter writer wanted him to dramatize the "persecution of the German people of Yugoslavia"). Most felt that the 50 percent good-Nazis-to-bad-Nazis ratio seemed a might high for reality's sake, and that the humane portrayal of the Holocaust perpetrators might weaken, however slightly, public condemnation of those historic events. The script, they said, had been a whitewash of history.

Serling answered the thoughtful letters thoughtfully— and the vicious letters ... thoughtfully. His heart may not have been in the fight anyway. He felt that Charles Laughton had been completely miscast in the role of the rabbi, destroying the credibility of the production and the subtlety of his writing. Rather than emoting quiet strength, Laughton could not convey the power of his faith. Instead of seeming a noble martyr, he left an impression of misguided weakness.

(Privately, Serling referred to Laughton as "that eminent British fag." His supermasculine personality was offended by homosexuality, and such homophobic epithets appeared regularly in his speech and letters, particularly when presumed gay actors had been cast in lead roles he imagined should be played by John Wayne. To his friends in the East, Serling took pleasure in confirming the homosexuality of certain male stars about whom there had been suspicions. "Incipient swishes," he once said, were common at Antioch. And when an old paratrooper friend proclaimed in the mid-1960s his admiration for Serling and signed his letter "love," Serling overreacted. In a responding letter he detailed angrily and explicitly how sick and perverted he thought him to be and suggested immediate psychiatric help.)

In early May General Foods told CBS it would no longer cosponsor "Twilight Zone." A few days later Kimberly-Clark pulled the plug. Serling again corresponded with executives at both companies, thanking them for their patience and efforts and calling them friends. The series appeared to be dead, until Serling agreed to several budgetary concessions—including the use of videotape, which cost less than film, for six of the episodes. CBS told him simply to take the 10 percent budget cut or leave it. He took it. Independent of that decision, General Foods (which used "The Twilight Zone" to sell Sanka) reconsidered.

Kimberly-Clark did not. As Serling thought, its sponsorship had been less committed from the beginning, when customers' letters complained about the twist endings. CBS agreed to find other sponsors and signed SOS, Colgate-Palmolive, and Ligget & Meyers tobacco.

Although "The Twilight Zone" attracted a devoted core audience and had been of unusual quality for weekly half-hour television, CBS decided the show needed a more visible running thread of consistency than just Serling's voice-over. First a repertory company of actors with whom the audience would identify, even as their roles changed, was considered—and quickly discarded. This left only a narrator, to be seen as well as heard.

The first name on everyone's list again—that is, with the exception of Serling's, which was the one that counted—was Orson Welles. He distrusted Welles and feared being overshadowed by the great man. Both were raconteurs, willing to assume center stage of any gathering. Both loved practical jokes. Both had achieved great success, fame, and fortune early in their careers (Welles completed *Citizen Kane*, still considered by many respected critics to be the greatest film ever made, before his twenty-fourth birthday). And, oddly, both would eventually become almost as well known for their voices as for their other achievements.

When production began in June, Serling elatedly added the role of on-screen host to his narration duties (as well as teasing the following week's episodes), for which he received Screen Actor's Guild minimum. He may have pretended to disdain the camera appearances, but he quite obviously enjoyed them greatly. In June he quoted writer Ben Hecht to a Young & Rubicam executive, implying that these words applied equally to him: "Every writer is a frustrated actor who recites his lines in the hidden auditorium of his skull."

"Rod was a frustrated actor—a storyteller," Dick Berg remembers. Although best friends, the two men never discussed Serling's job as host, about which Serling may have been embarrassed. "I kind of smiled at his need to be an actor and on camera. It would have been beneath our relationship to discuss that, to discuss his need to present himself. He loved his celebrity status; he loved being recognized. There was nothing bad about it, but I think he was somewhat chagrined, in our relationship, to acknowledge the frailty or hubris or whatever the hell he might have thought. I think he suffered. I loved the fact he was a celebrity, and we had great fun with his celebrity status."

Alden Schwimmer believes Serling liked nothing better in the world than introducing the show: "I know as a matter of absolute fact there were several times we discussed television series projects created by Rod, and got into very serious stages of discussion, where the condition came from Rod that he had to be the host—to the point where it jeopardized the sale of a couple of television series that might have gone had Rod not insisted that he had to be the host. . . . He loved being in the limelight."

Playing off of Alfred Hitchcock's penchant for appearing somewhere in each of his films (in *Lifeboat*, in which the action takes place only in the lifeboat, his image is seen in a newspaper read by one of the survivors), the directors, Serling, and Buck Houghton would invent clever ways for him to appear on screen after the opening teaser. They wanted to surprise and delight. The camera would pan quickly to find Serling in incongruous circumstances: panning off a rose from a garden, for instance, to focus on him apparently only three inches tall. "We thought them out very carefully," Houghton recalls.

As famous as he had been before, becoming an actual part of the story now would catapult Serling's fame into the—well, Twilight Zone.

Through the monstrous power of television, Rod Serling had become the most famous writer in America, if not the world (the show played in well over thirty countries) when the series ended its original programming in 1964. Only Rod Serling could be recognized by masses of people for his name, face, voice, or the title of a work. Shakespeare, Hemingway, Fitzgerald, Twain, Chayefsky, Arthur Miller, George Bernard Shaw—none was ever as readily recognizable. (One letter from the Midwest, addressed simply to Rod Serling—with no address or city— arrived without delay.) Three decades later, impressionists and actors in commercials still imitate his voice and style: tight, drawn-back lips; long, melodic sentences spoken in a chopped-off delivery; syllables overexaggerated for maximum dramatic effect; the slight cock of the head and narrowing of the eyes; elbow cocked, the cigarette held waist high, filter end toward the camera. "An impersonator's dream," Sammy Davis, Jr., notes.

"Rod's in the pantheon, recognized by millions and millions of people," Berg points out. "For that to happen to a writer is thrilling."

Whereas once he dined or traveled peacefully with his family and friends, Serling's face now brought gasps of recognition virtually everywhere. Unfailingly cheerful, he stood there—meal getting cold or family growing impatient—to sign autographs until no one else asked. Often people seemed surprised at Serling's small stature. On television, away from any relative yardsticks, he appeared to be of normal height, perhaps even tall. This may have been his most compelling reason for wearing elevator shoes, which he did at all times, in various styles—despite the fact everyone knew he wore them. ("I know that he worried a lot about being short, because we talked about it," Saul David remembers. "He would make jokes about being short—bitter jokes—before you could. When somebody does that you know that it's an open wound.")

Until 1962, when rights to air "The Twilight Zone" began to sell to foreign countries, the only places Serling could walk in public unencumbered by curiosity and/or autograph seekers were outside the United States. Yet then Serling missed the attention. Until the end of his life, he never lost his thrill over being recognized. One night in Tijuana, where he, Carol, and their friends Mary and Harold Arlen had driven down for the evening from San Diego, Serling heard his name called from afar. Against his companions' advice, he stopped and turned around. A teenage American boy he'd never seen before identified himself as his neighbor in the Pacific Palisades. Neither Carol nor the Arlens knew him. The boy claimed he had been caught trying to smuggle some firecrackers across the border; police fined him all his money. He asked to borrow enough to get home.

Once more against advice, Serling took fifty dollars from his pocket. They laughed at him; every time some poor little street urchin held out a hand, Serling accommodated. This was no different. The boy promised to repay him soon. Serling believed him, even as his wife and friends continued to snicker at his bleeding heart and naïvete. A week later the boy knocked at 1490 Monaco Drive holding an envelope with the cash inside. "I told you so," he said, waving the cash in their faces.

Another time the two couples went to the *Queen Mary*, docked in Long Beach, for dinner. Walking to the restaurant, they passed a large wedding reception in a ballroom. The bride and groom, attired in their finery, spotted Serling and immediately abandoned their guests to fawn over him.

Constantly in the public eye, Serling now felt more conscious than ever of his physical appearance. He dyed his hair jet black to cover the increasing gray strands, which he attributed to the stress of his job. And his infatuation with an omnipresent tan, begun while living in Connecticut and traveling frequently to California, became a bizarre necessity. "The maximum way to enjoy a good tan is to take it back to New York City with you in January," he said. During travels to the East Coast or anyplace where the sun shone infrequently, he took a sun lamp—baking his skin umercifully under the concentrated ultraviolet rays that turned his face into virtual leather by age fifty. He often worked by his pool, dictating into the machine or to his secretary, his face turned to the hot sun. When the sunshine didn't feel hot enough, even in Palm Springs, he held a reflector under his chin. "Rod, you're cooking yourself," John Champion told him. "Yeah," Serling replied, "it's going to be a beautiful color."

Actors and singers—celebrities of higher profile—held Serling in high esteem. At parties they, like the public at large, pitched their own stories (Jerry Lewis even offered a script written specifically for the show), and many sought him out for parts. Everyone, it seemed, wanted a role written by Serling. (Although he was under exclusive contract to CBS in 1961, NBC asked for and received permission for him to adapt Somerset Maugham's *Rain* as a ninety-minute special starring Fredric March; his wife, Florence Eldrige; and Marilyn Monroe, in her small-screen dramatic debut. After Monroe had emergency gall bladder and gynecological surgery in late July, she dropped out of the project. When the network considered Susan Hayward in her place, Serling backed out.) In this milieu he mixed well, confident of his own status.

"You don't know who I am, but I'm going to tell you," he said to Sammy Davis, Jr., at a party one night.

"Oh, my God, are you kidding?" Davis replied. He quickly looked Serling up and down. "I didn't know you were my size," he said.

Then, Davis remembers, "we went in the corner to sit down. The wives [Davis was married to actress Mai Britt] went right out the window. We were just sitting there in the corner of the living room, rappin' the night away. I was just fascinated with him."

Yet Serling did not quite fit the celebrity party crowd, at least not yet. Despite his close acquaintance with Davis and Frank Sinatra (which would engender a film, *Assault on a Queen*, in 1965; he also kept in touch with such celebrities as Hugh Hefner, Ann Landers, and Steve Allen) he felt ill at ease. What troubled him was precisely his celebrity status. While he enjoyed it, he still felt it somewhat unseemly, and he anguished guiltily over his enjoyment.

Rachel David—whose father, Saul David, as head of Bantam Books had guided Serling on the first *Twilight Zone* book collection before moving to California to produce films—remembers seeing Serling at several of the larger parties filled with celebrities, social climbers, and their children. A neighbor and the daughter of the Serlings' friends, she knew Serling's daughters, Jody and Nan, and often spent the night at the Serlings' home.

"Rod always wanted to leave these parties," she recalls.

"He'd stand back and watch things. If the kids came in, he'd say, 'Excuse me, let's go see what the kids need.' He'd want to get out of there with the adults and play with us. He loved kids, yeah, but he really just wanted to get out of there."

"He was an extremely gregarious man, a very social being, and very aggressively so," Dick Berg says. "He loved people, loved being noticed, loved fraternizing. But he was not a guy for mob scenes. His social life was very restricted."

When awards for the 1959–1960 season were handed out, "The Twilight Zone" won several, including favorite half-hour television series in a readers' poll; a Producer's Guild award; and a Hugo, annually bestowed by the World Science Fiction Convention. Yet winning his fourth Emmy in June (out of seven career nominations), for writing episodes of "The Twilight Zone" completely surprised Serling. "I don't know how deserving I am," he said. "But I do know how grateful I am."

Two days after winning the Emmy, Serling dropped identical letters to Hank Grant, columnist for the *Hollywood Reporter*, and Jack Hellman, columnist at *Daily Variety*, to note that he had received congratulatory telegrams from three NBC executives; Kimberly-Clark; Colgate; SOS; General Foods; McCann-Erikson, the ad agency handling Colgate; Young & Rubicam; Foote, Cone & Belding; and Ashley-Steiner—but not a single word from CBS, his own network. He then disavowed having written to them with this news.

After mailing off the letters, he received a congratulatory telegram and an invitation to a tribute breakfast the next morning, from Guy della-Cioppa. The afternoon after the breakfast, Serling wrote an embarrassed fawning letter, thanking della-Cioppa for flowers, as well as, completely dishonestly, the executive's friendship and support over the years.

Such unabashed sycophancy for a man whose taste and

judgment he did not particularly respect—*this* was the Velvet Alley.

A week later Ira Steiner relayed to him the details of a meeting with the CBS top brass, including president James Aubrey (who had also written him an effusive, if somewhat belated, letter of congratulation). "Never have I seen Jim friendlier, more respectful and happy in a relationship," Steiner wrote of the executive whom coworkers nicknamed the Smiling Cobra. "It indicated our relationship with CBS is solid, mutually respectful and stripped of what you described in your letter as the position of a hungry supplicant. I think the result is a helluva tribute to you."

That a four-time Emmy winner, a writer whose one-year-old television series had already inspired near fanatical devotion from huge numbers of people all across the country, would need such constant assurances and could be so sensitive to imagined slights seems ridiculous. "I think he had a great need to be loved and also to be admired," Berg says. "If that was an exaggerated need, maybe that came out of some insecurity. Maybe he always felt because of his size, because he was the runt of the litter, that he had to prove himself. I think it was an extreme desire to be loved. And yet it was never pathetic."

Not pathetic, perhaps, just pitiable. When he wrote in June to his cousin Rita, Ada Goodman's daughter, that he had partially hoped "The Twilight Zone" would be canceled so that he could work on a play or novel, he knew that "Requiem" would not be produced that fall, and probably not any foreseeable fall—or spring or summer. After reading the latest draft of the play, Leland Hayward, the great Broadway producer, suggested that Serling— whom he called a rare and extraordinary talent—should read "ten to fifteen certified-guaranteed-no-argument-about first-class modern plays. He must learn to discipline himself insofar as the use of words is concerned, and cut down to the bone all he writes. To me, the play meanders and wanders, and says the same thing over and over again.

"I don't know if Mr. Serling is willing to subject himself to the really difficult discipline that the theatre requires."

No, he was not willing. He lacked the patience. Although he did in fact take several weeks in early January 1961 to polish the play, he ignored Hayward's advice completely. The result, which he believed for a time was destined for production that fall season, reeked of the same overwritten, preachy, heavy-handedness that marked his previous eight efforts.

"He was an action guy," Alden Schwimmer says. "He wrote fast, did everything fast. . . . I used to have this discussion with him by the hour. I wanted him to really sit down and try to do something—write a play from the *kischkes*; a novel maybe. He talked about it from time to time. I guess he found it impossible or difficult, because he never really did it. It was all kind of surface stuff that he did."

John Champion attributes Serling's writing failures outside of teleplays, particularly with screenplays, to that same action addiction. Over the years Champion and Serling held dozens of conversations that lasted, owing to Serling's low patience threshold, at most ten minutes. Champion asked why he refused to study the screenplay form.

"Why should I?" Serling said. "It's the same as television."

"No, it's not," Champion replied. "They only appear to be the same. If you studied them you'd reach a different conclusion."

"Well, maybe next week," Serling said, time and again.

That particular next week never came. As Champion observes, the thought of learning a separate craft repelled him. "Rod was too busy at 190 miles an hour staying on the track he was on."

Serling's renowned impatience may have also been a shield for his deepest insecurities. For years and years, television stories simply bubbled out of him almost faster than he could write down the words. But these other writing forms did not come instinctively, as did television writing, and he may have feared digging down deep—from the *kischkes*, as Schwimmer says—to find nothing there.

"To find that a guy like that really doubted his own talents was scary," Saul David remembers.

The second season of "The Twilight Zone" premiered with "King Nine Will Not Return," a puzzling story about an army air force captain awakening in 1943 in the North African desert beside the wreckage of his B-25 bomber—alone, his crew mysteriously vanished. Robert Cummings, himself a major in the army air force during the war, played the character who tormentedly twists in a dream of what happened seventeen years earlier, when he missed the flight that proved fatal to the rest of his crew. Or has it been a dream? There's sand in his shoe.

All over America on Friday nights people held "Twilight Zone" parties. And Rod Serling was their host. For several months Cayuga Productions and CBS had received hundreds of letters a week describing various states of passion for the show or offering story ideas. With Serling's increased role as narrator, the letters began to get more personal. He seemed so sympathetic, so accessible, so much the godlike character who controlled the magical happenings of "The Twilight Zone" that much of the public targeted him as the man who could—and would—solve their problems.

"The spiritual vibrations we got from your show inspired us to contact you before anyone else."

"Since I alone have the responsibility of rearing our daughter, Melinda Ann, I am trying to plan a unique sixteenth birthday for her on July 31. I have chosen to write to you, a famous TV writer, and ask: 'What is a good way to have a happy life?'"

And this from the widowed mother of a two-year-old in Bedford-Stuyvesant: "I am in a box and can see no way out. This is a letter of desperation. My future stares at me often and all I can see is life ever after in Bedford-Stuyvesant or the like, raising a boy who won't stand a chance and me rehashing, day after day, those fatal words 'If only . . .' getting me more and more bitter and looking at everything with dead eyes. I need a sponsor."

So did Serling. In December General Foods informed him that the ratings had not improved adequately to continue its sponsorship. Colgate-Palmolive waffled too. At a broadcasting convention in San Francisco, Serling blasted sponsors, whom he called the ruin of television for the restrictions they imposed, and suggested that his own integrity in succumbing to these restrictions had been compromised. He also proclaimed that he planned to take "The Twilight Zone" off the air because it now strayed from his original concept. "We always had to have our yearly aggravation, that Rod didn't want to do 'Twilight Zone' anymore," Alden Schwimmer remembers. The protestations were disingenuous, in that Serling always corresponded pleasantly, if not obsequiously, with the sponsors—the very people and companies he lambasted at every possible opportunity.

The second season's shows had been generally well received. While overall they may have been a small step below the quality of the first year, many of the more memorable, if not the best, "Twilight Zone"s aired that season: "The Eye of the Beholder," in which a woman undergoing plastic surgery to make her less hideous is discovered at the end to be beautiful; "The Howling Man," about a traveler who frees the devil from a cell and then spends the rest of his life tracking down the demon, only to have his maid free him again; "A Most Unusual Camera," about three small-time crooks who steal a camera that takes photographs of a scene as it will look five minutes into the future; "The Invaders," in which a flying saucer filled with tiny creatures lands on an old woman's roof, and in the battle to the death we discover the creatures are not Martians or Venutians but Earthlings; "The Silence," in which a wealthy man bets a poorer man a half million dollars he cannot keep silent for a year—and when the year passes we find that the rich man is not rich at all and the poor man has cut his vocal cords to ensure winning the bet; "The Obsolete Man," about a totalitarian society that condemns people to death for being "obsolete"; and "The Odyssey of Flight 33," about a modern-day airliner that hits a freak tail wind and goes into the past, never again able to return.

The origin of "Flight 33" tells much about the way Serling's imagination contrived stories. Bob Serling had come to California to visit for a few days during the Christmas holiday season. One afternoon the brothers went to MGM to pick up Serling's mail, which happened to include a brochure from American Airlines offering for rent or sale a mock-up of a 707 airliner formerly used for stewardess training. "Rod just kept staring at that one brochure," Bob recalls. "He wouldn't open up the rest of the mail—just kept looking at that one piece. We got back to the car, his Continental, and he told me to drive home. I just looked at him, because he never let me touch his car. Now we're going down the San Diego Freeway, I'm driving, he's still staring at the brochure. Suddenly he says, 'Suppose you were in a jet going across the Atlantic and hit a freak tail wind, like something about six thousand miles an hour, and you went so fast you broke through a time barrier, and came back to New York City, and New York had disappeared, and then you keep going back to prehistoric times.' I said, 'Boy, that's a hell of a wild surmise,' and forgot about it.'" A few days later Bob received a call in Washington from Rod, asking him to research the cockpit dialogue that might occur in such a scenario. Bob consulted a friend, a TWA captain, who overcame his initial reluctance and drew up routes and contrived the dialogue that Rod eventually inserted into the script.

(Serling had learned that locale is very often the factor that lends a script the credibility it needs to transcend the audience's disbelief. In motion pictures locales can be built at great cost. In television they had neither the time nor the funds to construct physical replicas of the author's imagination. "Rod would talk story with me," Buck Houghton says, "largely to get production ideas: 'Where could we do this? How can we make this work?' He wanted to write to what was possible, rather than impossible. . . . I'd tell him that if he wanted to do a story about, for example, a gardener, an absolutely wild gardener who can't restrain himself from growing plants, fine, by all means go out to Busch Gardens, because that's probably where we'll shoot it. So he'd go there, look around, and say, 'Oh boy, there's a tiger lily out there I want to make sure we use.' If he wanted to see a tuna cannery, I'd arrange for him to go to one, or I'd point out a set at Metro he hadn't seen. . . . Rod also accepted as a premise that if you're going to ask for people's attention for something that's a little miraculous, you mustn't start changing scenes all over the place. With the exception of the pilot, 'Twilight Zone' episodes happen in two or three sets or locales."]

Serling loathed the six videotaped episodes—"The Lateness of the Hour," "Static," "The Whole Truth," "Night of the Meek," "Twenty-Two," and "Long-Distance Call"—the final six shows produced before the midseason hiatus. He felt that the savings of perhaps thirty-five thousand dollars had not justified the apparent drop-off in quality of videotape (transferred to film for broadcast purposes), and he did not want to go out, should the series not be renewed, on such a sour note. Early in the new year CBS granted a reprieve for thirteen new shows; Colgate had not pulled out after all, and Ligget & Myers picked up General Foods' spots. However, during production the network decided to pay for only seven of them—and only twenty-nine shows aired the whole season. This appeared to confirm Serling's suspicion that CBS cared less about the quality and legacy of "The Twilight Zone" than its sixty thousand dollar budget per show.

He was, as he told several people, "desperately tired." His schedule for the previous two years had been remarkably pressure packed and had taken a toll on his body. Besides frequent colds, flus, ear infections, and the

Berger's disease—whose symptoms cropped up from time to time during his life, depending on the number of cigarettes he smoked—he also developed kidney infections and a bad stomach; the former had kept him confined to bed for a week the previous fall. (Serling often took cat-naps at the dinner table if the talk did not hold his attention. "John, excuse me," he would tell John Champion—presumably among others—during after-dinner conversations. "He was not pretending, he was sound asleep," Champion swears. "His wife would be sitting next to him, my wife would be there, and the three of us would go right on with our conversation. Ten or fifteen minutes later, he'd wake up, shake his head, grunt, and ask, 'What's for dessert?' This happened not less than eight or ten times.")

It seems symbolic of his desperate fatigue that he would shortly abandon the pretense of ever seeing "Requiem for a Heavyweight" on Broadway. When Columbia Pictures came to him and offered a check for fifty thousand dollars for the screen rights to the play on the condition that it not be produced on the stage either before or during the theatrical run, Serling willingly agreed—in fact, with a notable sigh of relief. Tired of fighting for a project he knew in his heart of hearts lacked quality, a dearly and long-held dream disappeared easily. He would soon devote some time to developing "The Twilight Zone" as a feature film, but even then his treatment, which he dashed off quickly, fell short of acceptable standards. He apologized to Alden Schwimmer, whose job it was to sell the project, admitting he had done a poor job. "With Rod," Schwimmer notes, "you had to try to get something a little more qualitative and not let it go at being facile and slick."

"My perspective is shot," Serling wrote to Nolan Miller, his former Antioch writing teacher. In a brutally frank letter, Serling admitted that in the "bubble land" of Hollywood, he had lost perspective and was no longer the man he had intended in college to become, the man who wanted only the quiet pleasures of a family romping and playing in a large country home as he quietly plied his trade in the basement office, the man who cared more about quality, about "saying something," than about quantity or financial gain. To that end, he asked if Antioch might consider him a writer in residence for the fall of 1962—twenty months away, presumably after the cancellation of "The Twilight Zone." Miller initially doubted his seriousness, believing that the fatigue and depression had been speaking. He responded with a long letter detailing the drawbacks of academic life, not the least being the inadequate pay. After more letters, including correspondence with college vice president W. B. Alexander, they finalized Serling's five-month sabbatical, during which he would teach mass media to some of Antioch's brightest students. The sweet thought of that distant goal lifted Serling's spirits.

When the final batch of the season's "Twilight Zones" went into production in late January, McCann-Erickson, the advertising agency responsible for Liggett & Myers's sponsorship (it alternated shows with Colgate-Palmolive), suggested that Serling act as commercial spokesman once during each show for the company's Oasis cigarettes; however obliquely, the suggestion indicated the spokesmanship was a prerequisite to continued sponsorship. Serling reluctantly agreed, aware of inherent ironies: having mocked commercial television for so long, he'd now contribute himself to the commercial clutter. But CBS programmers balked, contending that unlike other actors who step out of character to do commercials, Serling really had no character to shed; they said the presumed loss of credibility would hurt the series. Not surprisingly, the ad salesmen prevailed, and on April 7 he performed in his first fifteen-second spot during the middle of "A Hundred Yards over the Rim" (an 1847 man on his way west in a covered wagon goes over a desert rim to find food and water and ends up in the year 1961.) Afterward, L&M declared itself pleased and pledged its sponsorship for the third season. To that, Serling proclaimed his hope for a long relationship and offered his willing servitude to their whims. (He then wrote to Al Weisman at Foote, Cone & Belding, with whom he'd established a friendship during Kimberly-Clark's sponsorship, complaining about having to do the commercials but rationalizing that the ordeal would be over in only twenty-six shows. He joked that he should have done on-air ads for K-C's Delsey toilet tissue.)

Come May, Serling again was surprised to take the Emmy for dramatic writing on "Twilight Zone." "Let's carve this one up like a turkey, guys," he said on the podium to his fellow writers, particularly Richard Matheson and Charles Beaumont. They had contributed six of the seven shows not written by him the first season, and seven of the nine the second season. Over the five years Matheson wrote seventeen episodes and Beaumont either wrote or was credited with twenty-two.

After "The Twilight Zone" had been sold to the sponsors in 1959, Serling wanted to tap what he assumed to be a bottomless well of creativity in the public at large and naïvely opened his show to all submissions—whether from established or unknown writers. Thousands of illegibly scrawled, pathetically amateurish, and otherwise unprofessional and unimaginative "scripts" found their way to Cayuga. He learned a powerful lesson: most people cannot write.

Buck Houghton then held a screening of the "Twilight Zone" pilot for professional writers. Two of the writers were Matheson and Beaumont, who happened to be best friends. Each man met with Houghton and Serling to pitch ideas. Many of those Beaumont pitched came from his own published stories. Matheson, however, generally stayed away from his published works until the series' final year.

Like Beaumont, Matheson had first made his reputation in the literary field. After dozens of published fantasy stories, he wrote "The Shrinking Man" and adapted it himself, in 1956, into "The Incredible Shrinking Man" for Universal. Meeting Serling for the first time in Houghton's office after the screening, he found him gracious, generous, and warm. "The Twilight Zone" became the first series for which Matheson wrote, and having no point of reference he did not fully appreciate the laissez-faire approach to scripts Serling himself had not written. "As far as I remember, he didn't ever touch a word," Matheson says. "I didn't realize till much later how wonderful that was."

"I'm a lousy story editor," Serling told William F. Nolan. "I always judged a story on the basis of how I would do it."

Once a mimeograph operator at Universal, where he met Ray Bradbury, Beaumont had made his literary reputation a few years before, mostly through *Playboy*, but also with his collection of short stories, *The Hunger and Other Stories*. By the late 1950s he was writing episodes for several television shows. After seeing the pilot, he became most excited about "The Twilight Zone." "It's gonna be great," he bragged.

Beaumont met Serling early in 1959 at a party given by a mutual friend, Ray Banks, and the exchange was typical of him. The moment Serling walked in, Beaumont approached. "Quite honestly," he said, "I must tell you to your face that 'Velvet Alley' was the worst piece of writing *I've* ever seen."

Serling, although taken aback, smiled broadly. Few people were ever that direct. When Beaumont began to write for "The Twilight Zone," Serling felt that the comment had been the cornerstone for a relationship—professional, if not also personal—founded on honesty.

Beaumont was a frenetic, exuberant meteor of a man. "We were all, even Rod, kind of in awe of Beaumont's energy," William F. Nolan recalls. "He moved like a firebrand through the world. Rod would work twelve to fifteen hours a day, but Chuck worked harder—as though he knew he would soon be dead. There was something in the psyche. Like Rod."

Beaumont suffered from persistently fierce headaches that led him to swallow literally gallons per month of Bromo-Seltzer (which he bought in the huge, novelty-size bottles). At age thirty-four he developed Alzheimer's disease and he died four years later, having wasted away terribly, to the point that he looked like an old man. When he became too ill to concentrate well enough to work, he hired Jerry Sohl, John Tomerlin, and OCee Ritch to ghost the assignments he had gotten. He wanted to maintain his status in the industry until he recovered from the disease, which he didn't understand and which no doctor could then diagnose. "I don't know what's happening to me," he lamented to his friends, head in his hands. (Defending his story "The Jungle" as a possible "Twilight Zone" script in a 1960 letter to Serling, Beaumont chillingly signed off: "Stop relaxing! Work! Get an ulcer! Die young!" The show did not air until the third season, by which time Beaumont had begun to experience his first symptoms of the disease.)

Nolan describes Beaumont as the hub on a large, metaphoric wheel, with the various spokes being he, Matheson, George Clayton Johnson, OCee Ritch, Ray Bradbury, and other creative men, particularly writers, who gathered often at Beaumont's house. On arriving, Serling, who came without his wife, would remove his coat and roll up his sleeves. He wanted to belong, be one of the guys. Despite his fame and accomplishments, these men, most of whom had written science fiction or imaginative fantasies long before he had, intimidated him; he relied on many of their works for inspiration, if not adaptation. He also knew they did not venerate him the way much of the rest of the world now did. And he understood clearly he had not yet earned their respect.

When Serling felt confident, the center of attention in a group that clearly admired him, he easily held court, offering an array of jokes and opinions guaranteed to infatuate others with this bright, passionate, macho, little man. When he lacked that confidence, as he did in Beaumont's crowd, he could embarrass himself. Like the prototypical social klutz who tries to top a joke and ends up laughing alone, Serling's attempts at humor almost always received only courtesy chuckles. "It was all as though he was making a big effort to be liked," Nolan observes. "He wanted people to like him and thought they'd like him more if he was funny."

Serling never did become very close with any of these men, not just because he tried too hard. Beaumont several times complained to friends, including Nolan, that Serling had stolen his stories, adapting them for "The Twilight Zone" without acknowledging the source story or offering payment. Each time, Beaumont avoided confronting Serling directly, but finally he no longer could. Face to face, he cited several stories that he believed had been appropriated.

Late that night, the doorbell rang at Beaumont's San Fernando Valley home. A special delivery messenger brought a single-spaced letter—typed by Serling—offering grief-stricken apologies. Nolan, who was there and read the letter, remembers Serling explaining that he read so much science fiction and came under so much pressure to turn out scripts that he rarely questioned where an idea came from when it popped into his head—and even if he did question, he could never trace it to the original through the devastating clutter of his mind. He said that he just now looked at the stories Beaumont pointed out and realized he did indeed read them years before; the theft, he admitted, had been completely unconscious and now caused him terrible pain.

Knowing Serling would still be awake, even at one in the morning, Beaumont called him. Serling had been pacing in the study, anxious for Beaumont's reaction. "I just read your letter, Rod," Beaumont said. "I understand your agony and your sadness over all this. Look, you're paying me enough just to write what I'm writing, and if any of my work slips through the back door, unconsciously through your brain, and ends up on the screen without credit, forget it. Let's just let it go at that." To his friends, who criticized his judgment, Beaumont explained, "I'm getting enough prestige and publicity and money and credits out of 'The Twilight Zone.' And I'm getting to adapt all my own best stories, so I'm not going to argue."

The dispute between Ray Bradbury and Serling was not resolved nearly as kindly. Serling had been a fan of Bradbury before ever knowing him, and when they did meet Bradbury was favorably impressed by Serling. An admitted neophyte in the loosely termed science fiction genre, Serling expressed his admiration and respect for the master; he paid him unabashed homage. Bradbury and the Serlings dined together, and Serling included Bradbury among those invited to attend occasional private screenings at his home. (At one screening to which he invited Richard Matheson, Serling showed Matheson's "The Incredible Shrinking Man," which Serling had long enjoyed.)

Both men intended that Bradbury contribute several episodes of "The Twilight Zone." Bradbury submitted his first effort, "Here There Be Tygers," an adaptation of his own story, in July 1959, shortly after production on the first season began. But when he saw the pilot, "Where Is Everybody?" he privately accused Serling of stealing his story.

They pored over both the story and script and Serling believed his innocence was established. Then after seeing "Walking Distance," in which the main character reverts toward his childhood with each turn of a merry-go-round, Bradbury felt Serling had stolen his "Black Ferris," about a man who returns to the past on every revolution of a ferris wheel. That Serling had named a character Bradbury seemed, to Bradbury, proof of the theft. Again they hashed it out. Serling contended Bradbury had not had the only happy childhood and admitted his own infatuation with the past; and anyway, Binghamton boasted more merry-go-rounds than any other city in the world.

Bradbury seemed appeased by the explanation, and the air cleared. One of the final shows of "The Twilight Zone" season that ended in June 1962 had been Bradbury's "I Sing the Body Electric," the only Bradbury-credited teleplay ever shown on the series. The show, about a widower who buys a lifelike robot grandmother to raise his children, was not particularly well done. Shortly after the show aired, Serling and Bradbury appeared together at a creative writing symposium at the Seattle World's Fair.

That September, however, Bradbury delivered a blistering off-the-record attack on Serling in the offices of *Los Angeles* magazine, which in its most recent issue had devoted several glowing pages, written by Constance Olmstead, to Serling. Olmstead, who had once worked as Serling's secretary, immediately phoned him with the gory details. Serling wrote to Bradbury, defending himself and urging Bradbury to confront him face-to-face rather than impugne his reputation behind his back.

Worse for Serling than the attack on him were the repercussions of his letter. Bradbury easily figured out who had passed along the report, and Olmstead was forced to either write a letter of apology to Bradbury or resign her editorship. "Connie, dear," Serling wrote, "I am ill because of this. . . . Who do I write to or phone? What step can I take to repay you for a hurt?" He explained that his letter to Bradbury mentioned "several people" who overheard Bradbury; in fact, he wrote there were two.

(In later years of "The Twilight Zone," Serling would be sued successfully three times for apparent plagiarism of stories he had written himself: "The Parallel," a story about a world parallel to Earth; "Short Drink from a Certain Fountain," about a man who regresses to infancy; and "Sounds and Silences," about a man who tries to shut out his wife's constant chattering with some surprising results. In all three cases a judge deemed the plaintiffs' original stories sufficiently similar to the produced scripts to warrant damages, but the final products as seen in the series seemed substantially dissimilar.)

As usual, Serling corresponded personally with the sponsors all during the third season, promising that high-quality shows were to be seen, even though he knew the quality had dropped considerably from the first two seasons. In one letter, dated early January 1962, he offered his complete services, from commercials to dramatic writing, to Larry Bruff, a vice president at Ligget & Myers.

He wrote twenty-one of the thirty-one scripts aired, far

above the minimum number specified in his contract. He largely imposed on himself the exhaustion that he understandably felt, and to which he alluded often when complaining about the grind of a weekly series.

A few of the shows stand out. "To Serve Man," an adaptation of Damon Knight's short story, is the favorite "Twilight Zone" of millions. Nine-foot-tall creatures land at the United Nations and leave behind a book, which crytographers soon decipher is entitled *To Serve Man*. Believing the aliens have noble goals, Earthlings soon begin to shuttle to their planet. In the end we discover the title refers to a cookbook. "The Shelter," which was included in Serling's second batch of short stories (published by Bantam in 1961) adapted from the series, focuses on a family locked in their new fallout shelter after hearing of UFO sightings—not because of an atomic bomb, the reason it had been built. Neighbors frightened for their own lives eventually break down the shelter door, even though there would not have been enough food to feed any of them. This show is notable for only one reason: Serling, himself fearful of the atomic war he believed to be inevitable, had been taking bids to have a shelter built into his home. He abandoned the project after writing to one manufacturer to ask what recourse he could possibly have if the shelter did not perform to expectations when the time came.

"Deaths-Head Revisited" tackled the Holocaust. A Nazi S.S. captain revisiting Dachau is forced by the ghosts of its former inmates to experience the tortures to which they had been exposed, driving him insane. "Cavender Is Coming" starred Carol Burnett, whose talents Serling greatly admired, as a hapless ex-usher. At Serling's request she had sent him the humorous details of the real ushering job she had had as a kid, and he incorporated elements into the script. Jesse White played an angel trying to earn his wings by helping her to fame and fortune. Reminiscent of "Mr. Bevis," "Cavender" had also been intended as a pilot; and like "Bevis," the show fell flat. One wonders, though: If Serling were as "desperately tired" as he claimed, and bored by the strain of weekly television, why would he undertake to begin a new series? Perhaps, believing that "The Twilight Zone" would be canceled, he needed something to assuage the addiction.

For the fourth season of "Twilight Zone," CBS wanted to schedule the show at 7:30 Wednesday evenings, a belated acknowledgement that the show attracted a faithful young audience but had a slot unsuited to peddling Liggett & Myers's tobacco products; L&M dropped its sponsorship in March of 1962, near the end of the third season. That appeared, once again, to doom the series. Even when Ralston Purina offered to buy half the show if only CBS would move it either up or back a half hour—they didn't want to go on with the heavily rated "Wagon Train" having a thirty-minute headstart—CBS would not budge.

One year before, CBS had broached to Serling the idea of making "The Twilight Zone" an hour show, and he said no—partly because he did not want the added responsibility, partly because he realized the show would not work as well in the longer form, and partly because he still believed then that other career avenues beckoned strongly to him. "One more season of 'Twilight Zone' will be enough," he told the *Los Angeles Times* early in 1961, "Three seasons is enough for any television show." Evidently, despite his fatigue and the upcoming Antioch sabbatical, he no longer felt that way. This time when CBS offered to make "The Twilight Zone" a one-hour midseason replacement, contingent on OK'ing two scripts, he agreed.

This decision signified a crossroads for Serling. What had begun, he rationalized, as a temporary way station on the way back to "art" had become a permanent residence.

"He probably enjoyed 'Twilight Zone' for a while—anybody would," Saul David says. "But after a while he probably thought that was all he could do. And he kept proving it, because every time he did a screenplay, it went bad."

That assessment certainly held true for *Requiem for a Heavyweight*, of which Serling had recently seen a rough cut. He admitted—as critics and viewers would say in October, after the film's release—that his screenplay had not sufficiently broadened the story to justify its thirty-five-millimeter incarnation. In fact, few did not think the original television version superior. At the same time, United Artists released his *Incident in an Alley*, which had been written and rewritten a number of times in the previous six years. Even though he received only story credit on the script, he took the criticism personally. "It belongs in an alley. . . . Yuck," said the *New York Times*.

With the new one-hour shows yet unwritten and his future apparently in jeopardy, Serling said yes to something once unthinkable: a commercial—for Schlitz beer, no less. He had been able to rationalize doing the Oasis spots on "The Twilight Zone" as the only means of keeping his series on the air. Yet for this there could be no other rationalization than money, three thousand dollars for a few hours' work. He must have known, given his history of attacking commercial television and the sponsors whose product plugging had often inflamed him, that becoming a bona fide pitchman—as opposed to relatively harmless hawking on his own show—would tarnish his reputation and undermine his credibility. He may have felt that the commercials—three fifteen-second spots— would pass largely unnoticed. But his hypocrisy came home to roost the night of May 23, when he attended the Emmy Awards, for which he was again nominated; he did not win—for only the second time in the previous seven years.

The Hollywood personnel in the audience had the benefit of a large studio monitor from which to watch the proceedings. There, during three commercial breaks, appeared Rod Serling, wearing a straw hat, for Schlitz. Groans, laughter, and murmurs traveled quickly across the industry crowd. Few did not appreciate the irony of what they had just seen. Even through his dark tan, Serling's blushing could be seen. He and Carol fled home after the ceremonies ended.

This incident, and his reaction to it, point up a dominant characteristic of Serling: driven apparently by severe insecurities, he rarely appreciated what he had until it appeared he'd lost it. Further, he did not, or could not, enjoy his accomplishments without romanticizing what else might have been or should have been.

"While I was tilting at those windmills I didn't realize how pleasurable it was," he had commented a year before, pining nostalgically for the pleasure during his "Playhouse 90" days of "getting into a good, solid, healthy fight to keep something intact—a theme, a comment; and as often as we lost we sometimes won, and this was exciting television." This from a man who had over the years shouted about both the horrors of commercials and the evil of sponsors.

Yet each time he had the opportunity to tilt again at windmills, he declined. And given the opportunity to make some fast money in a commercial, he willingly ate his words. Weeks later he explained to a woman who had complained about his huckstering that "I was not conned." He called it a "momentary lapse" not to occur again and promised never to do a commercial again—not for beer, nor cigarettes, nor anything else. ("I didn't realize how wrong it was until I sat down in the palladium among three thousand of my peers, and saw myself ninety feet tall on that screen selling beer," he told the *Los Angeles Times*.)

"I was conned," he pleaded in 1972, by which time he had done literally dozens of commercials. "They dangled a check in front of me. I didn't expect to see it up there on a screen ninety feet high."

Serling soon signed with producer Edward Lewis at Paramount to write the adaptation of a bestselling novel (by Fletcher Knebel and Charles W. Bailey), *Seven Days in May*, about a bizarre attempted takeover of the presidency by a right-wing general, the chairman of the Joint Chiefs of Staff who fears the consequences of the nuclear disarmament treaty that the president has just negotiated with the Soviet Union. John Frankenheimer, who'd recommended him for the writing job, planned to direct; he had just finished directing another political espionage drama, *The Manchurian Candidate*.

Serling also signed with CBS to continue "The Twilight Zone." (He wrote only one of the two sample scripts sent to CBS for network approval, "The Thirty-Fathom Grave"—about a seaman whose dead shipmates beckon to him from a sunken World War II submarine—hardly a well-crafted story and thematically reminiscent of a few previous shows; Charles Beaumont wrote the other script, "In His Image," an excellent story about a killer robot.)

So much for the so-called sabbatical. Besides writing the scripts and teaching three classes during his five-month term in Yellow Springs, Serling also hosted the Monday late-night movie on the CBS affiliate television station in Columbus, WBNS. He introduced the film, providing program notes and his own insider's perspective. The audience loved him. Unlike his persona on "The Twilight Zone," his natural affability shone through.

Typically, he described the hosting job to his Aunt Betty and Uncle Ed as an evil necessary to pay for food on his children's plates. His teaching salary came to only three thousand dollars for the five months, he said, producing "some very thinned down coffers." But this was blatantly false. He had received twenty thousand dollars to write *Seven Days in May*, and "The Twilight Zone" had started up production again, thus activating his executive producer's salary in addition to payment for scripts. If nothing else, the large checks he'd been sending regularly to the bank as strictly mortgage reduction payments testified to an enviable cash flow. Anyway, WBNS did not pay him for his hosting chores, other than giving him the use of a new leased car during the family's annual summer vacation at Cayuga Lake. The lie may have been necessitated by embarrassment over his unending need to prove himself—or to remain in the public eye: for the first time in four years, there would be no weekly dose of Serling on the tube.

(*Requiem for a Heavyweight* the movie opened in October with a strong ad campaign that included testimonials by Joan Crawford: "In all the years in my association with motion picture making, it's rare that I've seen as meaningful and as moving a motion picture story as *Requiem*. Its mood, its performances, its sheer power provide a gripping experience." Within a few weeks, its theatrical death had been pronounced, and Serling immediately began pitching to Kirk Douglas the idea of producing "Twilight Zone" as an anthology movie: three individual stories joined together "by a thread of location." He had discussed the concept at length with both Robert Parrish, who directed several episodes, and Buck Houghton, who would soon be rebuffed by Serling in his attempts to develop the project at 4-Star; he soon discussed it again with Herbert Ross.)

How and why he came to the hosting job defined the quintessential Serling. While visiting the Antioch campus early in 1961 to discuss his future position there, he stayed in a small Columbus motel, from where he could also visit Carol's grandmother. On Friday night, unable to watch "The Twilight Zone" because of the poor broadcast reception in the area, he telephoned WBNS directly. "This is Rod Serling," he said to the program director. "Are you planning on running 'Twilight Zone' this evening?"

"Well this is Clark Gable, and yes we are," John Haldi replied, promptly hanging up.

Serling called back again and identified himself clearly enough this time to satisfy Haldi, who invited him to the station to watch the program on studio monitors. Serling's good humor and obvious decency and his disdain of Hollywood affectations impressed Haldi. The two men struck up a friendship out of which was born the hosting job.

After choosing a film for the Monday-night airing from

the station's library of eight hundred, Haldi wrote the first draft of the weekly host notes and sent them for personalized editing to Serling. A few days later Haldi drove in his van the ninety miles from Columbus to Yellow Springs to pick up Serling and bring him back to the studio for taping. On one particularly bitter February morning, they started out early for what figured to be a slow and treacherous drive to Columbus. The VW's heating system, like all Volkswagens' of that era, might as well have been turned off for all the heat it produced. Serling sat shivering, a blanket pulled over and around him, only his beak-like broken nose showing; like "a little sparrow," Haldi remembers.

"Now I know why Hitler designed these microbuses," Serling said. "To kill us Jews."

(Their friendship kept Serling on the job long after he left Yellow Springs, until the fall of 1965; when time allowed, he flew in to Columbus to tape several shows at a time. Haldi recalls that Serling loved to rummage through people's medicine cabinets. One afternoon, before Serling arrived at his new home for cocktails, Haldi pasted behind the medicine cabinet door an obscene photograph of a naked man performing tricks with his unusually large endowment. After a few drinks Serling excused himself. Haldi heard the creak of the hinges and then an explosion of laughter.)

It's easy to understand how Serling could have felt such a special place in his heart for Antioch—enough to want to return there at the height of his career. Like Binghamton, Antioch reminded him of halcyon days. He told *Newsweek*, which sent a reporter to Yellow Springs to do a short feature on the unusual sabbatical of the most famous writer in America, that he had not wanted to leave school even after graduating. He must have romanticized the pleasures of the archetypical college professor's life: cardigans, pipes, fireplaces, and curious, questioning minds—Socrates leading the flock. Carol's influence, her family's lineage and ties to education, may have influenced that fantasy. And what more archetypal place could be found than Antioch of the early 1960s?

An island of radical liberalism surrounded by thoroughly midwestern towns and values, Yellow Springs—charming, quaint, and woodsy—burst with intellectual vitality. In the coffeehouses or on any street corner, people discussed subjects of great and minor import. Cinema, theater, dance, music, and art abounded. On campus the atmosphere conveyed a kind of mental euphoria. Students believed it their duty to question every belief, not with the idea of getting ahead in the business world—this was, after all, a liberal arts college—but of learning for learning's sake. Stereotypically the bright offspring of liberal New York families, they sought knowledge, not necessarily careers.

If Serling—the college's currently most renowned alumnus—expected a warm homecoming, he was disappointed. He saw no welcome banner across the door of their small, rented Victorian house on Whiteman Street the day of the family's arrival from Cayuga Lake in the WBNS-provided station wagon. Nor were his Drama in Mass Media (offered only in the fall quarter) and Writing and Dramatic Form (given both quarters) students awed in the least by this man from Hollywood. (The adults in town, however, sought him out constantly, making a weekly three-hour seminar/lecture in the evening a necessity.)

"A lot of people felt that television was not high art and looked down on it," recalls Walter Wanger, who took Serling's writing class. "There was definitely no one saying, 'Wow, we've got a famous guy here.' The media weren't integral to everyone's life—not the way they are today. There wasn't necessarily a feeling that he'd been a sellout, but there was a little bit of suspicion of him." Most of the students did not have televisions.

In his loosely structured class, Serling used his own works—"Patterns," "Requiem," and others, but mostly "The Twilight Zone"—to illustrate the form. He would leave the room during the sixteen-millimeter showings, then walk back in to mostly hostile questions. Despite the attacks, he answered honestly, sometimes brutally honestly. Many answers, he discovered, were indefensible, but he continued without defensiveness. "Nothing gets past these kids," he said. "I'll make a value judgment and they won't let me get away with it. I don't think I was quite prepared for the probing second-guessing." (Saul David notes that most writers want and expect applause after showing someone their work and argue with any negative points in the critique. Serling was different. "I knew there was something wrong," he would moan. Says David, "He expected bad news. He was the least secure writer I ever knew.")

But the students easily separated the so-called professor from the person who did not at all resemble the slightly foreboding figure on television. "It's impossible to imagine someone disliking him," says Wanger, who occasionally babysat Serling's daughters in Yellow Springs and later maintained correspondence with Serling. "He was not at all like a 'Hollywood' guy; he didn't have any of the Hollywood attitudes or mannerisms. He was normal, easy to talk to, and very, very nice." (Wanger's most vivid memory of Serling is of him smoking: "I have never, ever seen anyone," he says slowly, "smoke a cigarette with as much ferocity." Later after staying in Serling's home and even going to a party with him and Carol, Wanger's overriding impression remained "the cartons of cigarettes everywhere.")

Serling had sought out Antioch as a place to get away from it all, but instead he took it all with him; he was too insecure to do otherwise. No matter how much he complained, "he was really only happy when he was working," John Champion notes. "That explains the need for the cigarettes, the endless pumping himself up physically and mentally to be a work machine."

He dictated the second and third drafts of *Seven Days in May* in Yellow Springs on the Dictaphone and mailed them to his California secretary, Marjorie Langsford, for transcription; she sent them back to him in Ohio. They put together the pieces of the script like a puzzle over the phone. "I should have gotten a cowriting credit," she jokes. Meanwhile, production on the one-hour shows continued. Serling wrote four of his own and oversaw the other nine, again via the mails, with new producer Herbert Hirschman.

Buck Houghton had left "The Twilight Zone" rather than work on the one-hour shows, accepting an executive position at the new television division of 4-Star. "I told them that "Twilight Zone" is based on a willing suspension of disbelief," he recalls. "You can't ask people to do it for an hour. You can say, 'There's this fellow who can walk through walls,' and about thirty minutes later people say, 'What else you got?' 'Twilight Zones' work best as a two-sentence anecdote, not something that you say, 'And then.' You never say, 'And then.'"

Serling offered CBS the same wisdom, but the network insisted; in order to keep the show on the air, he relented.

Hirschman knew Serling from "Playhouse 90," where he'd been an associate producer and sometimes director. (He'd also produced "Perry Mason" and "Dr. Kildare.") As Houghton had discovered, Serling, technically his boss, was a pleasure to work for. Despite the two thousand miles between them, Serling trusted Hirschman's judgment in the choice of one-hour scripts and financial affairs. The new producer, charged with carrying on the status quo despite the rules having changed, turned often to Beaumont, Matheson, and Earl Hamner, all "Twilight Zone" regulars. Unfortunately, with the exception of Beaumont's "Miniature" (which starred Robert Duvall as an off-center man entranced by a nineteenth-century dollhouse that eventually becomes his home) and Serling's "On Thursday We Leave for Home" (when a rescue ship arrives to bring back to earth the survivors and their progeny of a marooned spaceship that had intended to colonize a brutal, unforgiving planet, the captain, James Whitmore—who has been their governor and god for thirty years—refuses to return to his life of relative unimportance), the one-hour scripts could not sustain the pace and intrigue of the best half-hour shows. After sixty minutes the idea seemed tired, and so was the viewer.

The fourth season of "Twilight Zone" opened January 3, 1963, with Charles Beaumont's "In His Image," about a psychopathic robot. It replaced the same series, "Fair Exchange"—a comedy about an American teenage girl and an English counterpart who exchange families for year—that had knocked it off the evening schedule in September. At the time, Cayuga Productions enjoyed a hiatus, awaiting the OK from CBS to shoot the final five shows of the season. As the approval seemed likely, the company also began searching for a new producer. Just a week before, his CBS contract now expired, Hirschman had exited "The Twilight Zone" to produce "Espionage" in England.

Before CBS chose the new producer, Serling demanded the autonomy to select the last five of the season's eighteen scripts and threatened to quit if he didn't get it—on general principle and because he wanted to adapt his four-year-old "The Happy Place." With vice president Hubbell Robinson gone (having been squeezed out in a corporate power play) and the show no longer carrying the significance of a pilot script, the concept of euthanasia for sixty-year-olds did not seem as shocking. Fearing that the network attributed the lower quality of the first thirteen scripts for the new season to Buck Houghton's departure and not his own absence, he explained to Robert Lewine, West Coast programming chief, that it had been he, not Houghton, who had selected scripts the first three years and that the choice of the next five scripts would be entirely his.

Serling and production manager Ralph Nelson favored Perry Lafferty, who had a long history as a television director, including three "Twilight Zones," as new producer. CBS chose Bert Granet, the man who had produced "Time Element" on "Desilu Playhouse" nearly five years before. "My feeling about Bert Granet is roughly the same as with Herb Hirschman," Serling told Lewine, who wanted to put in his own man to oversee script selection, just as Bill Dozier and Hubbell Robinson had years before. "They are both qualitative and intelligent gentlemen, well versed in production. But they are not versed in the concept of 'The Twilight Zone.'"

Granet may not have been versed in the "The Twilight Zone," but he certainly understood Serling's drawbacks as a writer, even as he admired his great talents. "Rod's biggest disappointment was that he wasn't a good screenwriter," Granet says. "He brought this up to me any number of times. He'd say, 'I don't get it.' Well, Rod was a man whose characters had to speak words. Never, even in 'Twilight Zone,' did he capture the visual; the directors got that."

"Isn't it great, teaching?" Granet mockingly asked Serling when they met again, Serling having flown in from Yellow Springs.

"Yeah, wonderful," Serling replied.

"Particularly," Granet added, "when you know you've got over a quarter-million-dollar income every year."

Granet had never forgiven Serling for not inviting him to produce "The Twilight Zone" after producing "The Time Element." He mistakenly believed that the show's popularity had inspired CBS to create the series, unaware it had long been in development.

"I think he should have come to me," Granet reflects. "'Look, Bert, since you produced it, I think you ought to be part of this operation.' I wouldn't have done it, because I was under contract to Desilu. I think he would have found a more difficult time handling me. Buck never raised his voice his whole life." Where Houghton rarely questioned Serling's writing, Granet was not so timid.

"Rod had one wonderful line every once in a while," Granet remembers. "'If I hit you, they'll have to put you in a bowl and spoon you out.' I'd get this every couple of scripts, cut it out, put it in an envelope, and send it back to him. But he was very easy to work with. If I didn't like something, I'd call him up. 'OK,' he'd say. 'I'll change it.' He seldom defended anything."

Serling departed Yellow Springs in late February, before the winter quarter ended; the date had been prearranged and his students were left to two fill-in professors.

He left probably refreshed, for two weeks in Hawaii with Carol, even though his work schedule had been only slightly less frenetic than usual. He also knew that *Seven Days in May*, a script of which he was particularly proud, began production in a month and that "The Twilight Zone," in its half-hour form, had been granted a fifth year—doomed to be its last. Ironically, the show received its earliest renewal during its least creative and most awkward season.

Renewed and refreshed, Rod Serling now began to realize how difficult it would be to escape from the trap he'd baited for himself: he was consumed by "The Twilight Zone."

In four years he had written almost eighty scripts for the series, with sixteen more to come in the final season; adapted stories from the scripts into two bestselling paperbacks; and begun developing the series as a feature film. He now sanctioned a third book of stories, this one a Grosset & Dunlap hardcover—to be ghosted by someone over whom he had no control and who'd not yet been chosen. (In a letter written later that summer, he admitted that writing prose was "the hardest thing in the world for *me* to do"). There were also the entities recently created by Cayuga's and CBS's granting merchandising licenses: *The Twilight Zone* magazine, *Twilight Zone* comic book, and "Twilight Zone" game. (Licensing income would add a significant sum to the ever-accumulating total, likely making "Twilight Zone" one of the most profitable shows in the history of television.) Anything that bore the words *Rod Serling* or *Twilight Zone*—that is, anything in the fantastical genre—sold like gold.

Serling knew it and quickly edited for Bantam later that year an anthology of other writers' previously published spooky stories called *Rod Serling's Triple W: Witches, Warlocks, and Werewolves.* By using his own name and not "Twilight Zone," he did not have to split with CBS what really amounted to a licensing fee.

Rogers & Cowan, the giant public relations firm, wanted to make Serling the centerpiece of its fall campaign for "Twilight Zone." "Rod Serling is highly respected by the press. . . . We plan to take advantage of both Rod Serling's reputation and the inherent news material in the show," wrote Henry Rogers in May 1963, pitching to supplement Cayuga's regular employment of Dancer-Fitzgerald-Sample. (Procter & Gamble, the new sponsor of "Twilight Zone," happened to be one of R&C's largest clients, and Rogers wanted to protect its investment.) Dancer-Fitzgerald-Sample rejected the proposal and decided instead to hire an Amazon beauty, "Miss Twilight Zone," to travel around the country for a series of personal appearances, some of them with Serling. In a letter to the company Serling called that kind of publicity "pretty cheapening" and instead opted for press conferences in which he could respond to presumably intelligent questions with honesty and wit. However, CBS allowed Virginia Trimble, a college student with an alleged IQ of nearly two hundred, to tour the country as Miss Twilight Zone. Even *Playboy,* the upscale bastion of liberal hipness, typecast him, insisting that he take part in an ambitious symposium discussing the far-off future: 1984 and Beyond. Having openly admitted to being strictly a Johnny-come-lately to science fiction, Serling protested the invitation when he heard the other participants included such legitimate futurists as Arthur C. Clarke, Isaac Asimov, and Robert A. Heinlein. (Serling's stab at 1984, a world dominated by telecommunications, came closer to reality than many of the other participants', who offered visions of daily life more in tune with "The Jetsons" than Ronald Reagan.)

Compared to the velvet alley, the dominance of "Twilight Zone" over his life was equally insidious and far more unyielding. In the velvet alley, he made the choices about what and how much to write; now the choices made themselves, without his consent. Before, no one attributed supernatural powers and Christ-like generosity to him. Now, with his face inseparable from the show, "fan" letters began to assume more predatory and desperate tones. A not atypical example from June 1963, written by a young man accusing Serling of stealing his unsolicited manuscripts:

> I have been cheated, lied to, hurt, stolen from, lonely, poor, unhealthy and tortured all my life. You were my last hope.
>
> I have completely turned away from God. I have been too lonely and hurt and now you complete my hell. I only have six months to live, I am completely broke, and though I am 22, I have never dated or kissed a girl. . . .
>
> Well, don't use my articles without paying me. Send them back so that I can send them elsewhere and try to sell them for enough money for my burial.

Rod Serling, the former future Arthur Miller, now appeared, perhaps to millions of viewers, as the kind of man who either got very hairy each night during the cycle of the full moon or had direct communications with little green men. Both Jack Benny and Garry Moore, on their respective shows, did humorous takeoffs on "Twilight Zone," with Serling playing the character people imagined him to be: the magical sovereign of a bizarre kingdom.

By the summer, when "Twilight Zone" went back into production, he had mostly completed his sixteen scripts for the year. In all, the company shot thirty-five original shows that last year; the French adaptation of Ambrose Bierce's *An Occurrence at Owl Creek Bridge* aired under a unique licensing agreement, allowing the series to come in under budget for the whole season. The job had become tiresome, and he looked forward to putting it behind him, at least for a while. In the fall he and Carol would leave on a six-week trip to the Philippines, Japan, and Australia, sponsored by the USIA, with which he had maintained contact over the years after meeting George Romney Wheeler, the agency's media director, at a cocktail party. Wheeler once asked him to write films for him whenever his time allowed.

Before leaving he set to work with vigor and enthusiasm on projects that he felt might break the stereotype he'd created. He intended to avoid the fate that had befallen Bela Lugosi after 1931, when no one wanted to hire the fine actor who played Dracula too well. But who would hire Edgar Allan Poe to write *Gone with the Wind*? Already, he discovered, many people had forgotten that he also authored "Patterns" and "Requiem."

Dick Berg had asked him to contribute scripts—as many as he wanted—to the new fall anthology series he was producing on NBC, "Bob Hope Presents The Chrysler Theatre." (Hope planned to alternate the anthology drama with variety and comedy specials on a weekly basis; the only other anthology show on the air was "The Richard Boone Show," produced by Buck Houghton, in which Boone and his repertory company of actors played different roles each week.) Both because of his desire to work with Berg and his need to write nonfantasy scripts, Serling jumped at the chance to return to his television roots. He quickly knocked out "A Killing at Sundial," his first non–"Twilight Zone" script for television since "In the Presence of Mine Enemies." The story was of a young Chippewa Indian who, after making a small fortune in oil, returns to his Oklahoma home intending revenge on the white men responsible for the lynching of his father. (Years before, lamenting his censorship problems to a newspaper reporter, Serling had flippantly commented about the Indians, as though the racism and discrimination they endured were justified. He meant no malice, and in fact he made the statement in ignorance, but several long letters castigated him for the statement and offered descriptions of the American Indians' plight. This script may have been his belated acknowledgement and apology.)

Bert Granet left "Twilight Zone," like Herbert Hirschman and Buck Houghton before him, for greener pastures: in this case the green of money. With its splashy "Great Adventure" series fast approaching bankruptcy under John Houseman's not-so-watchful eye, CBS aggressively went after Granet to assume the producing chores.

"Usually CBS said, 'Get your ass in the car and come over here,'" Granet recalls. "Not this time. New York executives drove out to see *me* at MGM, where we were doing 'Twilight Zone.' I knew then they were in trouble."

Granet asked the amount of Houseman's salary. The executives said they couldn't divulge that information.

"Fuck it," he told them. "I'm happy where I am." Two days later they came back to MGM with a copy of Houseman's contract.

"Double it," Granet said. They did. "I think they gave me a quarter of a million dollars to do ten of them," he notes.

When he informed Serling he would stay if his salary were raised to match CBS's offer—an impossiblity, he knew—Granet may have been getting back at Serling for not asking him to join Cayuga years before. Serling felt angry and abandoned. Only twenty or so shows remained—almost certainly, he believed, the series' last. CBS's handwriting seemed all too legible: By spiriting away the man they considered their top-notch producer to rescue a show they cared about deeply, while letting someone else stay home to babysit their aging dinosaur, CBS executives very clearly expressed their priorities. This time Serling did not fight for script control. He let William Froug, who had produced "Adventures in Paradise" and "The Dick Powell Show," among others, and had coproduced some "Playhouse 90"s, make the selections. Froug began by abandoning many of the scripts Granet had in development, including some by the show's long-time writers.

If this were the final year for "Twilight Zone," what then? Serling asked Froug to produce the new series idea still developing in his brain: "The Chase," a weekly espionage caper centered around McGough, an American James Bond whose office is in a "recessed cubby-hole" in the Pentagon. As conceived, each week McGough would be faced with a thorny problem—a Russian defector, for example, or an American spy, "or any one of twenty-five dozen other stories of intrigue, of suspense, and of jeopardy." The hook, Serling thought, was the last ten minutes of each hour-long show, during which, as the title implied, there would be an exciting, imaginative chase scene—either McGough escaping or pursuing. Serling wanted to shoot the series all over the world and believed it could be done easily, cheaply, and well. His two-page synopsis, sent to Alden Schwimmer, reflected his excitement for the idea, as well as his customary impatience; he wanted Schwimmer to commit CBS support based on a précis particularly lacking in details. If CBS liked the idea, he'd consent to write a pilot.

The final "Twilight Zone" season opened September 27, with Serling's "In Praise of Pip," starring Jack Klugman as a wasted man whose son, he's just been informed, lies dying from a bullet in South Vietnam. Besides the reference to American involvement in that far-off civil war at a time when few people could identify the Southeast Asian country, the script seems notable for the lamentation that becomes the story theme: a man mourning the father he never was. One has to wonder whether possibly his own guilt over his absentee role as father, not the war itself (which Serling knew little about), compelled the writing. In the end the man makes a pact with God to trade his death for his son's life.

The following day Serling left for the Australia-Asian tour. First stop, the Philippines—to confront the ghosts of his past. He visited many of the sites where almost twenty years before he had received his baptisms of fire: the Tellavista Lodge on Tagay-tay Ridge, where he made his only combat jump. He stood in the remnants of the resort and remembered how he'd lain on the floor, shivering with fright, never quite managing sleep. The memories flooded over him with a clarity he had suppressed these many years. He drove into Pasay, then Paranaque, then into Rizal Stadium, home of a baseball team, where he had shot a Japanese soldier in the infield. He entered the walled city and spoke to the people, some old enough to remember the Eleventh Airborne's heroics, some quite ignorant. He wandered through the military's Pacific cemetery, looking for names he knew—and found many. He stood before the Eleventh Airborne Monument, a decaying, barely legible concrete marker commemorating the Americans who gave their life for the country's freedom. And he wondered why, with such corruption and disintegration all around, the people ever wanted their independence.

In a remarkably revealing letter written immediately upon returning, he urged Bill Lindau, a buddy from the 511th who had shared the horrors of the war there with him, to make the trip himself. Being there, he wrote, forced him to acknowledge the bitterness he had long buried inside and tried to forget, and to recall the boy who'd gone to war and the emotionally battered man who'd returned. Not surprisingly after such an outpouring, he also noted that these feelings and revelations must necessarily be returned to that secret place where they'd been hidden all these years, as though a daily awareness of them would fracture his delicate emotional peace.

The visit must have stirred some deep passions in Serling. During a visit to Corregidor, where he felt he could hear the ghosts of dying and agonized soldiers (on walls and in the few remaining tunnels, scrawls could still be read, "Help me, dear God, please, help me"), he found himself imagining the filmic potential of the World War II history of the place: a thirty-minute anthology series, each show based on a different battle, shot right at the battle sight. Even before writing to Hunt Stromberg, CBS vice president, he investigated the use of Filipino facilities and crews. Total production costs, he concluded, would be at least 50 percent lower than in the United States. In expressing to Stromberg his colossal excitement for the project, he emphasized that this new idea in no way affected his desire to do "The Chase." He could, he said, easily do both.

"A Killing at Sundial" aired on "Chrysler Theatre" October 4, the first drama in the weekly series. Someone in the public relations department at NBC—someone, perhaps, who didn't like Serling—sent to his hotel in Manila a copy of the *New York Times* review. "For Mr. Serling and others associated with the production it was an hour of bleak adversity," wrote John Shanley. "It is difficult to believe that the gifted author of distinguished television dramas such as 'Patterns' and 'Requiem for a Heavyweight' could have been responsible for a work as shallow as 'A Killing at Sundial.'" Shanley went on to criticize the script's "large slices of bombast" and dialogue "that might have come from a bad, old movie."

The *Times* did not stand alone in its condemnation of the show, and although *Time* and a few newspapers in more minor markets praised it faintly, Serling's psyche experienced the damage. In a letter to Dick Berg, who had mercifully not sent him the reviews, Serling blatantly admitted that he'd never before felt such a sense of bewilderment and confusion as had suddenly overcome him. He offered to abandon, if Berg now preferred, the assignment to adapt John O'Hara's short story, "It's Mental Work." Berg, of course, had no intention of withdrawing the assignment and aired the show from Serling's script on December 20. (Berg believes the poor reviews for "Sundial" were an inevitable response to NBC's overpublicizing the "Chrysler Theatre" series.)

The confidence and enthusiasm that had bubbled from him since late summer suddenly drained away. Serling now began to believe that CBS shared little of his affection for either "The Chase" (although three years later another of Alden Schwimmer's clients, Bruce Geller, sold a somewhat similar series to CBS: *Mission: Impossible*) or his return-to-Corregidor idea.

"This was a man of extreme temperaments," John Champion observes. "He could get very happy, and he could get very low. And when he got very low, he would just cut himself off. He would just pull away from people."

Meanwhile, "Twilight Zone" had scored relatively well in the Nielsen ratings and was given an early renewal for production on the next thirteen shows.

A few weeks following Serling's return to the States, President John Kennedy was assassinated. Serling was in New York at the time, meeting with CBS. The day after, he received a call from the State Department, asking him to come to Washington immediately to write and narrate a short documentary about the new president, Lyndon Johnson, for foreign consumption. The department realized quickly, in the aftermath of the assassination, that they needed a type of propaganda to quell the attendant worries of allies, friends, and trading partners, most of whom knew little about Johnson; since there had not been an ordinary two-and-a-half month transition from election to inauguration—time enough for Johnson's aides, if not the man himself, to meet personally with them—a mass introduction was necessary. They chose Serling for his relationship with the USIA, which now intended to collect on his past-due promise to fit their media needs in with his schedule. This time, his schedule would have to wait.

The assignment, eventually called *The President: The Transition of the American Presidency to Lyndon Johnson*, became good therapy for Serling's grief over the death of Kennedy, a man he greatly admired. He saw in the assassination a symbol of a national breakdown in morality, perhaps even the incipient crumbling of the country itself. Although active in an incredible spate of social causes, particularly as a staunch supporter of the American Civil Liberties Union, he had still supported Kennedy's Bay of Pigs invasion and his conduct during the Cuban missile crisis; unlike many of the other pacifist liberals in Hollywood, he believed a ready military was less likely to have to fight than an unprepared one. After writing "In Praise of Pip" earlier in the year, he also began to investigate more about United States involvement in Vietnam; and again, unlike a growing number of Americans, he retained an ambivalence that tilted toward agreeing with the decision to prop up the South Vietnamese government in that civil war.

The film enabled him, as it would the intended audience, to become acquainted with Lyndon Johnson, a man about whom he harbored reservations. But after watching several hundred thousand feet of film of Johnson's speeches on file at the State Department, he understood the man's intelligence and gruff appeal, as well as his political acumen. Interestingly, he also realized that Johnson's image suffered not because of his own personality but because of the contrast to Kennedy's oratory skills and innate charm, and he developed a respect for the new president. The situation would have been much worse, he wrote to the Delavans, his neighbors at the summer house, if President Eisenhower had been assassinated a few years before, leaving Vice President Richard Nixon to assume office.

Three years later, when Ronald Reagan ran for governor of California against incumbent Pat Brown, Serling turned his active support to Brown. He felt no particular affection for Brown's record or abilities, only a dread of a professional actor manipulating the media; the public, presumably, would be sufficiently distracted by the actor's charm and glibness, while the real issues and the candidates' policies were obscured by the stage lights and greasepaint. Reagan, he feared, would use the governorship as a stepping stone to the presidency. At the time it seemed farfetched and paranoid. (As the head of a Hollywood contingent raising funds for Brown's reelection campaign, Serling solicited many celebrities. Marlon Brando, after receiving a personal letter from Serling, explained his refusal for funds: "If it's Brown against Reagan, I think I'll vote for Jack LaLanne.")

Away from home for most of the fall, Serling was confronted with a massive pile of correspondence when he
returned. Included were a few notable pieces: a letter from
Frank Sinatra inquiring after his availability to do a film
together; a letter from King Brothers Productions president Frank King, along with a copy of Pierre Boulle's novel
Planet of the Apes, to which King held the rights; and a
few letters from his old paratrooper buddy, Bill Lindau,
asking again, as he had in the fall, whether Serling might
be interested in making another jump next spring at Fort
Bragg. (Lindau, who lived in nearby Winston-Salem, North
Carolina, had made contact with the Eighty-second Airborne before broaching the idea to Serling.) Curiously, but
not surprisingly, Lindau's letters aroused his interest the
most. On Christmas Eve, the day before his thirty-ninth
birthday, he wrote to Lindau that it may as well have been
his ninety-ninth birthday for as old as he felt.

Serling's aversion to growing older was no act. Many of
his friends, as well as his brother, believed he had a
premonition of early death, and not solely because his
father had died at age fifty-two. He smoked four packs of
cigarettes a day, got too little exercise, and often took sick.
And despite his ever-robust appearance and cheerful persona, he was overwhelmingly tired, having spent fifteen
years compiling a body of work that the vast majority of
writers never achieve during even long careers. He felt
trapped in "The Twilight Zone"—not entirely unwill-
ingly—his own powers declining like atrophied muscles
for lack of real use in the previous five years. After so
many years of laying projects at the feet of others who
held control over his career—a career that dominated his
whole life—he needed something powerful to connect
him back to youth, to independence, to the original fierce-
ness of his dreams. A jump, like the sabbatical at Antioch—made for almost precisely the same reasons—might
be just the thing.

He told Lindau he'd contemplated the jump ever since
Lindau first pitched it and now found himself in the
position of *having* to prove himself to himself. Despite

his fear and trepidation, or perhaps because of them, he authorized Lindau to arrange the event.

The final season of "Twilight Zone" was not marked by a plethora of memorable shows, although "Nightmare at 20,000 Feet," written by Richard Matheson and directed by Richard Donner, certainly ranks among the best of all episodes. William Shatner starred as a man recently discharged from a sanitarium, who is the only person on a plane to notice a creature on the wing tampering with the engines. (In 1975, during a lecture to film students at Sherwood Oaks College in Los Angeles, Serling related that he once spent several weeks preparing with Western Airline employees to scare Matheson with a poster of a gremlin attached to the outside of Matheson's window during a flight to San Francisco together, only to have the hoax blown away by the blast of the jet engines. A good story, but apocryphal: Matheson notes he never had occasion to fly anywhere with Serling.) "A Kind of Stopwatch"—a bore who finds a stopwatch that freezes all matter, except for him, drops the device while robbing a bank and must live forever in a hellish limbo—Serling's adaptation of an unpublished story, also seems to hold memorable appeal. So does his "The Masks," in which a dying rich man forces his money-grubbing heirs to don grotesque Mardi Gras masks until the moment he dies; when he does, later that night, their faces are frozen into the shapes of the masks. "The Last Night of a Jockey," another Serling original, starred Mickey Rooney in a tour de force one-man show about a jockey who wishes to be tall after being banned for life from racing; granted his wish, he becomes taller and taller and taller, until he reaches ten feet—and is told he can indeed race again. "Living Doll," written by Charles Beaumont and his ghostwriter, Jerry Sohl, was about a child's talking doll who says to people she does not like, "My name is Talky Tina, and I'm going to kill you."

On February 5, 1964, Serling told *Daily Variety* that he

had canceled "The Twilight Zone." This was a dishonest, macho, face-saving claim: the series, despite its reasonably good ratings and devoted viewership, had not been included in the fall 1964 lineup of shows announced a few days before. On the very same day, Serling wrote to Alden Schwimmer, with a copy sent to CBS vice president Michael Dann, to explain the plans Cayuga had had for the series in year six. A greater emphasis was to be placed on space and extraterrestrials, and Vandenberg Air Force Base had already granted permission for location shooting; the shows themselves, Serling assured, would have been much more ambitious, telling stories on a broader canvas while recreating the urgency and allure of the series' first years.

Serling anxiously awaited the release of *Seven Days in May* later that month. He had seen the film but did not yet understand his own opinion; he needed the critical and public reaction for that. Perhaps, he thought, the all-star cast—Fredric March, Kirk Douglas, Burt Lancaster, Ava Gardner—would make up for any of the script's shortcomings. The book on which the movie had been based was well known and well liked, and he had been mostly faithful to it—which placed him in a double-bind: if the script did not capture the book, then he had failed; and if the script succeeded, well, then, he had only taken a form of dictation. This was his first film since *Requiem for a Heavyweight* almost two years before, and he needed the success. (It was not for the money that he worried, having just purchased a thirty-five-foot Chris-Craft yacht for Cayuga Lake.)

It seems likely, based on the subsequent chronology of events and Serling's habitual insecurities, that he would not have tried to sell "The Twilight Zone" to another network had he known that the movie would be well received and his career as a screenwriter apparently in flower again. (His agency, now named Ashley-Famous following a merger, certainly pushed hard for the resale, since they stood to lose $5,000 per show if the series went off the air.) He first chose NBC, which quickly said no. Tom Moore, the president of ABC—a network that then had few hits and was not unfavorably disposed to taking someone else's "dirty seconds"—got far enough into negotiations to work out a complete budget. Moore wanted to call the series "Witches, Warlocks, and Werewolves" (CBS would certainly not allow the use of the original name), after the title of the Serling-edited anthology, released a few months before.

Serling began work on a proposal, mutating "The Twilight Zone" into a form that later in effect became "Night Gallery." He called it "Rod Serling's Wax Museum." As conceived, each week a different bust in the museum would be unveiled, the bust of that episode's main character. It would be chilling but not horrific—the latter being the sense Moore evidently wanted to convey.

Following its premiere in mid-February, *Seven Days in May* received almost unanimously decent reviews and paying crowds (although the latter soon shrank each week). Whatever flaws were inherent in the script—for instance, Serling's occasionally stilted, dogmatic dialogue in which characters sometimes seem to give speeches rather than speak—were covered well by John Frankenheimer, whose excellent direction kept the far-fetched plot taut and exciting and did not allow it to disintegrate into unintentional satire or melodrama.

Bolstered now, Serling sent a rough first draft of the screenplay *Planet of the Apes* to Edward Lewis, the Paramount producer for whom he wrote *Seven Days*. And he no longer needed ABC, or at least he no longer needed to step so lightly. "Weekly ghouls," Serling told *Daily Variety*, is what Moore preferred—"C-pictures."

His remarks to the trade press severed the ties and killed "Rod Serling's Wax Museum"; after reading the paper, Moore canceled the project. This was uncharacteristic of Serling, to publicly denigrate a power broker's position. In the past he had commented publicly on numerous occasions over stupidities he perceived in the industry. But he had never before mentioned names—

particularly those of network executives—even when he disliked them or disagreed vehemently with their opinions. He knew he had offended Moore and sought to assuage, offering the standard I-was-misquoted explanation.

Two weeks later Serling flew to Fort Bragg, North Carolina, to jump out of an airplane for the first time in more than nineteen years. For the previous four months Serling and Bill Lindau had exchanged at least a dozen letters with each other and a like number with the headquarters of the Eighty-second Airborne Division at Bragg to work through the clearances and logistics. Serling viewed the jump as a method of revitalizing his spirit and repelling middle age. The army saw it as a terrific recruiting device: one of their own, the prodigal son, returned to make one final jump; there would obviously be a slew of newspaper reporters and network cameras. Only two major hurdles had to be cleared before jumping: CBS and Carol Serling.

Serling innocently told the network about his planned jump, believing the executives would find it rife with publicity possibilities. They didn't. His contract, like most exclusive contracts with "above-the-line" talent, apparently prohibited him from taking undue physical risks. Eventually, he convinced them that the positive press far outweighed the danger.

Carol Serling was probably not as easily appeased. For years Serling and she had not flown together on the same airplane for fear of an accident that would leave their two daughters orphaned (a year before, Serling had asked his brother Bob to act as guardian should anything happen to him and Carol). When Serling wanted to return from Palm Springs to Los Angeles in Jackie Cooper's small private plane in the early 1960s, Serling made Cooper promise not to tell Carol. How he convinced her that he would be safe jumping out of an airplane is unknown, but Lindau's wife was enlisted to call her directly with assurances, Lindau himself having recently made his own jump for the first time in more than eighteen years.

(Robert Goldsmith, a friend of the Serlings who had

grown up in Binghampton as a contemporary of Bob Serling, remembers being present in the Serling home one night for dinner when the couple heatedly discussed whether Rod should be allowed to make the jump. Carol argued against it, Goldsmith says, worried that an injury might interfere with their planned vacation in Italy. Rod believed the worst that could occur would be a broken ankle. "Hell," he said, "we'd be able to go even if I had a cast on it." Joking or not, they asked Goldsmith to make the final decision—saying they'd abide by his ruling. Tactfully, he avoided acting as judge and jury.)

In a letter to Betsy Lindau, Serling gratefully acknowledged the apparent influence she'd had in quelling Carol's fears for his safety and admitted that his own need to jump stemmed from the feeling that the best and most of his life now lay behind him. "The first rather pathetic clutch of the grown man . . . who tries to relive that moment," he wrote.

On April 1 a contingent of several dozen paratroopers, regular army, public relations people, and interested observers descended on Fort Bragg. After an all-morning refresher course, Serling and thirty-six young paratroopers, members of the Eighty-second Airborne, ascended in a C-124. He had been nervous and apprehensive, the nausea rising from his stomach into his throat. "It was World War II revisited," he told *Newsweek*. "You hear the old engines roaring, and you sit there in those bucket seats and look at the faces of the men, and the years drift away." The men checked their equipment, hooked their static lines, and jumped from twelve hundred feet. And then all too suddenly it was over.

Back on the ground, a group gathered around him. He signed autographs, posed for pictures, and gave television interviews while the real paratroopers filed quietly back to their barracks. In a sense he had recaptured his past, but the scene that played now poignantly emphasized, in a spare, wordless way that he never learned to express in a screenplay, how the years had changed him.

In at least one more way, he succeeded in capturing a bit of the old Serling that spring. Unexpectedly, he won his sixth Emmy for "It's Mental Work," the "Chrysler Theatre" adaptation of John O'Hara's short story about a bartender, a cocktail waitress, and the aging bar owner who suffers a heart attack; it was the script he offered not to write the previous fall after terrible reviews. The last time he had won an Emmy for something other than "Twilight Zone" had been in 1957, for "The Comedian," the story of a man who had found staying on top more difficult than getting there.

"Twilight Zone" ended with a whimper; the last of its 156 first-run scripts aired on June 19, 1964. "The Bewitching Pool," although written by Earl Hamner (a cowinner with Serling of 1949's second place "Dr. Christian" award, Hamner contributed many "Twilight Zone" scripts), was pathetically derivative and cannibalistic of the themes, elements, and plots that had once made the series so fresh: a young brother and sister escape from their parents' bad marriage by diving into their swimming pool, surfacing in a wonderfully idyllic spot where children never grow up and their parents never fight or divorce. The show seemed to justify why the series had been canceled and typified the admitted fatigue and boredom of its creators.

Two weeks later Serling and his family adjourned to Cayuga Lake for their annual vacation. In a July letter to Alden Schwimmer, written after a few weeks of sylvan tranquility and thought, he admitted that the quality of his work had dropped precipitously the previous few years. He felt that, despite the Emmys and other awards, nothing he'd written bore the mark of quality and that he no longer deserved his reputation for excellence.

That objectivity came by way of his hopefulness for the future: the belief that the world awaited his words eagerly and that given the time to carefully craft each script, he could still manufacture screen magic. He believed, incorrectly, that he would again live up to the gargantuan expectations created by his earliest—and greatest—artistic successes and that he could escape the powerful and far-reaching clutches of "The Twilight Zone."

"Fame is short-lived," he had told UPI in September of 1963. "One year after this show goes off the air, they'll never remember who I am. And I don't care a bit. Anonymity is fine with me. My place is as a writer."

7

SEASONS TO BE WARY

In his fantasies, Rod Serling dreamed of languishing at Cayuga Lake, taking long, pensive walks through the woods, trampling on the crisp autumn leaves, and then retiring to his study to write the Great American Novel or stage play; if perfection and greatness took two years, even three, so be it.

He had been in precisely that frame of mind when he wrote to Alden Schwimmer from the lake house during the summer of 1964, claiming he did not want to work for the next twelve months on any assignments: the blessed burden of "Twilight Zone" finally lifted, he had grown contemplative, reassessing his priorities for the first time since the production of "Patterns" almost ten years before. He questioned his assembly-line approach to work and looked back to find few scripts he admired or cherished.

Living in California, where the seasons blend almost unnoticed into each other, the years accumulate as if in a dream—and his fortieth birthday approached too rapidly. One month before his birthday he wrote again to Schwimmer, emphasizing his need to achieve a kind of

253

immortality—"a couple of monuments"—and not just accumulate a fortune in writing fees and residuals. Ironically, the letter had not been written to reiterate his plea for creative solitude but to terminate the agency-client relationship. Without the daily tether of a series or the pleasant desperation of assignments piled atop each other, Serling began to drift.

The actual task of writing slowly and carefully became much less attractive in the doing than it seemed in the romantic planning. After all, the two Bantam editions of his adapted "Twilight Zone" short stories had each taken more than eight months to write—and paid him ten times less than every other script he turned out in days or weeks. For a man accustomed to moving, as his friend John Champion notes, 190 miles an hour, the books' quality didn't justify the labor. Perhaps if he had been reasonably certain that the novel or play would be a true work of art, he would have devoted the time and care required. But the leisure time—the time to think—ate away at his confidence. He wanted the action—and needed a scapegoat.

The letter to Schwimmer implicitly blamed his agents for both his getting older and his not having these "monuments." He was disappointed that "Twilight Zone" had not yet been syndicated, when other shows that hadn't run as long, hadn't been as popular, or, in a few cases, had been canceled after "Twilight Zone" were then airing in syndication. He accused them of sacrificing his career to their agency's profits.

"Rod wanted a reaffirmation of our devotion to him," Schwimmer remembers. His long, detailed reply successfully refuted Serling's accusations with a litany of facts (after quitting the agency business at age forty-seven, Schwimmer attended law school and for ten years was one of Los Angeles County's top deputy district attorneys, prosecuting hundreds of criminal cases), including a reminder of his own personal advice, delivered many times, that Serling take time off to write a novel or play—highly speculative projects that likely would not earn the agency anything at all.

By ignoring this advice to create his own great works, Serling necessarily limited the types of jobs for which he was eligible: television pilots and perhaps film adaptations. Yet he could not accept that reality. He had taken particular offense to Schwimmer's suggestion that he become involved in the "Tarzan" television series then being developed by Ashley-Famous to star Ron Ely; he felt he was being treated as though he were just another hack writer. The suggestion, however, had been to bring him in as a creator of the series, with a proprietary interest. "You had to be very careful not to offend him with the kind of material he considered beneath him," Schwimmer recalls. "You had to constantly walk that tightrope. On the other hand, he wanted action and money. It's a little bit of juggling we had to do. . . . He would have made a ton of money [had he done 'Tarzan']."

After reading Schwimmer's letter, Serling dropped the matter with barely a word said again. He was embarrassed by his own intemperance and sensitivity. (In his letter, he complained that Ashley-Famous had grown too large for him, that he felt lost. He claimed that the sheer size of the William Morris Agency was why he "never" considered joining them when planning to leave Blanche Gaines; but this was patently untrue. He had indeed interviewed Morris agent Sam Weissbord, head of Morris's literary division, and preferred Ashley.)

One of Schwimmer's most repetitive jobs during his ten-year professional relationship with Serling was extracting him from commitments made at cocktail lounges or dinner parties, where producers or actors of questionable repute and motives often approached the famous writer with "wonderful" ideas. Serling rarely said no. "He really had no more intention of doing it than flying to the moon," Schwimmer says, "but he didn't want to be rude. He wanted to stay Mr. Nice Guy," so he orally signed on. (In 1967, soon after his novel *The President's Plane Is*

Missing climbed the bestseller charts, Bob Serling agreed to sell to a producer he met at a Hollywood bar the screen rights for five thousand dollars, a ludicrously small sum. He had been drinking at the time and was unaccustomed to the Hollywood come-on. The next day, feeling hungover and guilty, he told his brother of the encounter. Rod Serling became extremely angry and chastised Bob for making such a "stupid" deal. He then called Schwimmer, who broke the oral deal for Bob, just as he had a dozen or more times—and would again—for Rod.)

Serling's fantasies of idle walks and great novels did not jibe with his predilections. He spent the rest of 1964 trying again to develop "Twilight Zone" as a feature film. He also continued to peddle his first draft of *Planet of the Apes* and a feature-length version of his old CBS pilot script, "The Loner." For television he wrote two scripts: a fictionalization of his recent airplane jump for "The Chrysler Theatre" called "A Certain Sky Revisited" and a ninety-minute modern retelling of Dickens's *A Christmas Carol* called "Carol for Another Christmas."

"Certain Sky" (later aired under the title "Exit from a Plane") was a particularly bitter script about a famous and successful actor who wants to make the same sort of return-to-the-scene-of-the-crime jump as Serling had the previous April. The officer assigned to care for his needs happens to be an old friend from the war, married now to a woman whom both men had once loved. In the course of his twenty-four hour stay, the actor is shown to be a hollowed-out shell of a man with little to look forward to and no sense of pride in his accomplishments. Up in the plane, with the camera crews recording his every move, his fear grows more powerful than his "desperate need" to prove himself, and he refuses to jump. In an emotional sense, the script was every bit as autobiographical as "The Velvet Alley," depicting a man who held his Hollywood success in complete contempt and longed for the idealized serenity of the past. The actor, like Serling, had lived a charmed life until World War II, when the horrors of war and his own cowardice burst the bubble.

"Carol for Another Christmas" was written and produced as one of a special series of original programs, sponsored entirely and without commercials by Xerox Corporation, to help promote the image of the United Nations as a peacekeeping institution. The idea for such a series had originated with Edgar Rosenberg, a public relations executive (and husband of comedienne Joan Rivers), who had been approached by the managing director of the UN Special Fund, Paul Hoffman, a man concerned about the apparently poor national image of the United Nations. At the time, right-wing groups like the John Birch Society promulgated rumors that the UN operated with a secret agenda: worldwide Communist domination. Even if such rumors did not make a deep impression, the public at large still knew very little about the organization's goals, aims, and methods. Hoffman wanted to change that.

Rosenberg decided that a series of six commercial-free programs aired on television could more easily and quickly enlighten the masses than any other format. They would be written, produced, directed, and acted by high-quality talent, renowned or not for their social activism, working for scale salaries (Rosenberg got Joseph Mankiewicz to produce). After approaching several companies for seed money, Rosenberg was directed to Xerox, which agreed to fund almost the entire undertaking. Xerox president Joseph Wilson gave Rosenberg a check for four million dollars with no preconditions except that an announcement be made that Xerox enabled the programs through a grant. Rosenberg then had to find a network willing to sell prime time. CBS and NBC refused outright, but ABC, the third-place network, liked the association with top-name stars. Next step: the scripts.

The project was a natural for Serling, whose reputation as an outspoken, usually liberal, activist preceded him. The list of organizations to which he gave money generously or donated his talents, or both, included the ACLU, the Southern Christian Leadership Conference, NAACP, the Constitutional Rights Committee, the YMCA, United Jewish Welfare Fund, American Legion, Crippled Children's Society, and American Cancer Society. (Serling took his visiting brother to one Hollywood fundraiser, hosted by Marlon Brando, for ailing American Indians. After several impassioned speeches, a well-dressed young man began making the rounds of the crowded living room to collect donations. Bob Serling smiled when his turn came. Reaching into his pocket, he withdrew a twenty-dollar bill. The young man looked as though he had been shot. Later, when Bob and Rod spoke briefly on the terrace, Bob mentioned the man's rudeness. "Hell, I gave him twenty bucks," he said. Serling groaned loudly. "The minimum was five hundred.")

Serling had long been a frequent lecturer and speaker on a variety of topics, always political or humanitarian (he and Carol "adopted" a few underprivileged children in Korea under the Foster Parents Plan), and he enjoyed writing letters to newspapers, either to advance his own viewpoint or to counter one already published. His secretary, Marjorie Langsford, remembers that he very often took more care and derived greater satisfaction and pride from these letters than from his scripts.

For example, in March 1964, he wrote to the *Los Angeles Times*, which under publisher Otis Chandler was just then beginning to shed its bent as a powerful right-wing kingmaker (Richard Nixon, for example). Columnist Morrie Ryskind, one of the paper's old-time apologists for extreme-right causes, had just completed a series of columns in which he restated, with a wink and a nod, various reports of a left-wing conspiracy: that recently assassinated president John Kennedy and the late secretary of state John Foster Dulles had been Communist spies; that United States Chief Justice Earl Warren ought to be impeached—then lynched; and that former president Dwight Eisenhower had been disloyal to the United States.

"What was proven on that dark November day [the twenty-second, the date of Kennedy's assassination in Dallas] was that there is no more room for divisiveness in this country," Serling wrote.

The time has passed when Americans can attack other Americans with impunity, with emotionalism, and without a regard for the fact that democracy, by its nature, must not only countenance differences of opinions—but welcome them.

What Mr. Ryskind seems constitutionally unable to understand is that there is a vast difference between the criticism of a man or a party, and the setting up of criteria of patriotism which equates differences of opinion with disloyalty.

We have need in this country for an enlightened, watchful and articulate opposition. We have no need for semi-secret societies who are absolutist, dictatorial, and would substitute for a rule of law and reason an indiscriminate assault on the institutions of this republic that should and must be held sacrosanct. It was for this principle that a martyred young President laid down his life, the voices of hatred, discord and divisiveness notwithstanding.

A few weeks later, after a reader published a letter in the *Times* taking issue with him, he responded: "[The far right cannot] discount the fact that sitting in their parlor are the Ku Klux Klan, the American Nazi Party, every racist group in the United States and not a few of some Fascist orders that have scrambled their way up from the sewers to a position of new respectability."

Serling's reputation had also gotten him elected president of the National Academy of Television Arts and Sciences in June 1964, shortly after winning his last Emmy. While filling an unpaid, largely titular position, Serling believed he could move the academy—whose greatest concerns seemed to be the number of Emmys to be given and the format of the Emmy broadcast—toward the conception of the Academie Française: a true educational institution that would debate and define the role of television in society; of course, Serling hoped to make its role loftier and less indebted to commercial interests. He had long promoted this goal, ever since his earliest days in live television. Members from that time remember him reflecting his tremendous sense of enthusiasm onto the future of the academy.

In the mid-1950s the organization maintained its New York offices in the old Theatre Guild building on East Fifty-third Street, which is now the Museum of Modern Art. (Lawrence Langner, among a host of other accomplishments the founder and owner of the Theatre Guild, had donated the second-floor space, which was dominated by giant crystal chandeliers.) One evening Serling arrived late for the local meeting and found the street doors locked. He knocked and pounded to no avail; no one could hear him. Two hours later the academy members present began to file out of the building and found Serling sitting on the steps, waiting for them. Undaunted and in his usual intense fashion, he wanted to go for drinks or coffee with as many members as possible, to recount the meeting and offer his own input.

Perhaps if his tenure had been earlier in his career, Serling might have accomplished his aims. But since it came in the mid-1960s (his two-term presidency ended in 1966), when he felt himself floundering professionally, he largely abandoned his duties to executive director Peter Cott, who believed the job of president was intended to be ceremonial. "If Rod gave anything to the academy, it was his sense of values and morality," Cott says. "Unlike some other presidents I can think of, Rod was always responsive to me, always there for me when I wanted an answer." John Guedel, a trustee of the academy, recalls that Serling's oratory skills—"well-honed sentences, no ad libs, no wild sense of humor"—at least aroused the attention of members who ordinarily might doze during meetings. "But," recalls Guedel, "like so many people with great deliveries, you weren't quite sure what he said."

"Carol for Another Christmas," a fantastical tale, owed as much to "Twilight Zone" as it did to Dickens. Politically simplistic and naïve, bombastic and heavy-handed, it remains memorable only because of the circumstances surrounding its production and the reaction it engendered.

Daniel Grudge (played by Sterling Hayden) is a mean-spirited millionaire whose long-winded speeches recall Ayn Rand; he believes that the way to help poor and underprivileged people is to give them nothing. (Two years later, when Gentry International tried to develop a motion picture based on Rand's sprawling novel *Atlas Shrugged*, the author granted conditional rights. Her sole stipulation: that Gentry hire Rod Serling to write the screenplay. This was either a true statement of her admiration or a deliciously devious way of turning down the request—akin to "bring me the broomstick of the wicked witch of the west"—because Rand's self-determinate philosophy could not have been more opposed to Serling's. John Champion remembers that when Gentry pitched the request, Serling simply laughed—his laugh getting louder and longer the more he pondered it.) The story takes place on Christmas Eve 1964 (it was actually shown four days after that), the twentieth anniversary of the death of Grudge's son in World War II. During the night three ghosts (Robert Shaw, Steve Lawrence, and Pat Hingle) visit and convince him to change his hard-hearted ways.

A special UN commission had combed through the script, looking for any possible offenses its members might take; then the United States State Department filtered it again, forcing Serling to remove references to the burgeoning civil rights movement in America—the political issue dearest to Serling's heart. But because he was due to leave early in 1965 on a six-week trip to the Philippines and Hong Kong to give lectures on the media through a State Department cultural grant, he no doubt did not want to antagonize anyone there with stubborn creative insistence. (A year before, when writing the documentary on Lyndon Johnson, the department deleted the visage of a Hasidic rabbi from a filmed montage of life in America, so as not to offend Arab sentiments.) The stupidity of the demand was illustrated when Grudge and his nephew (Ben Gazzara), a college professor, argue over a foreign exchange program—certainly not an issue about which anyone could have credibly gotten heated; originally the confrontation had been over the nephew's participation in civil rights marches. The wonder, however, is that the department approved the script at all, for the image it presents of America, and American businessmen in particular, is woefully one-sided; this America, Serling seems to have said, is overloaded with greed and hate and venom, and lacks generosity and compassion.

The censorship for fear of offending sensibilities must have reminded Serling of his halcyon days writing for "Playhouse 90," and one can imagine him finding a sort of perverse pleasure by being back in the center of controversy. If so, then he surely enjoyed the public reaction to the program—which, for a variety of reasons similar to those Serling encountered writing the script, was the only one of the UN specials to be aired. (The most vicious criticisms of the program came from the *Evening American*, an Arizona newspaper published by Evan Mecham, who two decades later would be elected governor of that state and then ousted from office for severe improprieties and his racist views.) In fact, the length, breadth, and passion of some of the reply letters Serling wrote to viewers who had castigated him for, among other things, his "naïvete," his "furthering of the Communist conspiracy," and his "ignorance of history," suggest how much he still loved to fight the good fight.

Typical of the critical reactions to the show, based on politics, not drama, came from an Indiana woman who, until the show, had been a student of the Famous Writers School, a Connecticut-based correspondence school where Serling was one of twelve professional writers comprising the "faculty." In a letter to Gordon Carroll, the school director, she wrote that Serling's show, "put on by Xerox to glorify the United Nations," had "aided the communist conspiracy in this country, and being of this opinion I find

I have lost heart for my work. . . . He [Serling] apparently is not informed and I am hoping that he is another *innocent* American victim caught in the vast web of communist propaganda which has ensnared so many of our well-meaning citizens."

Carroll forwarded the letter to Serling, who replied directly to the writer. He noted that the basic difference between them was that his political and intellectual philosophy allowed room for all points of view, while hers considered any opinion outside her own to be subversive.

Saul David, who stood far to the right of Serling and most of the Hollywood community on the political continuum, was both amused and enchanted by Serling's bleeding heart. "He was unable to see any of the flaws in that kind of thing," David says. "He had this big gush of humanitarian sympathy, which was really very attractive on him." Though he referred to David affectionately as the "Jewish Fascist," Serling did not allow their divergence of political opinions to define the friendship, as did others, for whom the epithet was less affectionate than intentionally nasty. "Often," David remembers, "I'd find myself at his house, discussing politics, standing like a sheriff in one of those shows, with the lynch mob—all Hollywood liberals—baying and screaming at me. They were his close friends, and so was I. He used to think it was quite funny to see me firing back at them."

Bob Serling, also far more conservative than his brother, recalls several heated political arguments, at least one of which ended in shouting and name calling. Over dinner with their wives (divorced for ten years, Bob remarried in 1968) one evening, the talk turned to Antioch University, alma mater to three of them. Bob contended that the school had become too permissive and catered to minority special interests at the expense of quality education. Serling and Carol argued it had not and defended more liberal admissions policies based on "necessary" quotas. The debate soon erupted into a ferocious yelling match.

The next day Serling apologized, and the two brothers then resolved never to argue politics again, for fear their differences would ruin their relationship.

(Sammy Davis, Jr., with whom Serling spent a lot of time and money on civil rights fund-raising, recalls that he, the gentile converted to Judaism, and Serling, the Jew who became a Unitarian, only broached the subject of Jewishness, as though they both instinctively knew a discussion would lead to a rift. "It's a bone of contention either way," Davis explains. "It's a no-win. When you see someone so rarely and you genuinely like him, you don't want to bring up an unpleasantry." Serling hated direct, person-to-person confrontations.)

While in Manila in January, on the first leg of his State Department–sponsored lecture series (on all aspects of mass media writing, with emphasis on television and movie scripting, artistic creativity, artistic responsibility, and the ethics and morality of the writer), Serling received a cable explaining that producer Howard Koch had pulled out of the proposed *Twilight Zone* feature because his studio, Paramount, deemed the project too risky. Serling had left town two weeks before believing the contracts were all but signed and was now gravely disappointed— not least because the director on the film would have been his old friend Robert Parrish.

Given his druthers, Rod Serling, the president of the National Academy of Television Arts and Sciences, would have abandoned television at this point for a thriving screenplay career. He had hoped that *Seven Days in May* would establish his credentials as a screenwriter, but the studios had not rushed to sign him to projects. There was no longer any sustained interest in *Planet of the Apes*, aside from the King Brothers, the producers who held the screen option; they, and Serling, believed it could make a pleasant, relatively low-budget feature. Yet even with a projected budget of near one million dollars, studios repeatedly declined the "Twilight Zone"–like story of a space traveler landing on a planet where simians dominate and men are hunted.

Nor had "The Loner," under the title "The Violent Vespers," aroused any interest at all as a feature film. Serling began to get nervous. For the first time in a very long time, he had not a single project pending. (Before leaving on the tour, he had met in New York with Sam Spiegel, the tyrannical and marvelous film producer then looking for a writer to adapt the Hans Hellmut Kirst novel *Night of the Generals*, about a Nazi major general improbably tracking down one of his own officers for the crime of killing a prostitute in Warsaw. Serling turned down the assignment because Spiegel scared him. He later commented to Robert Parrish, who declined the job as director, that when Spiegel seemed to stare right through him after he said no, it actually hurt his feelings—and for that he'd like to see the old man tripped going up some stairs.)

William Dozier tracked him down in Hong Kong by phone. Now the head of his own television production company, Greenway Productions (named for the street on which he lived in Beverly Hills), with offices and facilities at Twentieth Century–Fox, Dozier asked if "The Loner," which he remembered from five years back, was still available; he dearly wanted to get back into production and away from the studios and networks as an executive. Serling said the project was still awaiting the proper buyer. Dozier proposed selling it to CBS as another joint venture. Serling agreed, and Dozier promised to get back to him.

Serling returned in late February to find that Dozier, Schwimmer, Michael Dann, CBS's senior vice president of programming, and William Self, the head of Fox's television production, had constructed the deal without his presence. This time Twentieth Century–Fox agreed to bankroll the production costs, with CBS buying the rights to air the shows for $62,000 dollars each. Greenway and Serling's unnamed production company would coproduce. (He had disbanded Cayuga Productions as a viable entity immediately after "Twilight Zone" ended its run, although the company still retained assets, including 50 percent ownership of "Twilight Zone," and legal obligations; the new company came to be called Interlaken Productions, after the name of their summer home's town.) Ownership divided 50 percent to Serling, 25 percent Greenway, and the final 25 percent to Fox (for contractual reasons, Dozier had to share his percentage with Fox).

"The Loner," a thirty-minute post–Civil War western to premiere in the fall of 1965, received an initial commitment of thirteen shows. Interestingly, Serling's deal with CBS differed from the one with Lloyd Bridges—Serling's neighbor and friend—who was to star as William Colton, the existential cowboy in search of life's meaning as he roams the new West. (Originally, they offered a net percentage to Bridges in exchange for a salary reduction, but he held firmly to his six-thousand-dollar-per-episode salary.) CBS obliged Serling to write a minimum of seven out of the first thirteen shows and an unnamed total of the remainder should the show be granted the go-ahead for an additional batch to be produced. According to the terms of his contract with Bridges, Serling had to write at least twelve of the first thirteen and "a majority of the balance." In addition, Serling would also act as executive script consultant—a largely academic title, considering he would be writing virtually all the scripts and thus have final say, but one that earned him an additional two thousand dollars per script to go along with his four-thousand-dollar writing fee.

Obviously, having to crank out these scripts as rapidly as on "Twilight Zone," Serling would not soon be leading the contemplative life of a novelist. "He wanted a series, he wanted that weekly bread," Schwimmer contends. "That was exactly what he wanted."

In early March Serling traveled to Washington, D.C., to debrief the State Department on his trip to the Orient and to address the local chapter of the National Academy of Television Arts and Sciences. "Television's greatest weakness," he told the Academy members, "is its reluctance to take positions. Historically, during times of greatest stress, during periods of greatest controversy, the mass media are the first to be attacked, the first to be muzzled, and also unhappily—historically and traditionally—the first to fold up their tent and look the other way."

Shortly after the speech, while driving with his brother to Bob's apartment, where he stayed, Serling began to complain of chest pains and asked to be taken to the hospital. "I think it's a heart attack," he said. At first Bob Serling thought his brother's hypochondria had surfaced again—he remembered, among other incidents, the time Serling believed he had "cancer of the heart"—but chest pains in the Serling family were not to be taken lightly. Bob called his personal physician, who checked Serling into Washington Hospital Center for tests and observation. Rumors circulated that he had suffered a heart attack, and within twenty-four hours, newspapers, television, and radio all over the country reported news of his grave illness. In truth, he experienced again only extreme exhaustion, aggravated by some mild form of food poisoning. The diagnosis, for at least the second time in his life, was greater relaxation. (The first news service to report his illness was Associated Press, the primary competitor of United Press International, Bob Serling's company. "I didn't phone it in," he says, "because I didn't connect it. He was my brother then. I was worried about him—I wasn't a newspaperman at that point." The next day his editors reprimanded him for getting scooped by AP on his own brother's illness.)

Serling ignored the prescription for rest except as a handy excuse to avoid attending parties, functions, and get-togethers he preferred to miss; rest took the place of going out of town, the excuse he usually gave to unwanted would-be visitors. To cut back on work now, at a time when he badly needed to reestablish himself, would have been a little death in itself. He knew before actually signing to "The Loner" that he had been approved to write the screen adaptation of *Assault on a Queen*, a best-selling novel by Jack Finney about a group of deep sea treasure seekers who come upon the sunken remains of a

German U-boat and decide to resurrect it for purposes of piracy; their first target was the *Queen Mary.* The film's star and its principal advocate was Frank Sinatra, with whom Serling had previously discussed a few film projects. What Serling did not know was that the project had been offered first to Richard Matheson, who called in his partner William F. Nolan for an opinion on how best to translate the novel into a film.

The two writers turned in to the studio, Warner Brothers–Seven Arts, a screen treatment that made light of the adventure. "We both read the book and agreed it would make a great comedy, that if you filmed it straight it wouldn't work," Nolan recalls. "We called it *Under the Bounding Main.* They read it and said, 'We can't make it a comedy.' We said, 'You can't make it a drama.' That's when Rod took it over."

Whether or not Matheson and Nolan had correctly assessed the book's potential, Serling was clearly the wrong writer to choose for the adaptation. In Hollywood, marquee value and fame very often win out over sound creative sense in matters of personnel. "It's the agent's mentality," says Saul David. "If all the ingredients that go into the salad are high-priced enough and wonderful enough, it doesn't matter that they may be ill-suited to each other."

Warner Brothers–Seven Arts—and Sinatra—felt that Serling had sufficiently proved his ability to write "action" on *Seven Days in May*—meaning that his writing had not failed, although it may not have improved the story much either. But they blundered in their thinking. What saved *Seven Days* was Serling's passion for the theme: that total nuclear disarmament is a goal to be devoutly sought. (Considering that his life was very likely saved by the dropping of the A-bomb on Japan, this seems somewhat ironic; few of his fellow paratroopers shared his pacifist tendencies). The film did not die despite his long polemical speeches. Consider the eloquence of Fredric March, as the president of the United States, who blames the attempted right-wing coup of his government on the technology: "Our enemy is an age. It happens to have killed man's faith in his ability to influence what happens to him. And out of this comes a sickness. A sickness of frustration." But *Assault on a Queen* intended no such message. It aspired to entertain strictly as adventure—a form in which Serling had neither expertise nor particular talent. As released in June 1966, *Assault on a Queen* was a ludicrous film; audiences laughed at parts intended to be gripping. One particularly painful line of Sinatra's stands out, reminiscent of the "gut" lines Martin Manulis usually excised from "Playhouse 90" scripts: "She's in my gut so deep we breathe together."

Serling turned in his final script to Sinatra late in 1965, shortly before production was due to begin. After reading it, Sinatra immediately called David, who'd produced his previous film then in release, *Von Ryan's Express*. (Sinatra had wanted Serling to write *Von Ryan's*, but the scheduling then could not be accommodated.) "We've got this script written by your friend Rod Serling," Sinatra said. "It's terrible. I want to send it over to you, and you've gotta tell me how to fix it." David reluctantly agreed and a messenger soon arrived with the draft.

"It had some terrible structural failures," David remembers. "It was very bad, but things could have been fixed—just a matter of resetting the dominoes. In a suspense picture, it's really like a fall of dominoes. Something that goes 'bang' in the first act has to go 'splash' in the third. Rod had simply not seen the structure." Without Serling's knowledge, David worked three days straight and sent the rewrite back to Sinatra, but by then the studio wanted to rush into production with the original script.

The previous March Serling had sold his 50 percent interest in "The Twilight Zone" back to CBS. After five years of constantly hearing about the show's budgetary problems, despite coming in at or near budget for each whole season, he believed the series would never be profitable in syndication. What a marvel of miscalculation. Why did he not wonder at CBS's interest in the series? Why would the network part with a chunk of cash for an unprofitable product? Of course, he did not arrive at the decision to sell alone. His accountant and his agents offered input as well. Nonetheless, the final decision surely fell to him.

Cayuga Productions sold all its rights, title, and interest in the series "Twilight Zone" and all the film masters for the paltry sum of $285,000 cash. Serling also received $225,000 as a buy-out for his services to Cayuga as host and principal writer of the series and $130,000 that Cayuga had in cash in various accounts. (It's doubtful that anyone at CBS or Viacom, the syndication company spun off as a wholly owned subsidiary of CBS in 1971 and which now owns the "Twilight Zone" package, knows exactly how many scores or hundreds of times its original investment the series has returned to CBS. As a point of reference, "McHale's Navy," says its creator John Champion, still earns profits of $300,000 a year.)

The same contract called for Serling to grant his exclusivity to CBS for the following three years, during which he would write nine pilot scripts for a total of $150,000.

It's likely that if the series had been sold to syndication immediately after going off the air in the summer of 1964, with the first syndication airing sometime that fall, Serling would either have held onto his interest or the price would have been increased substantially. "Twilight Zone" did not sell, Schwimmer explained to him in his November 1964 reply to Serling's plea to be excused from his agency contract, "because the network program department refused to release them through April [1964] in the hopes of a renewal and then in the hopes of repeating the film on a summer network basis. By that time, it was too late to do the proper sales job in syndication, which is substantially accomplished in February and March."

Interestingly, Serling knew "The Twilight Zone" would begin syndicated broadcasts in the fall of 1965, but he chose not to wait before executing the buy-out. Based on past struggles with Nielsens and sponsors, he cannot, of course, be faulted for not having the prescience to predict how phenomenally popular, and profitable, the syndication package would be. In his estimation, poor initial ratings might erase CBS's interest totally and leave him with nothing.

At the time, he was preoccupied with writing "The Loner" and, to a lesser extent, *Assault on a Queen*. By summer, when production began on the series, he had finished nearly a dozen scripts. He had exhibited all along a curious lack of complete interest in "The Loner" and told at least one critic, Bill Fissett of the *Oakland Tribune*, that he approached it with a distinct lack of enthusiasm; he explained—all too disingenuously—that he'd had very little to do with either the sale of the series or its direction. But when Dozier sent him the rough cut of the initial episode, "An Echo of Bugles," he knew that even his low expectations would not be met. Serling hated what he saw, directed by Alex March (whose work Serling had previously admired), and suggested to Dozier that they hire only three excellent directors for the entire series, rather than a different director for every show.

He also complained that Lloyd Bridges, who had been tinkering with the scripts and lines he didn't like when he felt other actors received better lines, should be instructed to accept the scripts as written, not least because his commitment to the series was based on Serling's writing talents; otherwise, Serling warned, he would quit the show. "I get a feeling, more and more pronounced as I get older, that actors think dialogue is like so much salami that you can either slice, eat or give away," Serling told Dozier. "It is for precisely this reason that I've never considered doing a series with a lead character before."

Serling returned to California from the lake house right after Labor Day (the family missed the Watts riots that August, which shook the entire city of Los Angeles and in fact the whole nation, although the violence was confined to a small portion of the south central area of the city) and met almost immediately with Dozier and Michael Dann, who had viewed several of the completed episodes. Dann was disappointed. Because the series lacked a pilot episode, he had based his expectations of the show on traditional westerns—or so Serling thought. In "The Loner," as in the majority of Serling's work over the years, the conflicts that propelled the plot were largely internal—the resolution of personal and emotional issues—as opposed to external, as in chases and gunplay. Dann evidently felt there should be more "action," which Serling understood to mean "violence."

Violence comes in many forms, only one of which is physical, Serling explained. Aiming to take the high road and trust the intelligence of the discerning viewer, he wanted to portray violence in terms of "tension" and emotional "jeopardy."

Dozier, who very much wanted the series to please both the audience and CBS, was conspicuously quiet during the meeting, which Serling took as a betrayal of their partnership and disavowal of their stated goal of quality over commerciality; Serling believed that Dozier's reticence had only amplified his disagreement with Dann—an uncharacteristic confrontation he found uncomfortable—and made him odd man out. This seemed to be confirmed by Dann's suggestion that Serling was too close to the material and ought to hire other writers as well.

Months later, with the series on the precipice of cancellation and his own patience almost entirely spent, Serling told Dozier that he regretted not having backed right out of the project at that meeting with Dann. Dozier, Serling discovered, had sent a letter to William Paley (whom Dozier had met years before; it was in fact Paley who had insisted Dozier leave filmmaking and get into television production), offering to change the concept of the show to make it less "cerebral," in exchange for a renewal and a better time slot. Saturday night at 9:30, against ABC's popular variety show "Hollywood Palace," was too tough.

A month later the matter became academic for Dozier: in January 1966 Greenway began producing a campy, twice-weekly, wildly popular version of "Batman."

It's possible, indeed likely, based on further correspondence between Serling and Dann, that Serling, his feelings terribly hurt by the opinion that other writers could write his show better than he, misconstrued Dann's feelings about the show. There's no doubt that their conceptions of the series differed, but if Dann had truly wanted a traditional shoot-em-up western, he wouldn't have needed to pay the price for Rod Serling to get it; any number of less skillful writers could have devised such a show for him. The value of "The Loner" was in its treatment of the cowboy as a thinking, feeling man, and that's the treatment Dann had bought; only Serling could have sold that without a pilot script. Further, memos from the censor relative to specific scripts for other shows as far back as the previous April indicated the network's discomfort with graphic violence: scenes of a saber entering a boy's chest and a bottle breaking against a man's face were instructed to take place off camera; the shot of a man murdered by hanging had to be "less gruesome"; in selecting scenes to be inserted into one show from footage of *The Red Badge of Courage*, a particularly bloody film, the censors urged them to "exercise caution in order to avoid excessive violence and carnage"; when a character lost his hand during a fight, the censors ordered them to use "your customary discretion"; and most significantly, at least twice the department of program practices demanded a reduction in "the number of violent acts." Still, the debate between Serling and Dann over the meanings of *action* and *violence* continued throughout the brief run of the show.

Serling carried the disagreement to the public, where he hoped his position would be validated by thousands of letters of support from the public, just as with "Twilight Zone" five years before. Unlike "Twilight Zone," though, "The Loner" failed to attract a passionately devoted following; in fact, it had hardly attracted a following at all, and very few cards and letters arrived. His ill-considered comments to the press, particularly to the *Philadelphia Inquirer*, exacerbated the rift between Serling and Dann, and Serling and the whole network.

"The Loner" premiered September 18, 1965, to poor ratings that never improved enough to convince Dann he had been wrong in his original assessment, that the show was too talky. Although Serling's exclusive three-year contract with CBS obligated him to provide nine pilots, he would not turn in a single script. In fact, after "The Loner" went off the air in April 1966, CBS never again aired his new work.

In early December he addressed a meeting of the Phoenix chapter of the National Academy—the visiting president offering his varying opinions. "Right now it's finger-pointing time," he said. "Everyone wants to put the blame on somebody else. And, much as I hate to say it, I must assume a portion of the responsibility for what turned out to be a bad show. Some weekends, I wish Friday would move into Sunday and skip Saturdays so there wouldn't be any 'Loner.'"

Serling had already begun a steady slide into a maelstrom of self-pity and doubt. "The Loner," he thought, would be his swan song in television (he wrote the Delavans, his Interlaken neighbors, that he was "persona non grata" at the networks) and *Assault on a Queen* the last movie script anyone would pay him to write. He had accompanied the cast and crew to Las Vegas for part of the production and spent a lot of time sitting at the crap tables with Sinatra, the star who evidently wished he were somewhere else, while the director, Jack Donahue, fretted over both the piss-poor shooting script he'd been handed and his recalcitrant star. In a letter written to Robert Parrish immediately after viewing the first rough cut, Serling called the film an "abortion," joked that the executives from Seven-Arts cried as the rest of the assemblage sat in stunned silence, and anticipated "suicides"—not unlike the reception that greeted their film *Saddle the Wind* in 1958.

Shortly before Christmas—his forty-first birthday—Serling received a letter from George Faber, the CBS director of client relations. Faber must not have known that Serling had sold his interest—financially, if not emotionally—in "Twilight Zone," otherwise he would not have informed him so gleefully that syndication ratings, after three months, were "sensational.... We naturally wish to pass on this information to the genius behind it all." Serling, no doubt, did not feel like a genius.

"It is quite apparent that I don't see eye to eye with the networks," he said two months later. "I may have outlived my usefulness with them. I think it is much better for them and for myself that I look for new creative fields."

The United States in 1966 was a nation involved in three civil wars, the combatants defined by skin color—white, yellow, or black. The fighting could be as ferocious in the streets of Selma, Alabama; Jackson, Mississippi; or Watts, California as in the jungles of Southeast Asia. In Vietnam, America had taken sides in what was essentially a civil war, fighting a mostly faceless enemy whose resolve was underestimated and whose strength of purpose was never understood. While the Vietnamese struggled for control over their homeland, America's purpose for being there seemed worse than dubious: what would victory mean, what would it prevent or accomplish? As the answers became less convincing to the children of the privileged middle- and upper-middle classes, mostly college students, they started passionately questioning authority, and soon a wave of civilian violence unprecedented in two hundred years began sweeping the country. One had to be either for or against the war—passions that increasingly threatened the nation's fabric. At the same time, and often in the same places, blacks battled whites—the have-nots against the haves—with a rage that had festered for nearly three hundred years. Unlike America the nation in Vietnam, black America's reason for fighting the white power structure felt clear and justified. At some point, to liberal white America, the antiwar movement and the Black Power movement intersected.

Serling, certainly, was actively committed to both. He genuinely believed that prejudice and racism were the worst sins Pandora had released. No one familiar with his work, "Twilight Zone" included, could think differently. He had met Martin Luther King, Jr., years before, thought him a great man, and gave time and money generously to virtually any civil rights cause (after the riots of the summer of 1965, he even helped conduct drama and theater workshops in Watts).

Serling's letter to the *Los Angeles Times* on April 8, 1968, immediately after the King assassination, probably stands as his most powerful piece of writing that whole decade—because it was heartfelt. When Serling was young and angry, even his lesser works reflected passion. As he got older and lost much of that passion, his work seemed emptier. "There is a bitter sadness and a special irony that attends the passing of Martin Luther King," he wrote.

Quickly, and with ease, we offer up a chorus of posthumous praise—the ritual dirge so time honored and comfortable and undemanding of anything but rhetoric. In death, we offer the acknowledgement of the man and his dream that we denied him in life.

In his grave, we praise him for his decency—but when he walked amongst us, we responded with no decency of our own. When he suggested that all men should have a place in the sun—we put a special sanctity on the right of ownership and the privilege of prejudice by maintaining that to deny homes to Negroes was a democratic right.

Now we acknowledge his compassion—but we exercised no compassion of our own. When he asked us to understand that men take to the streets out of anguish and hopelessness and a vision of that dream dying, we bought guns and speculated about roving agitators and subversive conspiracies and demanded law and order.

We felt anger at the effects, but did little to acknowledge the causes. We extol all the virtues of the man—but we chose not to call them virtues before his death.

And now, belatedly, we talk of this man's worth—but the judgment comes late in the day as part of a eulogy when it should have been made a matter of record while he existed as a living force. If we are to lend credence to our mourning, there are acknowledgements that must be made now, albeit belatedly. We must act on the altogether proper assumption that Martin Luther King asked for nothing but that which was his due. He demanded no special concessions, no favored leg up the ladder for his people despite our impatience with his lifelong prodding of our collective conscience. He asked only for equality, and it is that which we denied him.

We must look beyond riots in the streets to the essential righteousness of what he asked of us. To do less would make his dying as senseless as our own living would be inconsequential.

His reputation as an eloquent spokesman for reformation of the country's racial attitudes prompted *Playboy* associate publisher and editorial director A. C. Spectorsky to ask him for a simple letter defending the magazine's decision to publish a long interview with American Nazi leader George Lincoln Rockwell. (The interview was conducted by future *Roots* author Alex Haley, who had just finished writing *The Autobiography of Malcolm X*. Haley had called Rockwell's American Nazi Party headquarters in Arlington, Virginia, to ask for an exclusive interview. He did not speak in the manner Rockwell associated with blacks, so he did not have to identify his heritage other than to answer whether he was a Jew. When he later knocked on the door of the headquarters, there was great consternation among Rockwell's guards, who certainly did not expect to see a "nigger" standing there. Finally and reluctantly, Rockwell agreed to be interviewed by a black.)

"I don't believe for one minute," Rockwell said, in the *Playboy* interview, "that any six million Jews were exterminated by Hitler." He contended that the photographs of dead bodies of Jews seen in the liberated concentration camps were actually the corpses of German civilians killed in the Allied bombing raid on Dresden—and that the gas chambers were actually built after the war, by Jewish army officers. "We know this for sure: It was mostly Jewish Army officers who went in there to liberate these camps."

Rockwell, who called Martin Luther King, Jr., "Martin Luther Coon," went on to say that America's white youth were being perverted, by conditioned response, to black music:

> For instance, every time a white kid is getting a piece of ass, the car radio is blaring nigger bebop. Under such powerful stimuli, it's not long before a kid begins unconsciously to connect these same sounds with intense pleasure and thus transfers his natural pleasurable reactions in sex to an unnatural love of the chaotic and animalistic nigger music, which destroys a love of order and real beauty among our kids. This is how you niggers corrupt our white kids—without even laying a dirty hand on them. Not that you wouldn't like to.

After he became president in 1972, Rockwell said, he planned to solve the "black problem" by revoking the citizenship of all American blacks and giving them the choice of either returning to Africa, where they would be given "generous help and assistance in establishing a modern industrial nation," or being forcefully removed to reservations, "like the Indians were when they became a problem to the survival of the white people." Jews, he said, would be investigated by grand juries for unnamed crimes; if indicted, they would be tried, and killed if convicted. "I'd also purge the queers. I despise them worst of all."

Playboy took great pains to annotate the interview, correcting many of Rockwell's more outrageous allegations. In an editor's prologue, the magazine explained its reasons for publishing Rockwell's views: "The very virulence of Rockwell's messianic master-racism could transform a really searching conversation with the forty-eight year-old Führer into a revealing portrait of both rampant racism and the pathology of fascism." Yet as warned and predicted, thousands of people accused the magazine of allowing a sick man with sick views to have an important forum from which to spout his sickness. In the media the story of the reaction launched a secondary wave of stories debating the wisdom of granting such a forum. The outcry threatened to envelop the magazine and undermine its growing credibility as a voice of liberal reason.

For years Spectorsky had cultivated a professional relationship with Serling—an acquaintance of Hugh Hefner and sometime guest at the Chicago *Playboy* mansion—literally begging him to contribute to the magazine; as early as September 1962, Spectorsky wrote to him that the pages of *Playboy* "still hunger for Rod Serling material" (how beautiful those words must have looked to Serling during his Antioch sabbatical, a time when "Twilight Zone" was in a sort of Twilight Zone and his whole career seemed at a crossroads). Shortly after the interview's publication, he wrote again: "We've had some unpleasant static from people who feel it was a big, fat mistake for us to publish the George Lincoln Rockwell interview. . . . A letter to the editor from you, adding your prestigious voice to bolster our point of view, would be immensely appreciated. The honorarium for such a letter is nothing. I don't hesitate to ask it of you, however, since I think it is all part of the good fight."

With the magazine's long lead time between editions, it took two months before Serling's letter was published with the other letters, all of which condemned the magazine. "I anticipate that you people will probably be roundly roasted," he wrote.

> There is a breed of lay and social scientist who will forever cling to a concept of "defeating by ignoring." Hence, when out of the muck of their own neuroses rise these self-proclaimed Führers, there is this well-meaning body who tell us that if we turn both eyes and cheeks, the nutsies will disappear simply by lack of exposure.
>
> My guess is that, in this case, exposure is tantamount to education; and education, here, is a most salutary instruction into the mentalities, the motives and the *modus operandi* of an animal pack that is discounted by the one aged maxim that "it can't happen here." So might have said the Goethes and the Einsteins of a pre-war Germany, who thought then, as we do now, that civilization by itself protects against a public acceptance of the uncivilized. . . . What is desperately needed to combat any *ism* is precisely what *Playboy* has given us—an interview in depth that shows us the facets of the enemy. Yes, gentlemen, you may be knocked for supposedly lending some kind of credence to a brand of lunacy. But my guess is that you should be given a commendation for a public service of infinite value.

Serling's opposition to the Vietnam War evolved more slowly and with less passion than his commitment to civil rights. As a combat veteran and a traditional supporter of America's military and its role as the world's policeman, finding himself questioning the righteousness of United States involvement, as he did in 1966, was uncomfortable. And yet, as he told Bill Lindau, the alternative to American involvement so far escaped him. Vietnam was not a war in which the issues could be clearly defined, the enemy identified, the cause justified, and the morality uncomplicated, he wrote; it was not "our kind of war." By 1968, he would resign his membership in the Veterans of Foreign Wars because of its pro-war stance and his by-then blatant, committed, and outspoken rejection of such views.

While the intentions of this particular war may have still seemed ambiguous to him, his aversion to all wars as the ultimate evil—a logical outgrowth of ignorant prejudice—remained white-hot. By the spring of 1966 Serling had finished writing his first original Broadway play, *The Killing Season*, an antiwar drama set against a World War I backdrop that, unfortunately, went on too long, needlessly repeating the same points and suffering probably from Serling's most bombastic and heavy-handed writing ever. Like most of Serling's work, it offered at least patches of shining dialogue—but little else. He had written it from the seat of his pants, guided dramatically by the ferocity of his convictions, not by any skill or experience as a theater dramatist. What makes rousing speeches and incites crowds to action or riot usually causes theatergoers to fall asleep.

Driven by his messianic zeal, Serling was almost entirely unaware of the play's faults. He told *Variety* he believed it to be the best script, whether for stage, screen, or television, he'd ever written; Carol agreed, he said, but warned him it was "too stark and real" to be produced. Carol Serling, an intelligent woman with apparently excellent taste, probably knew how much the play meant to him and may not have wanted to upset his delicate confidence. Clearly and obviously, *The Killing Season* offered nothing different than *All Quiet on the Western Front* and was even written about the same war.

Taking Carol's lead, Serling told himself that the play, which he'd written on spec, could not find a legitimate Broadway producer because of its "controversial" theme. Through the spring he received only off-Broadway offers and refused them all, feeling he should not settle for less than the brightest lights. Staking his artistic ego entirely on the play's production, he simply had to wait for total legitimacy. So he waited. And waited.

When Emanuel Azenburg finally optioned the property with an eye to a fall production, Serling uncharacteristically told his closest friends, long before any kind of production seemed certain, that he would open on Broadway in October. Just thinking and hoping it felt pleasurable, and perhaps saying it could really make it so.

Serling had given up developing "Twilight Zone" as a feature film, in part because problems had arisen with CBS over the use of the title. The network did not seem willing to grant him permission to name a movie with his own words, which they now owned. But he had not given up on the three-story format. He joined two of the stories he would have used—one about an ex-Nazi on the run in South America and the other about a blind wealthy woman who buys a pair of eyes—with a third, one told to him years before by Sammy Davis, Jr., about a racist who meets a fitting fate. Davis and he briefly tried to develop them as a movie, under the title *Three Nightmares*, with Davis to star in at least one segment. But neither man, certainly not Serling, wanted to face turndown after turndown, so they quickly abandoned the quest.

The time had evidently come for Serling to discover whether he indeed had the talent to create long fiction, the only writing form he'd not yet tried. Remembering how difficult the adapted "Twilight Zone" short stories had been, he decided to start more slowly—with novellas, rather than a novel. Taking the *Three Nightmares* stories, he began "telling" them into his Dictaphone early in the spring.

He had always been a master storyteller. One minute after hearing a joke at a party or on a plane, he retold it in greater detail, with more subtlety and humor than the original, so the task did not appear too daunting. But it was. Stage directions and dialogue had always come easily to him, but now he had also to provide the voice of some invisible narrator who must be as articulate as he was interesting. Moreover, the narrator had to be omniscient—able to read minds, recount pasts, join scraps of disjointed information; none of these had to be done in the visual medium. His mind wandered easily. Usually the execution of a script flowed effortlessly into the Dicta-

phone once the story had formed in his mind. In writing
the book, however, he could concentrate no longer than
five or ten minutes before moving on to something else;
the drafts of these novellas are sandwiched onto Dicta-
belts between letters and other business.

Serling felt constrained by his past. Rather than opening up the freedom of the form, he was terrified by its
possibilities; he remained stuck in his conceptualization.
The stories themselves were mostly compelling enough,
but he executed them as though still writing for the
screen, telling each scene and then cutting to the next
with a double-space break. These were not novellas, they
were prose screen treatments with flair—"Twilight Zone"
episodes with the usual twist at the end, the scoundrel's
lesson horrifically learned.

The Escape Route concerns an ex-Nazi, Gruppenfuehrer Strobe, personally responsible for the deaths of
countless thousands at Auschwitz. After the war he fled
to South America, where, unrepentant, he lives in anonymity and dreams of his glory days killing Jews. When
he hears that Israeli agents have taken Adolf Eichmann,
also hiding in Argentina, back to Israel for trial, he knows
that his time is soon to come. Another of his Nazi acquaintances hangs himself, but Strobe insists on fleeing;
the thought of Jews exacting their revenge in an ironic
turnabout brings out his true loathsomeness. Believing
he's being followed, Strobe often takes refuge in an art
museum, where he develops an unusual affinity for a
pastoral painting of a fisherman in a boat on a lake. He
discovers that by sheer force of will he can replace his
own terror with the fisherman's perceived sense of peace.
Each succeeding visit to the museum, he develops a closer
affinity for the painting and soon believes himself able to
take the fisherman's place. One night, while running from
the Israelis, he breaks into the museum and heads for the
painting, determined this time to project himself fully
into it, thus escaping his pursuers. He runs to the spot in
the darkened museum and this time disappears into the

picture on the wall; neither the agents nor the museum guards can find him. However, one of them hears a distant noise, what seems to be a tiny scream coming from far away. They dismiss it. Not until one of the guards notes that the fisherman painting has been loaned out and replaced by a painting of a concentration camp (that ever-popular subject for a Buenos Aires art museum), do we see that Gruppenfuehrer Strobe is now the figure of a cruci-fied man in the picture—doomed to spend eternity screaming in pain.

The story seems too long, too needlessly detailed; the poetic justice would have had the same or even more impact had the writing been more terse. In some sense *The Escape Route* seems to be Serling's apologia for "In the Presence of Mine Enemies," his Warsaw ghetto story from "Playhouse 90" that had raised such a furor in appear-ing to absolve Germany. Here Serling offers his explana-tion of the mass evil that infected the country. The Jewish wife of the hanged man explains to Strobe that her hus-band realized on the night of his suicide, when looking into Strobe's face, what befell his country: "He said that there were normally decent Germans who had created a monster. But that the real crime came in that the monster was not created in their image . . . but the other way around. It was the monster who usurped and corrupted until it reached a point where Germany became a nation of monsters."

Color Scheme, the story told to him by Sammy Davis, Jr., he says in a short introductory note, takes place in a small, highly segregated Southern town. The white peo-ple, alarmed by the growing wave of black pride, summon King Connacher, a white racist preacher with the power to unite and incite them. The night of his sermon, a band of properly incited white townspeople set fire to the shack of the black preacher who has led the consciousness-raising, burning to death his youngest daughter. When the slimy Connacher drives away in his Cadillac convertible after finding the preacher walking aimlessly through the rubble of his shack, he runs into a concrete embankment. Not seriously hurt, he discovers the accident has somehow turned him into a black man—the worst tragedy that can ever befall someone, he has thought. Now Connacher gets a taste of life on the other side of the taunts and abuse. Unable to convince the white townspeople that he is in fact King Connacher, he is beaten to a bloody mess for his impudence—attempting to talk to the white woman he'd taken out into the fields earlier that night. Running away from the mob, he comes upon the black preacher, who is of course now white. For his repeated impudence, disrespecting the "white" preacher, he is killed by a shotgun blast, and his body is tied to the bumper of car and driven all through town, the flesh torn from his bones.

The story suffers badly from a lack of focus, and its resolution, with the black preacher becoming as nasty as the white townspeople, dilutes the message conveyed thirty pages before. His eulogy for Martin Luther King, Jr., written a year later, made his point more clearly, more poignantly, and in many thousand fewer words. (Sammy Davis, Jr., received an unexpected call one afternoon in September 1967. "I've got a gift for you," Serling said. "Let me bring it over." When he arrived at Davis's house, he handed him a wrapped package. "I can't give you a gold watch, like you give everybody," he said. Davis unwrapped the copy of *The Season to Be Wary*. Serling told him to turn to the dedication page: "For Sammy Davis, Jr., my friend. He has probably gotten just about everything possible out of life except a book dedicated to him . . . until now." Davis was visibly moved. "I'd never had anything like that dedicated to me—personally dedicated," he remembers. "It was wonderful—indicative of the man.")

Eyes is a simple story, laboriously told, of a wealthy and evil blind woman, Miss Menlo, who buys the eyes of a desperate man, Petrozella (no doubt named for one of his ex-army buddies who occasionally borrowed money from Serling), for transplantation into her own sockets; the experimental operation will grant the woman, blind since birth, twelve hours of sight—enough time to accumulate visual memories to last her, she believes, the rest of her life. (In January 1963, producer John Guedel sent Serling a short note with two story ideas—"free notions," he wrote—that he would like explored in "The Twilight Zone." He had recently spoken to a woman, blind since birth, who told him she "would give anything to be able to see for just one day. . . . Then she would store up the memories of that day and would know what so many things looked like." Guedel had been unaware that Serling apparently used his story idea as the basis for *Eyes* but felt flattered Serling found it meritable. "It's perfectly all right with me that he used it—I guess," he says.) Sometime after the operation, Miss Menlo sits in her New York apartment, anxiously anticipating the moment—precisely at eight o'clock—when the bandages come off. In anticipation of her night of vision, she has dismissed her household staff. The doctor visits her with final instructions, then leaves. She removes the bandages but sees nothing. Distraught, she finds her way down the stairs (the elevator does not work) to the street. But still, the darkness. In anguish, she soon returns to her apartment, pitifully resigned to her life of darkness. She awakens in the morning and sees the sun. Walking toward it, she tumbles over her balcony to her death. In truth, at the moment she had removed the bandages, a major power outage had plunged the city into darkness.

This story was by far the most ludicrous of the three, filled with plot holes and conveniences. Why, for example, does the doctor come to visit her before the bandages are removed; why does he not remove them himself, and wouldn't she want to see him? Why will her twelve hours be at night, when included on her list of must places to see are the Museum of Modern Art and the United Nations—both of them closed to visitors in the evening? And most baffling, why was she unable to see the headlights of the thousands of cars streaming by her Central Park South apartment?

Perhaps if he had actually written the stories with a pencil or typewriter rather than dictating them he would have seen their flaws—been more involved in their characters and less constrained by his established conventions. Writers who knew Serling and his work, from Budd Schulberg to William F. Nolan, say that dictation is anathema to quality prose; the rhythms and intricacies of prose differ from colloquial speech or even from stage monologues. Writing, they contend, must be done on paper (or even on word processing screens) for the writer to get the feel of the words that are meant to be read silently, in order to establish a personal relationship between writer and reader that is the hallmark of all good writing (especially fiction). The process of committing those words to paper is a jumble of writing, rewriting, crossing out, drawing arrows on the page where a paragraph is to be inserted, cutting, pasting, even throwing away. All of these are unavailable to the writer who dictates.

The Season to Be Wary could have been Serling's entry to that pastoral world where established fiction writers take long walks in the woods to find their stories and voices to tell them. But, as always, he had been in too much of a hurry to carefully craft a work of distinction. For as much as he complained about television writing, and as often as he pointed to other literary horizons, he obviously lacked the patience and commitment he needed to succeed in the forms for which he most desperately craved respect and validation. He wrote *The Season to Be Wary* because he thought he should, not because he wanted to; he couldn't develop the ideas as a movie, so he wrote a book, just as "The Loner" had become a television series when no one immediately wanted it as a film.

Sadly, for this man of forty-one who felt at least fifty-one, time seemed to be in short supply. If he lingered over a single manuscript for a year or two, and the manuscript still lacked distinction, he had no excuses for his failure. If, however, he wrote it quickly, rewriting as little as possible, he then had a ready-made excuse. Only writers who believe in their work, even if others don't, grant themselves the time. This was self-sabotage, a part of his personality that seems all the more pathetic because financially he could have afforded to take as much time as he wished. It was a shocking waste of a talent that should have been cultivated, not prostituted. He virtually guaranteed that he would end up writing for television, a medium he professed to aver.

By midsummer Serling knew that *The Killing Season* would not be produced on Broadway. Manny Azenburg's financial partner pulled out his money, aborting the production. In an outburst of anguish-inspired candor, he wrote later that summer to Julius Golden, one of his oldest friends, that recovering from the "shock" took weeks, because he had hoped and believed the play would allow him to authenticate the reputation for excellence he maintained but no longer merited. Realizing his failure as a playwright, he said, had been a trauma. (An advertising executive, Golden's Atlantic/Bernstein Associates handled Eagle Clothes, Inc., which provided Serling with twelve custom suits a year during "The Twilight Zone" seasons in exchange for a credit on the show.)

This revelatory admission still understated the extent of his suffering. "I knew Rod was riddled with self-doubt. I saw him cry over it," says Saul David. "He thought of himself as having failed. He thought of himself as a star that had fallen from great heights."

"A crisis of faith," Dick Berg calls it.

His agony began leaking into his private life. He questioned not only his talent but also his worth as a man. There are some circumstantial, yet convincing in context, indications that he was for a time made sexually impotent by his writing failures. Having tied his identity to success and adulation for so many years, he now equated his manhood with his waning creative powers and lack of acceptance for his work. Shortly before his death he gave an almost masochistically honest interview in which he appeared to make an unwitting admission of a sexual problem, drawing a parallel between self-doubt and impotence. "Everything that I wrote crumpled up, and then it became a self-destructive thing, when you begin to doubt yourself, when doubt turns into—it's sort of like impotence. Once impotent, you're forever impotent, because you're always worried about being impotent." The analogy seems a curious choice, even for as imaginative a writer as Serling: only a man who has experienced the pain of impotency would be aware of its insidiousness and self-perpetuation. While the period of self-doubt he referred to here had been earlier in his career, it's safe to assume that the sentiment also applied to the mid-1960s.

A somewhat more convincing piece of evidence was the off-handed remark Serling made to Gordon Carroll, explaining the horrors of his slavishness to wealth: a man and his manhood, he said, are better served by poverty. These weren't riches gained through the writing of great works, he felt, but through a reputation now undeserved—and expectations he could not live up to. Serling, who prided himself on his masculinity—and who abhorred homosexuality—now had a greater need than ever for acceptance and validation.

Not surprisingly, he turned outside his marriage for the type of fawning approval he felt he was not getting at home, where with his wife and children he was just Rod or Dad, not Rod Serling, super-celebrity, creator of some of television's finest moments. To others who didn't know him intimately, he could hide behind the persona he'd built on the screen, but at home he was just another vulnerable man whose world seemed to be crumbling— whose lifetime of insecurities, hidden until now by the frailest of covers, had suddenly grown into unavoidable monsters. With strange women he could bask in the glow of their admiration, their obsequious compliance, their devotion to the man they thought him to be, while with his wife he could not escape being the man she'd been married to for nearly twenty years. The exterior world abided his personal fantasies; his home remained a museum of glories long past and unretrievable.

Rod Serling's considerable philandering probably had nothing to do with his marriage to Carol, the woman he still loved. That he did not love himself, and therefore needed to turn elsewhere for confirmation of his masculinity and self-worth, likely is why he indiscriminately began picking up stewardesses on airplanes, "interviewing" starlets in Hollywood, asking friends in other cities to find him young females, staying at the *Playboy* mansion in Chicago (and later in Los Angeles). Stewardesses were the easiest to meet, and most readily available. When he flew, which he did frequently—sometimes on the flimsiest of excuses—they virtually threw themselves at him, offering to "show him around" the town when they landed (often he would write letters to stewardesses' supervisors, commending them for "service above and beyond the call of duty").

Friends, acquaintances, and colleagues of the Serlings, circumspect in their comments about his dalliances, will say only that the marriage occasionally strained under this weight. "He was a bit of a chaser," Alden Schwimmer admits. "I know he liked the ladies. And I think that they had little problems, he and Carol, on that score from time to time."

(Saul David remembers being at a dinner party in the Serlings' rambling home during this period. Even though every seat at the enormously long table was filled with guests, at one point a sudden awkward silence overcame the group—broken only by Serling, sitting at one head of the table, telling a joke to the people nearest him. Carol, from the far end of the table, said in a voice that carried all through the room: "For Christ's sake, Rod, are you telling that goddamned dumb joke again?" The tension between them was palpable.)

Since 1964 Serling had been a frequent celebrity guest on a variety of game shows, most often "You Don't Say" and "The Match Game." In a sense, these shows appealed to him in the way that casual sex did: he could act the part of the still bright, enchanting, beguiling writer of stature, the man who reshaped the medium. Competitive by nature and an inveterate game player of everything from pinball to bridge, he actually enjoyed the contests themselves. And the show producers loved him. Not only did he play enthusiastically but he also was Rod Serling; he lent an air of prestige.

Yet there was something unseemly about these appearances. Those who knew him well understood that he missed his appearances as the host of "The Twilight Zone" and wanted to replace them. These were performances he gave to satisfy his frustrated actor's craving for the spotlight.

The game shows, says his best friend, Dick Berg, were "an indignity" for which Serling apologized, at least to Berg. "I think he felt, and I think Carol did, too, that he had such dignity as a spokesman for writers, as the only identifiable writer, whose more important work was significant and provocative and compassionate. That he would get involved in daytime television, on game shows, frankly offends me—the thought of it, that he should have that need. And yet it was part of the excitement of the guy that he had all those needs. There was as much of the ham bone wanting to do game shows and be silly and function as an actor—being seen—as there was a need to be a seriously considered, critically fawned over artist."

If Serling could not get his required dose of fawning from adoring critics, producers, and the theater-going public, then he would get it from anywhere he could—including housewives, who in 1967 were the primary audience, besides sick schoolchildren, for daytime television game shows. Not so coincidentally, these women, judging by their reactions, still found him immensely attractive. "When he walked in a room, my heart would stop," says Eleanor Franks, an acquaintance. And that was at least as important now as his work: if they still perceived him as handsome and sexy, then the advancing years, which he constantly felt oppressing him, could be held at bay a little longer.

"Doomsday Flight," an NBC world premiere movie that aired on December 13, 1966, was a palpable expression of Serling's need for applause—which he rarely had heard since last winning an Emmy. When it became the highest-rated made-for-television film to that point, his criteria were met. Unfortunately, it had other ramifications that completely negated the positive—and confirmed his own piteousness.

A year before, his brother Bob had told him off-the-record about an incident related to him off-the-record by officials at American Airlines. The airline had received a call from a man claiming that, unless he received $200,000 in cash immediately, a pressure bomb placed aboard a particular American flight would explode when the plane's elevation went below a mile. Relayed this information, the plane's captain diverted the airliner to Denver, which American did not even serve at the time, because Stapleton Airport sat slightly higher than a mile above sea level. That no bomb turned up in the search did nothing to detract from the captain's ingenuity, and both the airline's and Bob's admiration for his skills.

When Bob passed this information onto his brother, it did not occur to him that the story would be turned into a script; he hadn't even reported the story himself, knowing that even hoaxes, if publicized, beget copycats. Soon, though, Serling asked Bob for technical assistance on something he called *Flight to Doomsday*. He wanted to know precisely where such an aneroid bomb could be placed on board without the air crew being able to find it. Bob cautioned him in a letter: "I hope you'll carefully ponder the possibility that somebody might get an idea from the story and actually try an aneroid bomb plot." But Serling insisted.

Within a week, at least three extortion plots based on the movie had been reported. Western Airlines, Qantas, and National Airlines were threatened, and real payoffs of $600,000—just in case—were made; in all cases, no bombs were found. The Airline Pilots Association asked that the film be withdrawn from circulation. (It was not, and five years later, when the film was reshown, three more copycats extorted money. This time, all prints were recalled from a syndication package.)

"I wish to hell I'd never written the damn thing," he told Bob, who says it was a regret he carried to his grave. Needing a good story, which this was, he had knowingly ignored the dire—and accurate—predictions.

"Can't a writer dry up? He can, you know," Serling wrote in January to Ellen Cameron May, a freelance writer whose story based on this written interview would not be published (in the *Los Angeles Times*) for another six months. "Talking to me is like dredging up the past glory of a major league pitcher who won the most valuable player award twenty years ago. He comes not with excitement but nostalgia."

His comments give credence to his brother's belief that he lived with a precognition of an early death. He was only forty-two years old, but his responses appear to have come from a much older man. At a time when he should have been at the height of his creative powers, as are many artists who with greater maturity begin to comprehend aspects of life that had before seemed mysterious, Serling believed he had little to offer: "The only thing, I think, that happens to a writer as the years go by is a disturbing sense of impatience that time grows short," he told May. "There's a built-in egotism to this. The quiet desperation a writer feels that he has yet to write the definitive play or book inside his head. It also assumes that a public waits with bated breath for his final and comprehensive word."

Few, apparently, were waiting for anything that Serling wanted to say in 1967, although many wanted to capitalize on his name and reputation. With Dick Berg, he tried unsuccessfully to adapt a satiric novel on race relations,

A Time For Glory, as a film; an ABC teleplay he attempted of *Dr. Jekyll and Mr. Hyde* met a similar fate, and producer Dan Curtis asked for his five thousand dollars back. He optioned *The Shamir of Dachau*, a novel about Bodo Cohen, a former prisoner of Dachau who may have killed camp commander Weiss in an act of vengeance; this too could find no takers. The projects being offered to him ranged from a proposed remake of *Citizen Kane*—starring Warren Beatty—to the screen adaptation of Herman Hesse's *Steppenwolf*; he dismissed the Kane project with a laugh and told Buck Houghton, who suggested Hesse to him, that he found the book lacked a single compelling element. His screenplay for *Planet of the Apes*, now owned by producers Arthur Jacobs and Mort Abrahams, who had a commitment from Twentieth Century–Fox for a production date later that year, failed horribly. This project, more graphically than any other screenplay of Serling's, illustrated his ignorance of the screenplay form.

In the book *Planet of the Apes*, French author Pierre Boulle sets up a wonderful conceit to illuminate mankind's general small-mindedness. A space traveler comes across a diary floating in space in a bottle. After retrieving it, he reads the first-person account of a man marooned on a planet in which the simians rule over men, who are literally beasts. When the man, Ulysse Mérou, finally establishes communication with a female ape scientist, learns the ape language, and astonishes her with his "ape-like" intelligence, page after page is filled with their epistemological discussions on the nature of ape versus man; by turning our notions upside down, Boulle exposes humanity's egocentricity. While fascinating, any film faithful to the book would have been marked by long stretches of preachy dialogue—unutterable and unfilmmable. And that's exactly what Serling turned in: *My Dinner with André the Chimp*.

Jacobs brought in another screenwriter, Michael Wilson, the Academy Award–winning writer of *Bridge Over the River Kwai*, to reconstruct Serling's work. (In what must have been a sardonic coincidence, Serling equipped his long, purple-colored 1931 reproduction of an Auburn with a custom horn that blared the theme song to *Bridge Over the River Kwai*. Carol never liked the car, feeling it overly conspicuous. The day he had the horn attached, he took her for a ride and waited until they stopped at a red light. With dozens of cars all around, he honked the horn. With the top down on the convertible, she had no place to hide from all the stares. He grinned from ear to ear.) Wilson completely rethought the book and used only the basic conceit of a man trapped in an ape's world. He made the character of Zaius—in the book just an ignorant and prideful scientist—a type of fourteenth-century grand inquisitor who refuses to accept the notion of man's equality, thus giving the film an evil character from whom the man must escape. He also invented the movie's surprise ending: finding the head of the Statue of Liberty washed up on the beach, the man discovers he has in fact landed on earth far in the future, after the atomic holocaust. In the book, the man escapes to earth in a crude spaceship; the surprise ending is that the space traveler who's been reading Mérou's first-person account is an ape.

Manny Azenburg, the would-be producer of *The Killing Season*, told him that the play had a chance for the following spring in London. Hope, springing eternal, buoyed him for about a month—then came the inevitable rejection and again despair. So the late July letter from Robert Reed, the director of the Hawaiian Educational Television Network at the University of Hawaii, could not have arrived at a better time. Reed, on behalf of the university, solicited Serling to be a writer in residence—a position similar to the one he had held at Antioch. Gladly and anxiously, Serling responded that he would be very much interested in such a position and even offered to visit the powers that be—as though he were a piece of merchandise on consignment.

A few days later A. C. Spectorsky unknowingly provided another kind of salve, asking what it would take to persuade him to think of *Playboy* first for his fiction. Serling playfully suggested that he would be glad to think of *Playboy* first, provided the company send him either "six Eurasian Playgirls" or an equity interest in the enterprise. He then admitted with almost heart-breaking poignancy that merely being asked reminded him that he was both loved and wanted, and it soothed his "stretched and put-upon ego."

Serling quickly contrived, created, and submitted his first piece to *Playboy*—a fantastical short story, "An Odyssey, or Whatever You Call It, Concerning Baseball." At the time, the New York Mets were the laughingstock of the major leagues: five years in existence and regarded as one of the most inept teams in history. Serling's story concerned the absolutely unthinkable: the Mets winning the World Series—two years before they actually did. Like his novellas, the story suffered from a lack of focus and a prose style that sounded exactly like what it was—a dictation.

His stretched and put-upon ego would soon be stretched and put upon even further. The rejection came not from Spectorsky but from his assistant, Robie Macauley: "Spec is ill—in bed with pneumonia—and has asked me to answer you about 'An Odyssey.' He feels that we must, with much regret, decline the story.... Though the outcome is disappointing in this case, we do hope it won't be a lasting discouragement and that you'll try us again with other fiction."

Embarrassed, Serling felt compelled to apologize, as though his bad writing had been a personal affront to Spectorsky. Not until he reread it when it came back in the mail, he said, did he realize how unfunny it was, and he wondered why he even wrote it.

Even judged by Serling's standards, this was remarkable obeisance, indicative of the letter he'd received the week before, which had torn away all remaining threads of his self-confidence: the University of Hawaii, upon further examination, had retracted its offer, deeming him not to have the qualifications the university required; that the University of Hawaii did not boast the finest academic reputation merely added to the already staggering humiliation. Only twelve years after "Patterns" the most famous writer in America, if not the world—the only writer people visually recognized—was being treated like a graduate student blindly sending out resumes.

Now an inhabitant of a purgatory not unlike the ones he'd created for his most despicable "Twilight Zone" characters, Rod Serling watched his wife and children return to California—where his daughters attended school— while he remained at the summer home. From there he would commute the short distance twice weekly to Ithaca College for the fall semester and again attempt to teach dramatic writing and mass media, this time to classes of students who held him in somewhat higher esteem than those at Antioch. ("TV coverage of the [Vietnam] war is unengrossing," he told the student newspaper, the *Cornell Daily Sun*. "Why can't we listen to Ho Chi Minh and hear his point of view?")

On the surface, teaching college students offered little hope of replenishing his track record, but Serling looked forward to the solitude of the few months. He would have at least five days a week to himself, and he wanted the time to think and work. He had another novel to write for his publisher (Little, Brown) and planned to adapt *The Killing Season* as a two-hour drama for the prestigious new "CBS Playhouse," the network's attempt to recapture its "Playhouse 90" glory days as the purveyor of quality anthology drama. He envisioned two of the novellas, *Eyes* and *The Escape Route*, as a "corker" of an anthology film and adapted both of them rather hurriedly under the title "Night Gallery" (as he had conceived during the aborted selling of "Rod Serling's Wax Museum," the thread of continuity between the stories would be the nightmarish art gallery on whose walls hang portraits of the protagonists—for example, Gruppenfuehrer Strobe, agonizing on the cross).

He had big plans again—and new agents to make them, he hoped, a reality. After ten years at Ashley-Famous he signed an eighteen-month contract with the giant William Morris Agency; it was a symbolic act, representative of his need for change, but as always the change was merely cosmetic. Rather than changing his attitude toward his work—concentrating on a single project at a time—he simply shifted the onus of marketing his aging reputation and imperfect products to a larger and more powerful agency.

But not even William Morris, he learned, could make *The Season to Be Wary* a success. All but ignored by the critics and public, the title had sold only five thousand copies by December. (Intentionally or not, the dust jacket copy says that "The three novellas . . . *betray* [emphasis added] the skillful hand of a master storyteller and prose stylist.") While he laboriously continued his television rewrite of *The Killing Season*, he stopped work on the novel *X Number of Days*, an intriguing story about a Jewish-American army officer commanding a detachment outpost in a small town in Germany a few years after World War II. When one of his own men, a loud-mouthed bigot whom he detests, is falsely accused of murdering a retired German army colonel whose Nazi past is well known, the commander must decide whether to expose the real murderer, a Jew in the town—whose culpability he discovers during the course of his own investigation— thus rekindling the strong anti-Semitism of the townspeople. In a sense, the moral dilemma harked back to his better, earlier scripts, and the complications would have made for an absorbing novel if handled carefully. Predictably, though, Serling thought two steps ahead: before completing even a single chapter, he pitched the story to Stan Kamen, Gregory Peck's William Morris agent, as a possible feature starring Peck.

In a letter to Bantam Books editor in chief Marc Jaffe, who owned the paperback rights to *X Number of Days*, Serling suggested a meeting to help get him back to work.

The problem, he admitted, was confidence; he wouldn't have minded being knocked by the critics over *The Season to Be Wary*, but being slighted seemed particularly brutal. It forced him to realize that his unofficial title as television's most famous and successful writer did not automatically confer on him the status—and praise—he craved in other fields of writing. And like the torment he suffered when *The Killing Season* was repeatedly rejected, the critics' disregard of his book taught him again that such early and stunning career successes as he had enjoyed may in fact be more curse than blessing, creating unrealistic future expectations and the anxiety of always needing to live up to those expectations.

Over the Christmas holidays, back home in California, he seemed overly preoccupied with his new Excalibur car. Whether it was parked in the garage or being driven down the street, he continually scrutinized every detail, every inch of paint, every imperfection—real and imagined. Coincidentally or not, he had just begun psychoanalysis three times a week with a Beverly Hills psychiatrist (analysis, he told Jaffe, was a synonym for "self-flaying"). After so many years of lying to himself and lying to cover those lies—piling layer upon layer—the process must have been terribly painful. The analysis was short-lived. A joke Serling began telling at this time seems to have reflected his misery, being more sardonic than humorous; he always laughed hard after telling the punch line:

> *An actor who's badly down on his luck during the Depression finally lands a very small part in a Broadway play. When the show goes into rehearsals he discovers that he's really not at all suited to his role. He figures that at any moment the director is going to fire him. But he's desperate. He needs the job, even if just for a few weeks, just to get back on his feet. The catch is, if he doesn't last a full seven days in rehearsals, they can let him go with just some pittance rehearsal pay. After the seventh day—well, the amount goes way up. And boy, does he need it.*

So every day, right after rehearsal finishes, he avoids the director by making himself as scarce as possible—dodging behind flats, sneaking through corridors, flattening himself against walls. Then, blending into the exiting crowd, he rushes down the back steps.

Well, down at the foot of the steps, on the sidewalk, is always this little, old, smiling Apple Annie. For good luck, everybody filing past drops a nickel or so into her basket. She just smiles this beautiful, kind smile and blesses them.

On the seventh day, the actor sweats out every single minute of the rehearsal. He's positive the director's going to yell out the bad news any second. Finally, they finish the work. He immediately dodges behind the flats, sneaks into corridors, flattens himself against the wall. But there's the director, near the back door, talking with a few people. So this time the actor runs into the john, where he waits a very long time, until everything seems to be silent. Now he figures he's got it made, and he goes to sneak out. Just as he gets to the outside door, he feels a hand on his shoulder. It's the director. "Gee, I'm sorry," he says. "We just can't keep you on."

The actor's whole world has been crushed. He opens the door and starts to walk down the stairs. As usual, there's the little, old, smiling Apple Annie. She's bending over, tying her shoes. He walks down the steps, suddenly rears back, and gives her a terrible kick right in the ass. It sends her flying into the street. She looks up in agony, tears in her eyes. She can't understand it.

"Goddamn you," he says. "You're always tying your goddamn shoe."

Saul David calls it the "black dog"—the self-perpetuating need to continue to make more money to pay for unwanted things. "The pressure of meeting the demands of big-money living are very great in Hollywood, and they chase you—like a black dog," David explains. "You get pulled if you're in a position like Rod, where you may dream of being Arthur Miller and you really want to be

Arthur Miller, but you've got this great big house and a lot of flashy and expensive friends and the opportunity presents itself to put that off and do this instead—it happens to all sorts of people. Take this contract, do this deal. And you always think, 'I'll do this and it'll buy me the time to do that.' Well, it doesn't. It only puts you onto another escalator. And pretty soon you're not buying time, you're buying another car."

Friends of Serling believe that money ceased to be a source of concern to him once he became established and began earning it faster than he could spend it. Even after he sold his rights to "The Twilight Zone" and understood the phenomenal loss in potential syndication income, it barely bothered him, they say. His years-old calculations for the cost per stroke in his huge, heated swimming pool and the dollar-per-minute rate to work at his desk in the poolside studio he'd built were good-natured satire. Yet when the writing became an unrewarding chore, and the money trickled instead of flowed, Serling decided to cash in on his celebrity, even beyond game show appearances.

Retaining Commercial Talent Agency to find him jobs in paid advertisements, he began an entirely new career as a highly paid huckster. The three thousand dollars he received in 1962 for the Schlitz commercial—the one that had embarrassed him badly enough to vow never again to do another commercial—paled in comparison to the money he began making hawking everything and anything. In the two years 1968 and 1969, Serling touted an almost unending stream of products, including Crest toothpaste, Laura Scudder potato chips, auto loans at Merchant's Bank in Indianapolis, B. F. Goodrich radial tires (one of his first commercials, in 1966, was for Goodyear), Packard Bell color televisions, Westinghouse appliances, Anacin, Samsonite luggage, Volkswagens, Gulf Oil, and Close-Up toothpaste (Serling actually introduced the product to the marketplace). He also got paid for his public service announcements for the National Institute of Mental Health (anti–drug abuse), CARE (for Biafran refugees), Epilepsy Foundation of America, United Crusade, the Des Moines Police Association, and the Save the Children Federation. He recorded messages for the Los Angeles Urban Coalition gratis.

Despite all the offers that rolled in for his services—which he authorized the agency to accept contingent only on price—Serling wanted more. He told his friend Al Weisman at the advertising agency Foote, Cone & Belding that he wanted to be considered for every commercial possible. "I have passed your name on to a number of people in the organization," Weisman responded with some disinclination. "If that's what you want, so be it." Evidently, his taste standards excluded only "housewives' products", like floor wax and hair coloring—that is, if he had to be seen on camera; voice-overs were fine.

All things being equal, Serling should not have been criticized or judged too harshly simply for taking the money probably only a few out of ten thousand people would refuse. No, what mortified him—and set tongues clacking—was the irony of television's former angriest young man, the one who had relentlessly assailed the commercialization of television, now succumbing to the seductions of yet another corner of the velvet alley. He felt discomfited and ashamed, knowing that these commercials further eroded his already declining image. "He did them at a time when he was slumping," Bob Serling says. "He was depressed. He wasn't selling scripts, and this was a damn easy way to make a lot of money."

Precisely and poignantly, the commercials indicated the true depth of Serling's desperation. For him to be willing to trade in what remained of his self-respect—to abandon the persona he had carefully created over the years, to disown the fights he had fought in public, to continue the ignominy of being a common pitchman—he must have faced nearly total despair.

Serling himself called his headlong leap into the world of commercials "crass" in a letter to Paul Treichler at Antioch in June 1969, a time when he more easily accepted the humiliation. His motivation, he wrote, was not to win some Zenlike, if-you-can't-beat-'em-join-'em contest, but simply the beckoning of "the bitch goddess," success; the allusion to the epithet, recalling Blanche Gaines's ancient warning, must have been his sardonic joke with himself. At the same time, he admitted to Robert Goldsmith, a friend who also hailed from Binghamton: "Look, when I'm hot I'm hot, when I'm cold I'm gonna be awful cold, and I'll make every goddamn penny I can make while I can make it."

Ironically, Serling owed his brief, final flirtation with greatness to his voice. Near the end of 1967, producer Alan Landsburg, working for David Wolper Productions, began searching for a narrator who could fill in the gaps between Jacques Cousteau's narration of the documentaries conceived by the great oceanographer, whom "The Undersea World of Jacques Cousteau" would make a household name. Landsburg knew that Cousteau's lilting French accent would not be understood by a large portion of the American viewing public. At the same time, these underwater stories delved into a nether world, an unexplored universe. Hearing Serling's voice one day in a commercial, Landsburg knew instantly that only one man truly bridged the worlds: he had both the presence in his voice and an ethereal identification; Serling's full baritone provided a perfect counterpoint to Cousteau's gentle, almost feminine quality. It was an inspired bit of casting and began a friendship between Landsburg and Serling that two years later would produce "Storm in Summer," his most memorable anthology drama since "Requiem for a Heavyweight."

Serling loved the idea of working on the Cousteau shows and said yes immediately. He would be well paid for the twelve shows produced over three years, the subject matter interested him greatly, and he could step back proudly into the limelight.

Landsburg rewrote the field producer's scripts that Serling would say. They were simple and clean, and Serling never changed a single word. "Rod had the most wonderful ability to read," Landsburg recalls. "We'd give him the script, and he intuitively knew where the commas were. We never rehearsed. After the first show, most 'Cousteau' narrations were cold readings." (This recalls John Huston's comment that Ronald Reagan was the best cold reader he ever knew.)

Serling read the scripts perfectly in a single take—using only half the studio time allotted for the taping—so the Wolper crew began inserting a single word of profanity into the scripts. "We just wanted to see if his eye would get it before his mouth said it," Landsburg says. "The classic was: 'And the albatross would return to find its nest raided, and he would be pissed off.' He would just break up at that."

The show debuted on NBC in early January to acclaim, and although Serling's part had been small, he willingly took whatever victory came his way. Meanwhile, "CBS Playhouse" summarily rejected his television adaptation of *The Killing Season.* When he decided to abandon forever *X Number of Days* as a novel and write it as a television script, he offered it to Wolper's company (owned now by Metromedia after a buyout) for production on NBC's upcoming anthology revival "On Stage," a series of occasional dramatic specials. The company bought the script, put it into development, and then abandoned the project.

Still trading on his fame and reputation, Serling received a steady stream of offers to speak to virtually any type of assemblage on the current sad state of affairs in American television broadcasting. For colleges and other student groups he would accept whatever fee they offered; private interest groups might have to pay two thousand dollars. On these occasions, standing alone on the stage or behind a lectern, Serling reveled in his role as the curmudgeonly gadfly, shaking his finger at the medium from which he could not escape. At a luncheon in Chicago honoring the "Hallmark Hall of Fame," his invective hit a frenzied pitch. Watching television, he said:

> I see things like "Let's Make a Deal"—a clinical study in avarice and greed where perspiring yo-yos go into convulsions trying to latch onto warehouses full of free acquisitions while the studio audience screams and gurgles and does a little vicarious perspiring on its own. I see things like "The Dating Game," where a vapid, mini-skirted second-place runner-up in a beauty contest throws out well-rehearsed, thinly veiled sexual fantasies to a trio of trick-or-treat Charlies who are obviously lusting for her body and the residual prizes that go with it. I see the dregs of television—the palpably indigestible, "Gilligan's Island" and "Hee-Haw," or the whole catalog of shows that offer up violence in lieu of any other language. On that little screen I can see all the havoc and damage that man can wreak on his fellow man.

By projecting himself as the secretary of quality without portfolio, Serling reeked of sour grapes; he dishonestly blamed his absence from the small screen on the medium's aversion to excellence, as though his offerings had been rejected for reasons other than their mediocrity. When CBS rejected "The Killing Season" for "CBS Playhouse," he told the Washington, D.C., chapter of the National Television Academy, in a speech at the Library of Congress, that he planned to stick to writing novels and motion pictures. Television, he said, too greatly restricts what a writer can say and concentrates only on "responding to the country's escapist mood." His brother Bob's great success in 1967 with the novel *The President's Plane Is Missing* had made him much more jealous than he let on. "When I was a kid, people used to ask me if I were Bob's brother," he said with an offhandedness that belied his ambivalence (he was at least as proud of Bob as he was resentful). "Then I made it big and for ten glorious years people asked if he were my brother. Now it's reversed again. People are asking me if I'm Bob's brother. I'm going to have to write a novel." (A few years later, when Serling introduced his brother, then visiting the summer home, to the wife of the president of Ithaca College, the woman complimented Bob on his work: "Oh, I just loved your book—*The President Missed His Plane*.")

But despite countless assurances and public pronouncements to the contrary, Serling wanted television and needed it to want him back. Every facet of his life connected to television. Even if he had truly wanted to, he could not have disentangled himself. His commercials aired only on television, as did the game shows and talk shows; his part-time career as a college lecturer and guest professor revolved around discussing his television works; the only scripts he knew how to write well were teleplays; the speeches and lectures that he got paid to make criticized television. Television allowed Serling to be a professional celebrity; it was his flypaper.

Serling liked Landsburg and the people at Metromedia. Landsburg found Serling exceptionally charming and was enchanted by his jokes and stories. (Coincidentally, Landsburg's wife had been raised in Binghamton.) They had an easy rapport, which allowed Serling to let down his guard, and Landsburg could see the pain and tenderness just under his skin. In the next few years the two men would get together often, usually just the two of them, for drinks and dinner and laughs and chats.

On one occasion they met at a topless bar. Topless had just begun in Los Angeles, and Landsburg wanted to see what it was. Serling took him to a place he already knew. The two men sat down and were immediately approached by a beautiful topless waitress Serling had obviously met before. "She leans over me, her tits falling on my shoulder," Landsburg recalls.

"Oh, he's so wonderful," she said, looking at Serling. "He's helping me with my poetry."

Landsburg bit his glass to keep from laughing out loud.

"No, really," she said. "He really is." Serling nodded calmly, suppressing a smile.

Still Landsburg refused to believe the story until she brought him home and proudly showed him the work; Serling really had helped her. (A few months before, a young man Serling had met while in Florida visiting his Aunt Ada sent him several poems composed during a brief stay in a mental hospital for depression; they had been written, he explained, as a form of catharsis, and he wanted Serling's opinion. "Poetry rarely moves me, no matter how good it is," he said. "I don't understand it. Never did.")

Serling wanted to return to writing what he knew best, and he wanted to work with Landsburg, particularly on the NBC anthology series. He pitched an original story about corruption in the Congress, "Certain Honorable Men."

If the pitch had not been accepted, Serling might never have returned to Landsburg with another story, despite their budding friendship. "Rod hated going to pitches because he hated being turned down," Landsburg says. "There are some writers you can turn down in meetings. They say, 'OK, what would you like?' Rod never did that. If you turned it down, Rod got very stiff-lipped and went away."

That had not been his reaction during his career's earliest days. Turned down on one story, he would fire off another, and another, some of them occurring to him as he sat across from the producer or story editor. These days he had no backlog, no overflow of ideas. Each one came slowly.

"The worst job in the world is writing," Landsburg says. "You're alone, you're with yourself, and either you trust your own judgment or you don't. And if your judgment is questioned enough times, you begin to question your own judgment as a writer. If enough people turn you down, you begin to question your own skill. Who else do you have to depend on? It's you against them. In Rod, because of his great early success, this was even a bigger sense of insecurity than most other writers."

The plot of "Certain Honorable Men" was basically "Patterns" transferred to the political arena. It revolved around an elderly and decent congressman, Champ Donahue, whose career is destroyed by his ambitious young aide, who, impatient with Donahue's old-time patronage and quid pro quo methods, dredges up ancient and forgotten scandals. As in "Patterns," the line between good and evil seems terribly thin: the aide's motives are idealistic, and he sees Donahue as an impediment to the process by which complete social justice will be done; and Donahue's scandals are only business as usual, the price of getting anything accomplished in a body politic where backs require scratching. Again, Serling pointed to everyone's ultimate corruptibility. Do the aide's methods justify his ideals? Does Donahue's desperate attempt to stay in power justify his motives? Unfortunately, few cared.

The show (recorded on color videotape and aired September 12, 1968) offered nothing the viewer hadn't seen before, particularly those familiar with Serling's "Playhouse 90" work. Serling hated the production and in fact told his friend Bill Rega that film, whatever its faults, was still better than live videotape, which now seemed to him to look cheap and amateurish." The particular object of his disdain was Peter Fonda, who he felt had failed to convey the subtext written into the character. Two years later, after Fonda's American motorcycle odyssey *Easy Rider* began grossing tens of millions of dollars, Serling told a student audience at the University of Missouri that Fonda and costar and director of the film Dennis Hopper "left me with this unalterable feeling that [they] should start a Honda agency and get out of the acting business."

Before the show began rehearsals in New York during the late summer of 1968, Serling told Landsburg and director Alex Segal that he preferred not to be involved in any rewriting except for major changes—which the script had not needed, in Segal's and Landsburg's estimation.

Nonetheless, he left the Cayuga Lake cabin for a few days to make himself available should any problems arise and checked into the Hampshire House, where the rest of the non–New York cast and crew had taken quarters.

One morning Landsburg picked up Serling for breakfast. Between Serling's penthouse and the ground floor, the elevator empty but for the two men, Serling pitched Landsburg a story. It had to do with a young black boy from Harlem who, through unusual circumstances, spends the summer with an elderly Jewish delicatessen owner in upstate New York.

"That's awfully familiar stuff," Landsburg said. "There's a French movie that just came out that deals with the exact same material. [*The Two of Us* was about an anti-Semitic French farmer hiding a young Jewish boy during the Nazi occupation.] I think I've seen it all before."

"You're wrong, you're absolutely wrong," Serling told him. "And I'm going to prove it to you. I'm going to write the script."

Two months later a script entitled "Storm in Summer" arrived on Landsburg's desk. Landsburg picked it up skeptically, prepared not to like it. Instead, the reading made him cry. "It was just beautiful, a beautiful piece of work," he recalls. He called Serling that afternoon with his opinion and sold it "in about a minute" to "Hallmark Hall of Fame." (Originally the script ran sixty minutes, for which Serling was to be paid fifteen thousand dollars, but when his William Morris agents later told him that he would receive an additional ten thousand dollars for an extra half hour, he expanded it to ninety minutes.) The show aired in February 1970.

Planet of the Apes, released in February 1968, was an immediate and surprise hit. For his services—the first drafts of the screenplay—Serling had received seventy-five-thousand dollars. The deal he turned down and, in retrospect, should have taken, would have paid him $25,000 less in exchange for 5 percent of the producer's net. Seeing the long lines at the box office and reading of

the enormous amounts being returned by the exhibitors
to the studio, he could only shrug it off as another incredible lack of foresight. At the time it seemed the right
move. When, six years earlier, David Susskind had offered
him a similar choice on the film *Requiem for a Heavyweight*, Serling took the lower figure in exchange for the
profits; the film, of course, lost money.

Although Serling's versions of *Planet of the Apes* had to
be considerably rewritten, he took great pleasure in the
success. Sensing a natural sequel, he immediately set to
work on its plot. His ludicrous effort, which he pitched to
Apes producers Mort Abrahams and Arthur Jacobs,
pointed up just how miserably Serling understood the
screenplay form and perhaps explained why he concentrated on adaptations of other writers' stories. The un-
titled plot concerns Charlton Heston (who played the
human survivor in the original) being chased for no apparent reason by the apes who have just let him go. In the
course of his escape the man comes upon remnants of
man's long-ago civilization on earth and begins to remember, almost genetically, how life had been when hu-
mans ruled instead of apes. Always too conveniently, he
comes upon the weaponry and transportation he needs to
single-handedly win back control of the planet for his own
kind . . . until, after he is apparently defeated when his
Piper Cub airplane crashes, another space ship filled with
men and women wipes out the marauding apes. Then the
men and women do what men and women do, as in the
Garden of Eden, and poof, Heston becomes Adam and the
world is reborn.

Abrahams and Jacobs rightfully rejected it, turning over
the plotting to Pierre Boulle, the author of the original
novel.

Serling wanted to adapt *Eyes*, *The Escape Route*, and
another story, *Cemetery* (about an evil nephew who
murders his rich uncle, only to be haunted by a painting
that every night progressively reveals his uncle emerging
from the family crypt), into a full-length anthology film

under the title *Night Gallery*. He sent the book, along with a short précis of *Cemetery*, and his recommendation that Rod Steiger play the lead in each of the three (Steiger, the star of several Serling-written teleplays, had just won a best actor Oscar for *In the Heat of the Night*) to virtually every studio. (He also recommended himself as narrator.) Only Universal expressed interest.

In his follow-up letter to Arthur Joel Katz, Universal's head of production, Serling included what he felt to be an interesting selling point: the possibility that the movie could spin off into a horror, fantasy, occult, and science-fiction series.

Five months later an interviewer asked Serling whether he would consider devising another weekly television series. "When Tris Speaker goes back to baseball, I'll go back to a series," he said. Two months after that he sold *Night Gallery* to Universal as a one-shot television special, rather than an anthology feature.

The following March, after writing the pilot script of a series called "The New People" (about a group of college students marooned on a desert island, it was an idealistic cross between William Golding's novel *The Lord of the Flies* and "Gilligan's Island" and was producer Aaron Spelling's idea), another interviewer asked what it would take to get him back into weekly production. "After five years of my own show," he said, "I wouldn't get involved in another series for eighty-million dollars."

Within a year, either Tris Speaker, dead since 1958, had begun playing outfield again for the 1920 Cleveland Indians or Serling received $81 million dollars: "Night Gallery" began as a weekly series. It would prove to be the most painful and humiliating working experience of his life, driving him out of both television and California.

8

LAST STOP

A commercial huckster who no longer apologized for his ubiquitous pitches. The frustrated ham actor, abandoning all pretext of literary decorum. By 1969 Rod Serling, a writer without a story to tell, had become a caricature of Rod Serling, the professional celebrity.

The previous fall Ralph Andrews, one of the established masters of the game show industry, had asked Serling to host "Liar's Club," his comedy game under development for syndication to independent stations. The two men had known each other fondly for several years, since Serling appeared on Andrews's shows, notably "You Don't Say." On "Liar's Club," each of four celebrities described the actual purpose of objects or inventions they'd probably never seen before. One of them had been briefed with the true answer ahead of time, while the other three invented wild and funny bluffs. Picking up the sigmoidoscope from the table, for example, Peter Lawford demonstrated how zookeepers force-feed vitamins down the throats of wild animals.

By all appearances, Serling enjoyed his six-month stint as host. He worked one day a week, shooting five shows for which he received five hundred dollars; clearly, he did it more for the exposure, and the fun, than the money. The job came almost entirely without pressure. Regardless of how many mistakes he made, Andrews thought him the best possible host for the show; in fact, Andrews and his staff, like the taping crew on "The Undersea World of Jacques Cousteau," purposely placed obstacles in his path, just to see him respond good-naturedly. "He screwed up more than any host I ever worked with," Andrews says happily.

The show revolved around Serling, focusing on his reactions to the outlandish explanations. Never knowing in advance which celebrity knew the real answer, he spent most of the time laughing. He laughed easily and readily, the perfect audience. His enthusiasm glowed and made him utterly charming and appealing to the camera. The host of "Liar's Club," it seemed, shared no genes with the host of "The Twilight Zone." He heard jokes and told jokes, and in that sense the public Serling and the private Serling were identical.

"My wife said I looked like a constipated Sicilian prize-fighter on that turkey," he told the *Los Angeles Times* two years later. "I laughed at everything—even though nothing was funny. I always seem to break up when I'm involved in something that isn't going well. Nerves, I guess."

Whatever emotions agitated under the surface, he always maintained the image of a cheerful, happy kid, and almost everyone who knew him or came into contact with him developed a genuine fondness for his kind nature.

Priscilla Serling, Bob Serling's wife of one year at the time, learned slowly that her brother-in-law's insincerity was so practiced that no one could detect it until knowing him better. "Rod would say, 'Oh, that's interesting,' or 'That's funny.' But it was a facade," she remembers.

During Serling's Cayuga Lake sojourns, the cartoonist Johnny Hart ("B.C." and "Wizard of Id"), who lives in nearby Ninevah, sometimes met him for drinks at local bars. He recalls Serling as "always friendly, smiling, ready to laugh and have fun." When an autograph seeker or well-wisher approached, Serling would smile broadly and whisper through his teeth into Hart's ear: "Help me avoid this guy," or "I hope he falls over a chair." But he always signed the autograph or shook hands, making appropriate small talk as necessary. (At the Embassy Club one evening, Serling spotted a woman with whom he'd grown up; as a child, she had the unfortunate reputation of being "the ugliest girl in the school." Serling walked up to her and planted a big kiss on her cheek. Being kissed by him brought tears to her eyes, not least because he remembered her, she said. Walking back to his friends, he whispered, "How could you forget her? She's the ugliest thing I've ever seen.")

Serling felt lost, a sense of desperation clawing at him. In February he signed with Universal to write and host the three adaptations of *Eyes*, *Cemetery*, and *The Escape Route* under the title "Night Gallery," for airing in the fall. As he had told the studio's Arthur Joel Katz, their primary value to Universal would be as the pilot to a "gothic horror" series. The studio told him these shows would not strictly be considered a pilot, although ratings and audience response might determine its future life.

Serling had just returned from visits to Cornell University and Ohio University to research the film that producer-director Stanley Kramer had hired him to write about the student uprisings then shaking many of the country's campuses; the working title was *The Children's Crusade*. At Cornell Serling watched fierce antiwar protests and black militancy meetings, while at OU, a more traditional and conservative school, the small antiwar gatherings reflected much less passion than the black separatist meetings. Serling came away believing he had witnessed the beginnings of a black-white civil war. The young black touting "black power," he wrote to Kramer, "is outraged, prideful, unyielding, and a smoking bomb."

Accordingly, Serling's rambling first-draft screenplay,

delivered a month later, concentrated on the race issue. In his accompanying letter he called it the most difficult job of writing he'd attempted since entering college. It did not please Kramer at all. He envisioned a film delving into the so-called "generation gap," the apparent inability of parents and children to communicate, as well as the antiwar issue around which white middle-class students especially had congregated; he wanted a more "white" film, probably believing that few adults would pay to see a film in which white adults suffer the collective guilt of three hundred years' worth of black oppression.

Over the next few months Serling wrote at least two more drafts, enough to convince Kramer that little would be gained by succeeding versions. On a Saturday morning, Michael Zimring, William Morris's West Coast literary department head and the man who had negotiated the deal that paid Serling $180,000, accompanied Serling to Kramer's Beverly Hills home. Serling argued in defense of his latest draft and offered to rewrite again and incorporate the necessary changes. Kramer, unyielding in his criticisms, ended the meeting. Walking back to the car, Zimring was struck by the writer's obvious anxiety. "How do you think it went?" Serling asked repeatedly. He soon found out when he received a phone call from Kramer advising him that his services were no longer necessary.

Kramer's rejection hurt him deeply, as though it confirmed his waning talent. (A year later Serling sent a note to Kramer stating that he would forever regret failing to live up to Kramer's expectations.) "He was crushed," Zimring remembers. "You would have thought that he had more confidence than that. I knew a lot of other writers who didn't have a tenth of his talent but had a lot more confidence. Confidence is everything in this business. Here was this famous writer, Rod Serling. I was really surprised. . . . Although I never knew him that well, I always got the feeling he wasn't very happy, that with all his successes, he never achieved what he wanted to achieve."

Kramer hired Erich Segal (*Love Story*) to write what

became *R.P.M.* because he was a college professor and was assumed to have his finger close to young America's pulse. (Knowing that Serling spent much more time than the average Hollywood writer on college campuses, Kramer had originally wanted him for the same reason.) Released in the fall of 1970, starring Ann-Margret and Anthony Quinn, the film did not bear Serling's name. It bombed. "Segal didn't do a very good job for me either," Kramer recalls. (Serling, Carol, and their friends the Arlens attended an early evening show in Westwood. Playing at a theater in such close proximity to UCLA, which manifested its share of turmoil in the late 1960s and early 1970s, a film about campus revolts and uprising should have attracted a sizable audience. But the Serlings and Arlens had practically the entire movie house to themselves. Serling gloated over both the empty seats and the quality of the film he hadn't written.)

Soon after being fired himself, Serling fired his William Morris agents—five months before the termination date of the contract he'd signed after leaving Ashley-Famous, the agents he had originally chosen because they seemed to care about him and his career. Ten years later he'd signed with the biggest agency, William Morris, hoping that some of its grandeur would rub off. Now, disenchanted (he had in fact been disenchanted with them for several months already and called them "mongoloids without class, without taste and with damned precious little honor"), he wanted the most aggressive agency, Creative Management Associates, run by Freddie Fields and Sue Mengers.

Although Fields would be his agent, it was Mengers's prominence that lured him to CMA. She had built a reputation for being shamelessly ferocious in both pursuing and serving her actor and actress clients. Years before, when launching her own career, she had begun a correspondence with Serling (as no doubt she did with many, many industry people while building up a successful network of contacts), writing him notes of congratulation for shows and movies and reminding him to think of her clients when casting "Twilight Zones." (Serling rarely offered casting instructions, unless the part had been written specifically for a particular performer, like Carol Burnett.) "Please hurry so that I will really know that it is not just a dream," Mengers wrote him in March, urging him to sign the standard agency contracts, which would not take effect until September. (Not so ironically, perhaps, Serling angrily left CMA two years later, after Mengers referred to him in a printed article as an agency chaser.)

The move to CMA reflected Serling's increasing desperation: change for change's sake. He drank more now than ever, and his relationship with Carol evidently hit its nadir. Vern Hartung, with whom he had grown up and entered the army, remembers that during the summer, when Serling visited Cayuga Lake, they would meet for drinks, occasionally with Johnny Hart. Serling would drink astonishing amounts for someone his size; at closing they'd go to private clubs that allowed them to drink liquor they carried in themselves. "Rod used to go to the phones every hour on the hour and call home to report to Carol," Hartung says. "Every hour. She worried about him. . . . He just kept drinking and smiling." (Hartung recalls the night he had dinner at the Scotch 'n Sirloin with Serling, Hart, and Hart's partner, Grant Parker. Serling had wanted to pick up the check, as he almost always did when dining out with friends, but Hart had prearranged payment. Angry, Serling asked the waiter if he knew how to stand on his head. The waiter tentatively said yes. "Then go ahead," Serling demanded. This was Mr. Rod Serling giving him an order, so he complied, his feet wiggling in the air next to the table for several seconds. When he got back to his feet, the four men laughing uproariously, Serling handed him three one-hundred-dollar bills as a tip.)

In California at a party for Frank Sinatra, Jr., Serling spent most of the evening talking to Pamela des Barres, nineteen, the singer in a rock band called the G.T.O's and almost twenty years later the author of *I'm with the Band: Confessions of a Groupie.* "He was incredibly drunk, drinking all night," she says. "He seemed very interested in me and was kind of interviewing me, asking all sorts of questions. He seemed like a poor, pathetic old man." Des Barres suffered his incessant questioning. This was Rod Serling, one of her cultural heroes. She told him that she also made shirts for a living—hippie-looking shirts that would have looked completely ridiculous on the almost forty-five-year-old, ivy league–tailored Serling, but he asked her to make him one anyway. Smiling, she gave him her number.

The next morning his call awakened her at eight. Hearing Serling's voice at the other end of the line, des Barres kept thinking, "I can't believe 'The Twilight Zone' is calling me." He asked for her address and directions, to have his shirt fitted, he said. Believing he only used the shirt as a ruse to be with her, she was surprised he never showed up.

As much as anything else, his unhappiness showed in his abandonment of politics. In a March letter to a man with whom he had corresponded over the years on various political issues and who now asked for his support in publicizing an effort to reduce antiballistic missiles, Serling told him that he had decided to give up the fight and pass on the baton to the younger people. This was a startling admission. All his adult life Serling had viewed politics as a metaphor for hope—the hope of a better world. Now he had given up that hope, both literally and figuratively. Similarly, his letter several months later to his friend Jules Golden made no effort to sugarcoat his ongoing commercial deluge, which he called "the refined art of extended prostitution. But I say, fuck them all—I hope to die with a sizable residue of comfort left to loved ones."

He wanted to work and needed to be wanted, regardless now of whether the work had major literary, cinematic, or social significance—or indeed, whether it violated the canons he had expounded ceaselessly for fifteen years. He believed he had to take advantage of whatever currency still remained to the name of Rod Serling. He even pitched the idea of an hour "Twilight Zone," in color, to Perry Lafferty, CBS's programming vice president. "Liar's Club" had not attracted enough stations, and Ralph Andrews terminated the show's production. (A year or so later it would be resumed as a network show with Allen Ludden as host. Interestingly, Serling, Ludden, and Hal March— who was the original host when the show aired only in San Francisco—would all suffer early deaths, while a fourth host, Bill Armstrong, nearly died in an airplane crash.) So when the Los Angeles–area CBS affiliate, KNXT (now KCBS) called him to narrate an offbeat weekly series, he said yes.

Dan Gingold, the executive producer of "Rod Serling's Wonderful World Of . . . ," was surprised that Serling agreed to host the program, which each week explored such topics as congestion, crime, prejudice, propaganda, and snobbery. For the previous six years Gingold had produced another nonfiction series called "Ralph Story's Los Angeles," in which the local news anchorman narrated visual features about local life. Eager for a change, Story had quit, leaving talented writers and a production crew without work. "In those days," Gingold says, "you just didn't let people go. It was more family-oriented." After searching for a replacement show, they settled on the idea of discussing subjects rarely spoken of in polite conversation. To carry it off though they needed a marquee name. Serling's name appeared at the top of their list for potential hosts, despite their certainty he would laugh at the offer.

To Gingold's astonishment, Serling took his call and met him at the Polo Lounge of the Beverly Hills Hotel. Serling began the meeting with a joke, which Gingold believed was indicative of the writer's self-effacing grace and charm. "He was one of the greatest dirty joke tellers

I've ever met," Gingold says. Even the price, about twelve hundred dollars a show, did not bother Serling. When he half-heartedly expressed doubts about his ability to carry the program—explaining that on "The Twilight Zone" he had been on camera for only a few moments—Gingold put him at ease. Each week he had only to read over the well-written script that would arrive in his mailbox, make any comments or corrections he wished, then come into the studio for the taping. There he would introduce the topic, narrate the film and video inserts, and close with a comment; the taping ran continuously, without editing. In obvious ways, Serling's commercials, his voice-over work on the Jacques Cousteau specials, and his hosting of "Liar's Club" had been a training ground for "Rod Serling's Wonderful World Of. . . ."

Serling showed up promptly every week and promptly began telling dirty jokes. "It became such a routine that I eventually decided it was just a kind of cover, that it was covering an insecurity or something," Gingold remembers. "It was very difficult to engage him in any kind of ongoing, significant conversation. Whatever we talked about, he interrupted with a joke."

Gingold and his crew had been thrilled with Serling's agreement to host the show—even if they were less than thrilled with his performances. "We were probably a little in awe, that here's this guy who was at the absolute pinnacle of fame, who somehow graced us with his presence—and that was enough," says Gingold. But eventually everyone's infatuation with Rod Serling, the famous writer, turned to a kind of morbid fascination. His relentless dirty joking evolved to the threshold of embarrassment. They dreaded the inevitable joke and formed amateur diagnoses behind his back.

Gingold had visited the Serlings' home and been impressed by Carol's almost "patrician" quality, which contrasted boldly against the self-deprecating image Serling had provided. "He was famous and successful, but somehow it didn't rest well on his shoulders," Gingold says. "He gave me the impression that he felt he never deserved it. Maybe that's the reason for the dirty jokes and the kind of lower-class wallowing. Here's a guy that deserved to show a little more class and didn't." Wave some money in his face, Gingold believed, and Serling would do almost anything.

After thirteen shows, Serling, aware of his shortcomings as host, asked to be let out of the contract.

Serling left his writing and media students at Ithaca College in the fall of 1969 to spend three days in Palm Springs with Alan Landsburg and Buzz Kulik, the director Landsburg chose for "Storm in Summer." Under the warm sun, they worked through the minor problems remaining in the script Serling had written about the elderly Jewish delicatessen owner who befriends the young black boy from the inner city. Sitting by the pool, Landsburg and Kulik outlined every dialogue, plot, or character change they felt necessary, and Serling took notes.

This seemed a far cry from previous rewriting sessions with the writer: Landsburg on "Certain Honorable Men," for which Serling expressed a desire to be omitted from small changes, and Kulik on the 1963 film *Yellow Canary*. Twentieth Century–Fox had hired Serling in the late 1950s to adapt the novel *Evil Come, Evil Go*, by Whit Masterson, but set aside his script and abandoned the project. A few years later, required to pay Pat Boone a few hundred thousand dollars whether or not the picture was shot, production quickly began under director Kulik, who'd made only one other low-budget feature film after many years as a television director. At the time, Serling had left for his Antioch sabbatical, and when Kulik called him to rewrite, he first agreed to tinker then backed off. "Listen, Buzz," he said, "I really didn't want to do this in the first place. I don't think I can contribute anymore. I've done the best I can, and there's nothing else I can contribute to the project, so—good luck." ("A common, not a rare bird," said the *New York Times* review of the film.)

Serling knew that the script to "Storm in Summer" was a good one; and if it could be improved, so much the better. Even his legendary impatience yielded this time to his desperation for a success on the screen.

The script now polished to everyone's satisfaction, Landsburg began casting and chose Peter Ustinov for the role of Shaddick (Serling took the name from the protagonist of his abandoned novel, *X Number of Days*), the Jewish deli owner—a decision Serling abhorred. "Peter," Landsburg said to Ustinov over the phone, "you know there's a particular tang to this story that's Yiddish." Just like that, Ustinov replaced his British accent with the melody of an old Jewish man who'd lived his life behind a corned beef sandwich counter. Landsburg was enchanted, but Serling preferred a Jewish actor and if not that at least one American-born. After hearing Ustinov on the set, not in character, refer to the "pastram-eye," Serling only hid his displeasure.

"Storm in Summer" aired on February 6, 1970, and received nearly unanimous praise for story, direction, production qualities, and acting. Serling had not enjoyed such a renaissance in a very long time. Steve Allen contacted him immediately, believing the script lent itself very well to a stage musical. Serling said yes very quickly. He and Allen had known each other somewhat over the years, both of them active in many of the same liberal causes. On the flight from New York to Los Angeles that marked their move to California in 1958, the Serlings happened to sit next to Allen, who entertained Jody with jokes and tricks until she threw up in his lap. (Invited once to speak at a book and author dinner in Los Angeles, Allen accepted and was then told by a member of his staff that Rod Serling would be the other speaker on the program that evening. On arriving, he saw that it was not Rod Serling but Bob Serling. In his otherwise prepared opening remarks, Allen inserted an ad-lib: "I was informed that Rod Serling was supposed to be here tonight, and now I find out it's Rod Serling's brother. If I'd known that, I would have sent my brother." The remark got a big laugh, Allen recalls, "but later I thought that it sounded like a terrible put down to him, and I hadn't meant it that way.")

Allen told Serling that "Storm in Summer" would not need too much adaptation, just some simple cutting, because books for musicals must leave room for fourteen songs. He wrote the songs rather quickly and assisted Serling in lopping the narrative to the bare bones. They found no takers in New York or even Los Angeles; the Off Broadway Theater in San Diego planned the premiere production.

Before rehearsals began, Allen received a letter stating Serling's regrets: he'd thought over the matter carefully and decided he wanted to see "Storm" produced as a straight play, not a musical. Allen never questioned him about it again. Two years later, while plugging the premiere, Serling acknowledged to the *Los Angeles Times* that the idea of adapting the teleplay for stage had been Allen's idea, "but as we worked on it, it became obvious that music was doing nothing to further or enhance the play, and Steve very graciously bowed out." It's likely that Serling did not want to share his stage debut with anyone else. In musicals, the composer is the one who receives most of the acclaim and bows; the writer is generally shunted aside.

The original three "Night Gallery" episodes aired as a two-hour NBC world premiere movie November 8, 1969, to very high ratings; in fact, it was the highest rated program of the evening. William Sackheim, hired by Universal as a staff producer, had discovered the outlines of the three stories Serling submitted some months before to Arthur Joel Katz, who bought and then shelved them, believing two insurmountable strikes were against them: they were anthology and not horrific enough in the traditional sense of horror entertainment. Sackheim brought them to Sidney Sheinberg, president of Universal's television division (and now president of MCA, the entertainment conglomerate that includes Universal), and after pushing hard for the project was granted production funds. When the studio hurried him to finish, Sackheim hired three directors and three crews to shoot the stories concurrently. Sheinberg saw an opportunity to make good on the promise he'd made to twenty-year-old Steven Spielberg: to direct something before his twenty-first birthday. Sackheim chose Spielberg to guide "Eyes," the segment starring Joan Crawford as the treacherous blind woman who pays for twelve hours of sight—a script Spielberg did not much like.

Crawford had long carried on a correspondence of professed mutual admiration with Serling, whose original teleplay adaptation of the novella changed the character of Miss Menlo to Mr. Menlo; the actress's expressed interest in the part caused him to change it back. (*Mommie Dearest*, Crawford's daughter Christina's book about her published after her death, makes the casting choice appear nearly to type: tyrannical, ruthless, and somehow pathetic.) The adaptation focused almost solely on the character of Menlo (Spielberg's direction did nothing to solve the question of why cars' headlights weren't visible to her), while the novella gave much more space to the sad character of Petrozella, the man forced into selling his sight. For "The Escape Route," Richard Kiley, who'd first met Serling during the production of "Patterns," played the hunted Nazi who meets a fitting end in an art museum. "The Cemetery" starred Roddy McDowall as Jeremy, the nephew who kills his rich uncle for the inheritance, only to be outdone by the uncle's longtime houseman—next in line to the fortune—who himself inexplicably falls victim to supernatural justice.

Discussing the casting with Sackheim, Serling outlined his choices for the key roles (only Crawford and McDowall actually starred) but joked that "Night Gallery" would probably star Minasha Skulnick, Molly Picon, and Nelson Eddy's nephew.

Despite his repeated public statements feigning disgust with the rigors of weekly television, Serling was very anxious to make a return. Tired, distressed, depressed, and increasingly nihilistic and irascible, he found himself waiting for the phone to ring, bringing adaptation offers. Where once original story ideas for movies or long-form television had popped into his brain faster than he could write them down, he now felt a peculiar void. Both "Liar's Club" and "Rod Serling's Wonderful World Of . . ." had been canceled, and while the commercial offers continued, the film-writing offers had all but stopped—at least for anything he wanted or felt qualified to write; marginal projects carried by so-called producers who could get studio financing only if Rod Serling said yes were always available. His career seemed to have ground to an ignominious halt. He clearly needed an outlet similar to "Twilight Zone," in which his throwaway ideas could be expanded or other writer's stories adapted.

Given the high ratings for the three-part show, it seems logical that Universal and NBC would have quickly added "Night Gallery" to the schedule, either for the following fall or as a midseason replacement. But they did not. NBC told him, and Universal concurred, that audiences wanted continuing characters, not anthology. Even his hosting the show, appearing on camera to introduce every segment, did not satisfy the requirement.

In desperation Serling began searching files and crates for old stories that might be adaptable in any form. He found an episode of "The Loner," called "Mourners for Johnny Sharp," and sent it to William Dozier with an eye to a ninety-minute "Hallmark Hall of Fame," which had just aired "Storm." Dozier politely rejected the idea. His short story, "Clean Kills," met the same fate at *Playboy*. (Within a couple of years, he would try to sell "Leave It to the Kids," a program idea he'd had in college—a panel show in which the "experts" are precocious children answering their peers' questions.)

Serling pressed CMA to press Universal and NBC even harder for the series. Their eventual approval, Serling wrote, "was like pulling impacted wisdom teeth with cardboard pliers." It came with severe restrictions; Serling's acceptance of them indicated how badly he wanted the series on the air. To start, only six episodes would be produced, to be alternated with three other series— "McCloud," "The Psychiatrist," and "San Francisco International" (on which brother Bob Serling was a technical adviser)—under the name "Four-in-One." And someone other than Serling would be the boss. Even as creator of the series, he had to give up control. His contract called for him to act as host and write a number of episodes; Jack Laird, Universal's own man, would be responsible for the show. Sackheim had withdrawn as producer because he wanted to avoid the rigors of weekly television.

"Storm in Summer" won the Emmy in June as best dramatic show of the year, while Peter Ustinov took the best actor in a dramatic special. How, Serling asked several friends, could it have been the best show without being the best-written show? He felt hurt at the perceived slight, which may have been an unorganized reaction by the Academy's voting members to published comments he had made predicting the imminent extinction of the National Academy of Television Arts and Sciences, "an aging dinosaur." A year later, nominated for an episode of "Night Gallery," he called the Emmy awards "repugnant and ridiculous" but added he would not have the courage to reject one—as George C. Scott had just done with the Oscar earned for his portrayal of General George Patton.

Despite being just a hired hand, Serling looked forward to "Night Gallery" with great zeal. He would again be on-camera host, a job he had particularly missed, and, most important, he would be working regularly at a job he knew well. "Night Gallery," unlike "Twilight Zone," was not restricted to a single twenty-four-minute script. The sixty-minute show sometimes had four separate stories of varying lengths, from forty minutes to a thirty-second blackout sketch. For the first six shows, which began airing in December, Serling wrote ten scripts. Only one was memorable: "They're Tearing Down Tim Riley's Bar," an emotionally autobiographical story of a man (played very well by William Windom) whose best years now lay behind him and whose career has descended far from its apex. He finds little joy in living, except for reliving past joys and triumphs.

Fired by his boss, he goes to the neighborhood bar, targeted for demolition to make room for progress. A business executive, he is in many senses Staples, the young man in "Patterns," twenty-five years later, who wonders where the time went and why he made the choices he did, after finding himself replaced by a younger, hungrier version of himself. But the story is also taken from "Twilight Zone": the ghosts of his past call to him, and he revisits his own homecoming from the war as a paratrooper, when all the world lay before him. The sounds of jackhammers and the wrecker's ball drag him reluctantly back to the present, and he yells for the past not to leave him stranded in this world he detests—and which he thinks detests him.

If Serling had been at the series' helm, the story would have ended bleakly right at that point, with a resignation and poignancy not unlike "The Velvet Alley," which closed with the writer, Ernie Pandish, sitting in the snow, crying for what has become of him. But Jack Laird tagged on a pseudohappy ending, reminiscent of It's a Wonderful Life. The man has been rehired, and a surprise party is given in his honor. As much as anything, this creative usurpation described Serling's experiences on the series, which was picked up for a full season the following year and a half season—in half-hour form—for the year after.

Jack Laird exercised virtually complete dominion over "Night Gallery" and was apparently dedicated enough to the show to sleep much of the time in his office. Although Serling was being paid a weekly small fortune, Laird rewrote virtually everything to satisfy his own taste (by contrast, Serling rarely rewrote any of his other writers on "Twilight Zone") and refused to defer. "When I complain, they pat me on the head, condescend, and then hope I'll go away," Serling said. He had wanted "Night Gallery" to embrace the gothic as a means to an end, not an end in itself, as "Twilight Zone" had told stories that instructed and entertained. These did not necessarily have to carry sharp moralistic subtexts, but he felt compelled, possibly because of his commercial indulgence the previous few years, to write stories that had a strong point of view— like "They're Tearing Down Tim Riley's Bar." "I wanted a series with distinction, with episodes that said something; I have no interest in a series which is purely and uniquely suspenseful but totally uncommentative on anything," he told Universal. A single other script of Serling's on the show, "The Messiah on Mott Street," came close to his original conception of the series. In it, an elderly Jewish man, who believes he'd been visited by the Angel of Death, tells his grandson that he is dying. Despondent, the grandson goes in search of the Messiah, to save his grandfather's life. While it certainly had touches of the supernatural, the purpose of the story was not to shock.

By the end of the series' run, Serling was only a front man, his scripts either entirely rewritten or ignored. To his friends and family, he made no secret of his anguish over the turn of events. "I'm fucking furious," he told his friend John Champion. "These people are taking what could have been a good series, and are so commercializing it, it's not going to turn out to be commercial."

"In all the years I knew him, 'Night Gallery' was his worst working experience," says Champion. "If you're paying someone ten thousand dollars a week, and you won't let him go near the typewriter, and you make yourself deaf to everything he says, and you tell your secretary that you're not available. . . ."

By 1971 Serling had been all but driven out of California, spending at least six months a year at the summer home and teaching as often as possible at Ithaca College. "One of the reasons he wanted to go back to Ithaca and teach was the realization that in Hollywood, in show

business, if you're not at the top, you're nothing," says Bob
Serling. "I think the strain of trying to keep up at the top
finally got to him."

He still had the commercials and an increasing number
of well-paying speaking engagements, which he'd hired a
speaker's bureau to procure for him; college campuses,
where he decried the current state of broadcasting and
morals, became his second home. "Night Gallery," which
he continued to write from afar, as though putting distance between him and what the finished product was
likely to be, seemed a metaphor: all the bad choices made
out of desperation, anxiety, insecurity, or for money in the
previous twenty years now came back to haunt him. He
felt the world had passed him by. Producers and studio
executives, who once thrilled to meet with him over their
projects, now thought him just another well-known television writer. This was a time when the power base in the
industry began to shift, and the younger producers and
executives drove out the aging moguls. The first of the
baby boomers had come of age, bringing with them the
sensibilities needed to communicate—or so went the
thinking—to the emerging generation that would dominate the nation's viewing and spending habits for at least
twenty years. While these young people knew "The Twilight Zone" intimately, they felt no particular reverence or
allegiance anymore for its creator. What had he written
lately? they asked without irony. Their ignorance and
callousness aside, he had only himself to blame for being
in that predicament; by not generating his own original
stories, he was at their mercy. He was not some hack
writer who could no longer get hired by these young
turks; he was Rod Serling, a writer of great distinction
who had squandered his enormous talents.

That summer he adapted for ABC Irving Wallace's 1964
novel *The Man*, about a black man, a not particularly
respected cabinet member, who becomes president of the
United States through a coincidental series of deaths.
(Through its ABC Circle Entertainment division, the net-

work also released the film theatrically for a brief time in 1972.) Serling's version, embarrassingly "updated" to reflect the tenor of the times, hinged on a plot point involving a black assassin from South Africa who seeks sanctuary in America, thus dividing the nation into two camps: one in favor of his staying and one opposed. In the end, the president (played by James Earl Jones) makes a very Serlingesque speech condemning the politics of violence and then deports the assassin.

There was a time when this type of story aroused him, stirred his passions, made him anxious to extol his social gospel. That time had passed. Like the protagonist of "They're Tearing Down Tim Riley's Bar," at times he would stare at the bound scripts on his shelves or flip through scrapbooks containing reviews he no longer got—or deserved. "Now I know why people keep scrapbooks—just to prove to themselves it really happened," he said. He knew too well that he had thrown away an immense talent and had "not a helluva lot" of which to be proud. With more duty than eagerness, he began writing "Storm in Summer" as a novel. Whether it deserved to be novelized was beside the point: it was his last good story. He never completed it.

On New Year's Eve 1972 Serling attended a party at the home of Jerry Paris. He walked up to Sy Gomberg, an old friend he hadn't seen for some time, and put a hand on his shoulder. Gomberg turned and saw Serling, then pushed him arm's length away. "Rod, what did you do?" Gomberg angrily asked. Serling turned white. "Rod, tell me something. Did you do a story about a Jewish grocery store man who takes in a black boy?"

Gomberg, the screenwriter of *Imitation of Life, When Willie Comes Marching Home,* and *Summer Stock,* had been the creator and sole writer of ABC's classy lawyer series in 1960, "The Law and Mr. Jones," which starred James Whitmore. Serling had admired the series for its integrity and intelligence, and when ABC announced its cancellation, he stepped forward in an unsuccessful effort to save the show. From that, he and Gomberg became friends, and they and their wives shared several intimate dinner parties with, among others, the Whitmores.

Often at these gatherings, Gomberg related stories of his unusual family members. He'd written short stories about his younger brother for *Colliers* and *Cosmopolitan* and had offers for a novel, which he kept always on hold, waiting for the day when he would actually write it.

Gomberg was a natural storyteller and captivated Serling with his tales. (Perhaps afraid of losing the competition, Serling rarely held court, as he usually did, around other writers whose work he represented.) One story had particularly infatuated Serling. Gomberg's father, a small grocery store owner in Newark, New Jersey, had virtually adopted a twelve-year-old black boy from the inner city. The boy's father, a track worker for the Pennsylvania railroad, often left for three or four weeks straight, while his mother, a schizophrenic, sometimes tried to set fire to the house or ran out naked and screaming into the street. Tommy, the boy, needed help both physically and psychically, and Gomberg's father provided it—despite catching him stealing from the store. Eventually, after Gomberg's brother died from the delayed effects of a war wound, the boy took his place in the family.

Another story Gomberg told concerned his grandfather, Itzik, who believed the angel of death visited him frequently, just to remind him the end could come at any time. One time Itzik solemnly declared that the angel had visited him in the night to announce he had precisely two weeks to live. For the two weeks he sat ashen-faced in bed, refusing to eat, refusing to go to temple, refusing to do anything. He called to his side, one by one, his most beloved: Gomberg's father got the watch, Uncle Bill the *tallis*, and Gomberg the dominoes. "Hey, Curly," he rasped weakly to Gomberg, handing him the set after their last game together. "They're marked."

The night before Itzik's presumed death, the entire

family from the New York–New Jersey area congregated in the small New York City apartment to pay their last respects. Twenty-one young kids, the grandsons and granddaughters, nephews and nieces, each kissed the old man good-bye then lay on the floor to sleep, lined up like logs in a lumber mill. In the morning, Itzik sat up in bed. Everyone gasped; it was a miracle. "The angel of death visited me again last night," Itzik proclaimed. "And he said to me, 'Itzik, they love you so much, how can I take you?' So he left, so I'm here." To Gomberg he said, "Give me back the dominoes."

That night with the Serlings and Whitmores, Gomberg related other tales as well. As they would whenever he finished, the assembled guests urged him to write the stories for publication or viewing. He planned to, he assured them. Around Hollywood, the small, industry town, Gomberg developed an inside reputation as the writer who told these apparently true stories of his interesting and eccentric family. He was often introduced to people who'd heard them secondhand as "the guy who told those great stories I told you about."

Serling, particularly, kept on Gomberg to publish the stories. Neighbors in the Pacific Palisades, they would sometimes pass each other on Sunset Boulevard. Serling would honk and wave from his convertible and at the red light yell, "Have you written 'Itzik' yet?" "No, not yet," Gomberg would say. "Hurry, hurry," Serling said in jest, "'cause I'm gonna write 'em."

Early in February, a few days after "Storm in Summer" aired, James Whitmore called Gomberg to ask if he'd seen the show. Gomberg said no. To everyone else who related details of the plot and asked whether he'd sold Serling the story, he said no, absolutely certain that Serling would not "steal" it.

"Hallmark" presented an encore presentation of "Storm" the following April. Again Gomberg missed it, again people asked him whether he'd sold Serling the story, and again he defended Serling. In December his sister called, inquiring if he'd sold Serling a couple of stories. "A couple?" She told him that "Storm in Summer" reminded her of their father and that an episode of "Night Gallery" she'd recently seen, "The Messiah on Mott Street," seemed very much like their grandfather.

Gomberg had before felt reluctant to accuse Serling of theft, believing "Storm in Summer" to be a coincidence; but when he heard that not just one but two stories bearing suspicious resemblances to his own tales had found their way onto television—and both of them written by Serling!—his pent-up anger caused him literally to shake when he saw Serling at the party.

"You're completely mistaken, absolutely mistaken," Serling told him.

"God, I hope so," Gomberg replied.

Serling explained that "Storm in Summer" came about when a deli owner he knew in Ithaca had taken a young black boy from the inner city for two weeks on the Fresh Air Fund, a New York program that relocates disadvantaged youths out of the city for some part of the summer, placing them with families in less urban areas. "Come on, Sy," he said, "you know I would never do that." He refused when Gomberg asked for the name of the Ithaca deli owner.

Serling, who hated confrontations, wrote Gomberg a long note two days later. Enclosing copies of the two scripts for Gomberg to read, he reiterated the differences in his "Storm" script from the one Gomberg had told him years before, and pointed out that in "The Messiah on Mott Street" the elderly man has no family except the grandson. The script also introduced a "creature of fantasy," the Messiah; the angel of death, he said, has always been a prominent character in Yiddish literature. He closed by challenging Gomberg to sue for plagiarism if the explanations seemed untenable.

Gomberg immediately wrote back, admitting his own anguish at not having written these stories of his family before now: "For these were among my favorite 'nuggets' filed for future writing, along with the story of Itzik. . . . I realize the gestation period had been long. But then it often is with me." Having finally found, he said, a framework for the novel, he planned to begin writing in the near future. But now, although the two scripts were not "exactly as I told you," he felt these stories no longer belonged to him. "If I now write anything about a Jewish delicatessen owner who took in a black ghetto waif and what followed, or about a bearded old Jewish grandfather bedded down with pleurisy who had a favorite grandson and a pipeline to the Angel of Death, then what? Will I be accused of plagiarism or a lack of originality by those who remember those characters from the shows?"

Serling's letter that followed shortly, besides alluding to his novel in progress, an adaption of *Storm in Summer*, acknowledged the obvious: an impasse. Gomberg, calling the revelation of the novel "excruciating," suggested a way out of the dilemma: arbitration by the Writer's Guild. Serling refused for the obvious reason that he had nothing to win out of it and said he regretted only that the disagreement could never be settled in a way that salvaged what remained of the friendship. He again challenged Gomberg to sue.

Before Gomberg received Serling's last letter, he read in *Daily Variety* that "Shaddick," a midseason thirty-minute pilot based on "Storm in Summer," had been ordered by CBS, with Serling to script and Alan Landsburg to be executive producer. He wrote to his attorneys for an opinion and dropped the case. From then on, he ignored Serling, and when invited to a party by mutual friends, he refused to attend if informed Serling planned to come. (Gomberg recalls he later met Ray Bradbury. After Gomberg related the events, Bradbury told him that Serling had admitted having taken his story for the pilot of 'Twilight Zone,'" Gomberg says.) Still later, when Serling took sick, Gomberg sent him a pleasant note, intimating that all hard feelings had passed.

Gomberg's anger and frustration were certainly understandable. Yet his naïveté seems incongruent in such a veteran writer. Telling the same stories over many years to dozens, if not hundreds, of people—most, if not all, of them in the entertainment industry—the wonder is that these obviously enchanting stories were not used sooner. In Hollywood, as in any industry in which ideas are gold, a creator must either produce his own stories or copyright them carefully in detail, before telling them indiscriminately. Either careless or too trusting, Gomberg had done neither. Further, one has only to look at the networks' prime-time programming to see that few, if any, truly original ideas can still be found. While an individual series may be praised for its originality of thought or fresh writing, generally the weekly plots or situations are recognizable to those with good memories or a sense of history. Even Shakespeare "borrowed."

For Serling's part, it's entirely possible and plausible that, desperate for strong material that otherwise eluded him, he remembered these stories of Gomberg's; perhaps the "theft" occurred unconsciously. If so, it was not the first time. For a man who wrote and read as much and as quickly as Serling, locating the source of an idea may have been nearly impossible. The tragedy is in the desperation he felt; this was his motivation. Compelled to write quickly, he usually failed to write well. Lacking the emotional equilibrium necessary to nurture his extraordinary talent, he wrote far below his potential. And he knew that very well.

Working on the series "Shaddick" for Alan Landsburg, a man he liked and whose taste he trusted, would have been good for Serling, providing him an opportunity to do quality work on a weekly basis—or as often as he chose. The pilot, starring Herschel Bernardi as Shaddick and directed by Carl Reiner, was ahead of its time as a form. Comedy-dramas, now called "dramedies," would not find their way into mass acceptance in prime time for fifteen more years. The show, like the "Hallmark" special, was a mixture of laughs and bittersweet tears. Serling could write straight drama, but despite his prowess as a story-teller and jokester, he could not write funny lines; his humor derived from character.

Alan Wagner, CBS's vice president of development, called Landsburg into his office. "We need a laugh track," he said.

Landsburg phoned Carl Reiner. "Carl," he said, "do you want to put a laugh track in?"

"What?" Reiner asked, amazed at the request. A laugh track gave the audience no credit for intelligence, as well as being completely inappropriate to the type of laughs in the show.

"I don't know either," Landsburg said. He then called Wagner. "Alan, I don't know how to put it on."

"Too bad," Wagner said.

The pilot was never sent to New York and never shown to top CBS executives, all because it lacked a laugh track.

NBC cancelled "Night Gallery" around the same time, ironically allowing Serling a measure of retribution. Universal wanted to enter the series into syndication but felt it didn't have enough episodes to make it truly valuable. The previous year another Universal series called "The Sixth Sense," starring Gary Collins in stories of the occult, had aired for a single season. The studio took that series and included it with the "Night Gallery" episodes, dividing the whole package into thirty-minute shows. But to provide continuity with the addition of the "The Sixth Sense" shows, Universal needed Serling for some additional on-camera introductions and wraparounds.

Serling had left CMA and signed with International-Famous, the newest incarnation of the original Ashley-Steiner agency and the immediate predecessor of what is now called International Creative Management. Bob Broder, his agent there, negotiated a deal whereby Universal paid Serling not only for a day's work filming his spots but also a $200,000 advance against his syndication profits. "With the standard Universal definition [of profits] at that time," says Broder, this was money he would probably have never seen any other way. The studio needed him, and it had to pay.

A few months later Broder negotiated another deal that paid Serling considerably less money—for the stage production of *Storm in Summer*. The total, Broder recalls, was about $750 for a four-week run. "We don't even know who these guys are," he told Serling, unaware the play represented a partial realization of the writer's dream.

"Take it," Serling told him, perhaps feeling that a success at the Off-Broadway Theatre in San Diego could lead to Broadway in New York. "Poverty knows no pride," Serling joked when asked by a columnist from the *Los Angeles Times* why San Diego.

James Burrows was the director at the Off-Broadway. A graduate of the Yale Drama School and later the director of both "Taxi" and "Cheers" on television, he had been instrumental in convincing Serling to drop Steve Allen's songs and return the play to its dramatic roots. Sam Jaffe starred as Shaddick, the deli owner, and Rodney Bingley played the young black boy. (Also in it were Edd "Kookie" Byrnes of "77 Sunset Strip," the show "Twilight Zone" knocked off the air, as Shaddick's nephew; and Patty—*The Bad Seed*—McCormack, as the gentile girl Byrnes's character wants to marry.)

"It's a thrilling new experience for me," Serling told the *Times.* "I feel I've run out of gas in the mass media. The beauty of being totally untyrannized is absolutely terrific. I feel liberated; free to add or take away things; free from the shackles of the clock."

It was entirely a measure of Serling's name and reputation that the *Los Angeles Times* allotted him so much space to plug the show three days before its opening, then sent its number-one drama critic, Dan Sullivan, to San Diego (at a time when the paper did not have a San Diego edition) to review opening night. Serling probably wished he had neither fame nor reputation. He had always been terribly pained by bad reviews, particularly those that

dismissed his hard work in a line or two; he felt he bene-
fited by longer, more incisive reviewing. Sullivan's detailed review, which ran many column inches, started
badly—and got worse.

"There were some honest snuffles in the audience as the
old Jew and the young black boy said goodby in the last
act of Rod Serling's *Storm in Summer* . . . and you had to
respect the reaction, but not the material that provoked
it," Sullivan wrote.

It continued: "A paradox: Serling has long been an advocate of 'maturity' in TV drama. Yet given a medium where
real maturity is possible—the stage—he reverts to 'Abie's
Irish Rose,' as retold for the *Hallmark Hall of Fame*. Freedom, it would appear, can be as inhibiting to a writer not
used to it as censorship."

Noting that the show's publicity handout referred to the
production as a "serio-comedy," Sullivan suggested that a
better word would be "tripe—or, in this context, Hebrew
National Baloney." Even worse: "A real playwright can
create characters who ring true as individuals yet also
carry something of the archetype about them, a good
example being the old furniture dealer in Arthur Miller's
The Price."

The show closed out its run, and Serling never again
contemplated a stage play.

Serling now spent more than half his time away from
California, lecturing at colleges and teaching classes at
Ithaca. Except for commercials and voice-over work, little
held him there. He became in essence an amateur professional, who approached meetings at the studios and with
producers more as a curiosity than an ambition, as
though writing were simply another trade, like welding.
He wrote scripts as favors for producer friends like Landsburg and Aaron Spelling. Spelling, the exclusive property
of ABC and the network's single largest supplier of programming—some executives and producers nicknamed
ABC "Aaron's Broadcasting Network"—called him one
time to punch up one of three one-hour scripts, each

about a different kind of doctor, which he and partner
Leonard Goldberg called "The Practice." Two days before
shooting, the producers received the original writer's
rewrite and hated it. At three o'clock in the afternoon,
Spelling called Serling's house. "Help," he said, asking
Serling to improve the dialogue. "I'm burned out, and the
script's just not as good as the other two." One of them
was written by Reginald Rose.

"No problem," Serling said. No doubt he felt wonderful
being asked.

Spelling sent the script by messenger and the next
morning received almost a completely rewritten draft—
much improved over the original.

"This is terrific," Spelling told him. "God bless you. I
want to pay you."

"Don't be silly," Serling said.

"Rod, you can't do this. I want to pay you."

"No, we're friends."

"Come on, producer to writer, what should I pay you?"

"Send me some fruit," Serling finally said with a laugh.

That afternoon a truck parked in the driveway of Serling's home. Two men got out and began unloading crates
of grapefruits, oranges, apples, and pears, finally covering
his entire lawn with fruit.

Shortly thereafter, Serling and Spelling tried to revive
"The Twilight Zone," Serling for the umpteenth time with
the umpteenth producer. He could not have been too
surprised when ABC said no. "It broke my heart," says
Spelling.

The next time the two men talked, a year later, it was
long-distance, and Serling was in the hospital. "Boy, have I
been in 'The Twilight Zone,'" Serling said. "I'm telling you,
Aaron, don't work so hard. It's not worth it."

The Rod Serling who arrived at Interlaken, New York, in
May 1975 for a summer and fall of relaxation and regener-
ation looked at least ten years older than his fifty years.
His skin, too long exposed unmercifully to the ravaging

sun, had deep lines in the forehead and cheeks and was the consistency of leather. His eyes lacked their characteristic sparkle and charm. He was very visibly tired—not just from lack of sleep, but from a tiredness in spirit.

On arriving, he called Dick Berg for no apparent reason. He just wanted to talk, to hear his friend's voice. Berg thought the call strange; they had just spoken in person twelve hours or so before. This was not like Serling at all.

While carrying luggage out to the car in California the day before, Serling had felt sharp chest pains, which passed when he let someone else take over. Now, two days later, while mowing the cottage lawn, overgrown under the spring sun, the pains returned, worse than ever. He sat down in the grass, clutching his chest, and Carol called the ambulance.

As heart attacks go, this one had been relatively mild, the doctors said, prescribing rest and a diet that banned cigarettes. During his two weeks in the hospital, Serling bribed nurses and orderlies for smokes, hiding them when necessary. One day while smoking, he heard Carol's voice saying hello to a nurse. He was surprised; she was an hour early. Not knowing what else to do with the lit cigarette, he stuck it into the back of his radio. If Carol could smell the cigarette, she said nothing—until smoke began to pour from the radio wires, which had caught fire. "I'm like a killer, caught with a smoking gun in my hand, standing over a corpse," he said.

When he was released the doctors and his family expressed optimism for his recovery chances. They felt that bypass surgery, then relatively new, would not be necessary as long as he took better care of himself: worked less, quit smoking, got reasonable amounts of exercise.

He did work less, accepting only a job narrating a documentary Bob Serling had written for the Air Transport Association. Bob sent the script to the cottage and Serling recorded the narration on a tape recorder.

If he smoked less, it was only because, with others around, he could not light up at will. He had stashed cigarettes all over the property—in the eaves of the buildings, where boughs came together in trees, behind posts. (Carol would not find them until after his death.)

Yet the doctor's prescription had not cured the patient. The family discussed transferring him to Los Angeles to have familiar, big-city specialists perform the now necessary bypass. But moving him would have been too risky. His Ithaca heart specialist recommended taking him to Rochester for surgery at Strong Memorial Hospital. Surgery was scheduled for eight o'clock the next morning. When the ambulance arrived at the cottage to take him, Serling handed the Air Transport recording to the ambulance driver and made him promise to mail it to his brother in Washington, D.C. He could have given it to Bob himself, but he didn't know that the entire family would be gathered that night around his hospital room.

Serling was afraid—afraid of the operation, afraid of dying. "That's what I anticipate death will be," he said: "a totally unconscious void in which you float through eternity with no particular consciousness of anything." He had cried weeks before, the first time Bob and Priscilla Serling came to visit him in the hospital, and now he cried again. Then, Priscilla had beat him at gin so that he wouldn't think he was dying. This time, Bob jokingly asked whether he could have the Auburn, Serling's latest expensive roadster, if he didn't pull through. Serling laughed appreciatively. Four years before, when his serious triglyceride problem seemed potentially lethal, Bob had asked his younger brother to take care of his wife and two small children in the event of his death. Serling willingly agreed, returning the promise Bob had once made to him.

At seven in the morning, June 28, 1975, he called Carol at the hotel and asked her to come early to his room. They talked for an hour, while he was prepped for the surgery. They kissed good-bye and promised to see each other soon.

Carol, Bob, Priscilla, Nan, and Jody and her husband of a

year and a week huddled in the waiting room. The doctor had said to expect him at about ten o'clock. By 2:30 no one had told them anything. Their repeated nervous pleas to the nurses for news met the same answer: "When we know, you'll know." At last, the grim-faced doctor walked toward them.

The operation had been an apparent success. But while the doctor was sewing him up, he had another heart attack right on the table. The surgical team opened him again, intending to perform yet another bypass. One surgeon cut into his other leg to remove the saphenous vein for the transplantation. The vein crumbled in his hand, leaving them helpless to save him. These were the veins of an eighty-year-old man.

In death, Serling moved from one of his most memorable characters to another. At the end of his life he had become Mountain McClintock, the boxer who fought one too many fights and struggled to find honor in a world that was no longer entertained by him; unlike the original Mountain, though, Serling turned professional wrestler, a sideshow freak, because he didn't know where else to turn. Now, his heart having failed, he became Andy Sloane, the aging executive who died because he didn't know any other way to quit the job he should have quit long ago.

Serling could easily have written the scene: Standing next to the sheet-draped corpse in the operating room, a cigarette in his hand, the dispassionate narrator, gently pointing out the ironic moral at the end of the episode, sums up this man's failed expectations: "The writer of 'Patterns' and 'Requiem for a Heavyweight' got waylaid, it seems, in the Twilight Zone."

EPILOGUE

In death Rod Serling actually achieved what he unsuccessfully sought in life: a measure of immortality for
his work and for himself. He remains to this day,
nearly a decade and a half since his passing, the only
writer whose name, face, and voice are easily recognizable
to the masses. In fact, he has become something of a
cultural icon. Imitators of varying skill, attempting to
emulate his distinctive voice and mannerisms, pedal a
long list of products, from bank loans to washing ma-
chines, on television and radio.

Thirty years after its debut, "The Twilight Zone" continues to play in syndication in virtually every major
United States television market. It has also been seen in
nearly one hundred foreign countries. There can be no
overestimation of the impact that Serling's series has had
on popular culture. His editorial influence can be seen
clearly in the work of a whole generation of filmmakers,
most notably Steven Spielberg and George Lucas. Even the
term "Twilight Zone" has fallen into common usage.

Yet among the same masses who know him so well, few

can name a single title from his immense body of work—
more than two hundred television plays alone—aside
from "The Twilight Zone." Unfortunately, his greatest
scripts, written in the 1950s for such shows as "Playhouse
90," have all but faded from view. If they are seen at all it
is usually during PBS retrospectives of television's so-
called golden age. Yet being rarely seen, or barely remembered, does not tarnish their lustre.

Serling's great mistake was to judge himself more by his
failures than by his successes. Because his successes
came early in his career, he spent the rest of his life trying
to live up to that original rush of acceptance, and at the
same time fearing he would not. Writing under that burden
of desperation only served to emphasize to him the disparity between what he later turned out and what he felt
capable of writing. While he may not have climbed as
high on the artistic ladder as he might have intended, he
should be, and will be, remembered for his successes and
not his failures.

In the spring of 1985, Serling's lifelong dream of making
it to Broadway finally came true. *Requiem for a Heavyweight*, starring John Lithgow as Mountain McClintock, ·
opened a brief run at the Martin Beck Theatre.

METHODOLOGY
AND SOURCES

I first became interested in writing a biography of Rod Serling in about 1985 after watching an episode of "The Twilight Zone" I'd seen probably ten times before, including its original broadcast in the early 1960s. This time when Serling's closing narration ended, I began to wonder whether his narrator persona had really matched his off-screen personality; I knew of him only that he had authored such early television plays as "Patterns" and "Requiem for a Heavyweight" and that he had hosted "Night Gallery." The next day I walked through a large independent bookstore, searching unsuccessfully for a biography that might answer my wonderment. Nor could I find a volume listed in *Books in Print*. Incredibly, ten years after his death not a single book had been written about one of the major cultural icons of the technological era. Rather than wait for someone else to do it first, I began to explore the possibility of writing Serling's biography.

My first step was to spend a few weeks in the Special Collections Department of UCLA's Research Library, looking through the many boxes of correspondence, manuscripts, and other memorabilia that Serling and his wife, Carol, had donated to the university. I wanted to see whether he seemed sufficiently complex and compelling to occupy two years or so of my life. By the second day, I became fascinated by the hundreds of so-called fan letters written to him—which he'd saved—particularly the letters of desperation; it soon became evident, at least to me, that the public adored a man who, in some senses, did not feel worthy of their admiration. Armed with this belief and a few other salient facts about Serling, I approached my publisher.

After receiving the go-ahead, I began a long process of investigation—following any lead I could find with any new ones that might develop and using a great deal of intuition—by first calling Buck Houghton, producer of "The Twilight Zone" for its first three years; a kind soul at CBS referred the call to him, and Houghton, who is a very intelligent and gentlemanly man, agreed to meet with me. After a particularly long interview, he gave me Carol Serling's unlisted phone number. She and I soon had the first of perhaps fifty phone conversations—all of them off the record—about her late husband, me, and my intentions. She referred me to the extensive collection of Serling's papers at the University of Wisconsin Center for Film and Theatre Research in Madison, to which Serling himself donated the bulk of his written memorabilia.

During the next two years, I spent many weeks in the archives reading room of the Wisconsin State Historical Society (which administers the collection), poring over every letter, memo, report, and script in the huge collection. Serling apparently saved almost everything that crossed his desk from 1955, when huge success first enabled him to hire a secretary, to his death twenty-three years later. His correspondents included a veritable who's who of show business and politics. Fortunately, his able secretaries also saved copies of his return letters and notes. As much as anything, the letters provided a nearly palpable sense of place, enabling me to chronologize Serling's activities and whereabouts; an inveterate letter writer (rather, letter dictator), Serling left a very revealing paper trail.

In researching and writing this book I relied on the memories and reminiscences of a number of people, some of whom knew Rod Serling very well, others less well, still others only vaguely. I always weighed the information according to the subject's relationship to Serling, his or her reputation, whether or not he or she might have a figurative ax to grind, and apparent memory recall (in interviews containing information that I knew to be wrong or later discovered to be wrong, I discarded everything but that which I later confirmed elsewhere). Several other interviews were granted on the condition that they be on background only, and I accepted information from sources who requested anonymity only if those persons had already established, to my satisfaction, a record of reliability on other information.

Anecdotes in which one of the people listed below is a participant were related to me by him or her; the use of quoted dialogue comes directly from the participant as he or she recalled it.

In chapter one, my sources were boyhood friends of Serling, acquaintances, teachers, and family. They included: Ed Abram, Pat BeGasse, Helen Foley, Dr. V. Garabedian, Sybil Goldenberger, Ann Goodman, James Haley, Eileen Haley, Lloyd Hartman, Suzanne Hersch, Robert Keller, and Bob Serling. The historical information about Binghamton, New York, came from the Binghamton Chamber of Commerce, a Binghamton Public Library research librarian, the Broome County historian, Broome County clerk, Seneca County clerk, the Seneca County recorder, and the Seneca County historian. Research materials included the *WPA Guide to the Empire State*, *Who's Who in America* (1920–1940), *Encyclopaedia Britannica*, and *World Book Encyclopedia*.

For chapter two, I was able to reconstruct much of

Serling's World War II experiences from the recollections of many members of the 511th Airborne Infantry: George Doherty, Charles Feureisen, Lieutenant General (retired) Edward M. Flanagan, Kenneth Haan, Vern Hartung, Richard Hoyt, Peter Hurst, Richard Loughrin, Buzz Miley, Fred Sciarapa, and Jerry Shea. Most of them knew Serling well. In addition, Alonzo Bouie, Department of the Army, National Resources Center, provided me with much useful information about Serling's war record, as did the Veteran's Administration records division, which sent me a copy of his V.A. file. The larger details about World War II came from a variety of books and sources. I turned often to *World Book Encyclopedia*, *Encyclopaedia Britannica*, the *New Columbia Encyclopedia*, and to a number of biographies of Douglas MacArthur. The smaller details, particularly with regard to the 511th, most often came from General Flanagan, who has himself chronicled the war in the Pacific in several books.

Individuals interviewed for the remainder of the book tended to offer information pertaining to various periods in Serling's life, so to confine them to a single chapter would be unfair. Their roles are clarified here only if they are not mentioned specifically in the text or not otherwise generally recognizable. They are listed in no particular order: James Burrows; Dick Berg; Buck Houghton; Saul David; Martin Manulis; Richard Kiley; John Champion; Michael Pipher, Rod Serling Memorial Foundation; Peter Cott; Alden Schwimmer; Sammy Davis, Jr.; Sonny Fox; Reginald Rose; Connie Hirschman, daughter of the late Herbert Hirschman; Marjorie Langsford; Robert Goldsmith; Ralph Andrews; Bert Granet; Bob Broder; Perry Lafferty; William F. Nolan; Rachel David; Harry Ackerman; Ann Weisman, wife of Serling's late friend Al Weisman; John Guedel; William Self; Aaron Spelling; Johnny Hart; Dr. Harold Arlen; Mary Arlen; John Bloch; Irv Kupcinet; David Eagle, film producer; Hall Bartlett; Robert Lewine; Budd Schulberg; Richard Matheson; Roger Anker; Earl Holliman; Henry Blankfort; Norman Corwin; Michael Zimring; Earle Reynolds, an Antioch University professor and neighbor of the Serlings; Barbara Reynolds, Earle's wife; Tim Reynolds; Thomas Goff-Brennan; Pamela des Barres; Dr. Ernest Pipes; Dr. Albert Schrut, a friend of the Serlings; Allan Jonas, a friend who worked with Serling on some ACLU fund-raising; Jackie Cooper; William Dozier; Steve Allen; Bob Schiller; Sy Gomberg; Walter Schwimmer; Marc Scott Zicree; Kenneth Leedom; Alan Landsburg; Dan Gingold; Buzz Kulik; Syd Cassyd, the founder of the Academy of Television Arts and Sciences; John Haldi; Priscilla Serling, wife of Bob Serling; Eleanor Franks; Ernie Kaufman, an actor from the era of live television; Stanley Kramer; Carlin Weimer, Ohio State University engineering department; Roger Conklin, station manger WNBF, Binghamton; Walter Wanger.

Others who did not know Serling personally but provided information and guidance included: Elizabeth Adkins, archives manager of Kraft, Inc.; Barbara Hatch, FBI information officer (Freedom of Information Act division); Randy Dolnick and Ronald Simon at the Museum of Broadcasting; Tappan King at *Twilight Zone* magazine; and Harry Miller and George Talbot and the Wisconsin Center for Film and Theatre Research. Institutions that provided a great deal of assistance and information included: United States Information Agency; Santa Monica Public Library; UCLA Research Library and Special Collections Department; Duke University; Writer's Guild of America; Director's Guild of America; Academy of Motion Picture Arts and Sciences and its extensive library; American Film Institute; Viacom, Inc.; Herbert Mitgang, the *New York Times*; Beth Knizly, USIA; Stanley Kauffmann, *The New Republic*.

NOTES

CHAPTER 1: WALKING DISTANCE

Page 28. **"It was the first time . . ."**: *TV Guide*, June 3, 1972.

CHAPTER 2: REQUIEM FOR A BOY

Page 48. **"[War] is separated . . ."**: First draft of *Good Housekeeping* article in manuscript form at UCLA Research Library, Special Collections Department.

Page 56. **"His wife . . ."**: "Life With Rod," *Rod Serling's Twilight Zone* magazine, August 1986.

Page 53. **"I was bitter . . ."**: Marc Scott Zicree. *The Twilight Zone Companion*. New York: Bantam Books, 1982.

CHAPTER 3: A MOTH TO A FLAME

Page 64. **"I was convinced . . ."**: "Rod Serling's Last Interview," *Writer's Yearbook*, 1976.

Page 65. **"And perhaps across his mind . . ."**: Zicree, *Twilight Zone Companion*.

Page 66. **"I never had a master plan . . ."**: Interview with Ellen Cameron May. *Los Angeles Times*, June 25, 1967.

Page 68. **"I really didn't know . . ."**: William F. Nolan, "The Gamma Interview," *Gamma*, number one, 1963.

Page 68. **"massive compulsion"**: "Serling's Last Interview," *Writer's Yearbook*.

Page 68. **"We all strive..."**: Interview with William F. Nolan, June 1961.

Page 75. **"an incredible event"**: "Serling's Last Interview," *Writer's Yearbook*.

Page 87. **"These weren't bad..."**: Rod Serling. *Patterns*. New York: Simon & Schuster, 1957.

Page 87. **"a piece of your flesh"**: "Serling's Last Interview," *Writer's Yearbook*.

Page 87. **"beer mug at twenty paces"**: Nolan, "The Gamma Interview."

Page 89. **"a period of about eight months"**: "Serling's Last Interview," *Writer's Yearbook*.

Page 89. **"ex-tent revivalist"**: Nolan, "The Gamma Interview."

Page 89. **"an audition show"**: Serling, *Patterns*.

CHAPTER 4: SLAVE TO A BITCH GODDESS

Page 94. **"I had the strange..."**: *Ibid*.

Page 101. **"In the strangely brittle..."**: Motto of the Rod Serling Memorial Foundation, Binghamton, New York; quoted from the *Binghamton Press*, which reprinted the remarks several times from an interview in the late 1950s.

Page 102. **"a very solid dame"**: Interview with William F. Nolan, June 1961.

Page 103. **"wanted to believe"**: "Life with Rod," *Twilight Zone* magazine, August 1986.

Page 104. **"In retrospect..."**: Serling, *Patterns*.

Page 107. **"One minute after..."**: Nolan, The Gamma Interview.

Page 112. **"the price tag"**: Serling, *Patterns*.

Page 115. **"twenty-three bids"**: Interview with William F. Nolan, June 1961.

Page 115. **"with the expert conciseness**: Review by J. P. Shanley, *New York Times*, April 17, 1955.

Page 116. **"Success is not..."**: William F. Nolan, "No Requiem for Rod," *Rogue*, January 1962.

Page 117. **"I suddenly found..."**: Interview with William F. Nolan, June 1961.

Page 117. **"Anne Edwards, as the girl..."**: Review by J. P. Shanley, *New York Times*, June 17, 1955.

Page 117. **"The pieces of the plot..."**: Review by J. P. Shanley, *New York Times*, June 24, 1955.

Page 117. **"dictated by economic considerations"**: Gilbert Millstein, "'Patterns' of a Television Playwright," *New York Times Magazine*, Dec. 2, 1956.

Page 117. **"I took assignments..."**: *Ibid*.

Page 118. **"not a good writer"**: *Ibid*.

Page 125. **"dies at the hands"**: Nolan, "No Requiem for Rod."

Page 130. **"You rehearse a show ..."**: *Los Angeles Times*, Sept. 1957.

Page 135. **"did not have a very auspicious"**: Review by Jack Gould, *New York Times* Oct. 5, 1956.

Page 137. **"The first thing I had to do..."**: *New York Times*, Oct. 7, 1956.

Page 139. **"overwhelming force and tenderness"**: Review by Jack Gould, *New York Times*, Oct. 12, 1956.

Page 140. **"The money's in the bank..."**: "Patterns of a Television Playwright," *New York Times*, Dec. 2, 1956.

Chapter 5: A Thousand Dollars a Week

Page 145. **"*not one* redeeming feature"**: *Ibid.*

Page 156. **"It can be said safely..."**: Rod Serling, "TV in the Can vs. TV in the Flesh," *New York Times Magazine*, Nov. 24, 1957.

Page 167. **"chopped it up"**: Nolan, "No Requiem for Rod."

Page 168. **"a romantic Mexican youth"**: *Time*, June 30, 1958.

Page 168. **"My sheriff couldn't..."**: "No Requiem for Rod."

Chapter 6: Another Dimension

Page 206. **"maximum way to enjoy"**: Rod Serling, "Somebody Asked Me, Therefore...," *Journal of the Producer's Guild of America*, January 1960.

Page 225. **"belongs in an alley"**: *New York Times*, May 17, 1962.

Page 226. **"tilting at those windmills"**: interview with William F. Nolan, June 1961.

Page 226. **"sat down in the palladium"**: *Los Angeles Times*, May 31, 1962.

Page 226. **"I was conned"**: Dwight Whitney, *TV Guide*, June 3, 1972.

Page 229. **"had not wanted to leave school"**: *Newsweek*, Oct. 28, 1962.

Page 231. **"Nothing gets past these kids"**: *Ibid.*

Page 248. **"Weekly ghouls"**: *Daily Variety*, March 12, 1964.

Chapter 7: Seasons to Be Wary

Page 272. **"Violence comes in many forms"**: *The Valuator* (Official magazine of the California Teachers Association), Winter 1965.

Page 275. **"It is quite apparent..."**: *Ibid.*

Page 281. **"he believed it to be the best script"**: *Variety*, Dec. 8, 1966.

Page 289. **"Everything that I wrote..."**: "Serling's Last Interview," *Writer's Yearbook*.

Page 293. **"Can't a writer dry up?"**: Interview with Ellen Cameron May, *Los Angeles Times*, June 25, 1967.

Page 297. **"TV coverage . . ."**: The *Cornell Daily Sun*, Sept. 19, 1967.

Page 305. **"country's escapist mood"**: *Variety*, Jan. 17, 1968.

Page 305. **"When I was a kid . . ."**: "TV Times," *Los Angeles Times*, March 2–8, 1969.

Page 311. **"When Tris Speaker . . ."**: Interview with Aleene Mac-Minn, *Los Angeles Times*, Sept. 11, 1968.

Page 311. **"After five years of my own show . . ."**: "TV Times," *Los Angeles Times*, March 2–8, 1969.

CHAPTER 8: LAST STOP

Page 313. **"constipated Sicilian prizefighter"**: *Los Angeles Times*, April 1971.

Page 316. **"mongoloids without class, without taste"**: From a letter to his cousin Rita Goodman dated May 7, 1968.

Page 323. **"as we worked on it"**: *Los Angeles Times*, Dec. 24, 1972.

Page 325. **"was like pulling impacted wisdom teeth"**: From a letter to John Urie dated March 16, 1970.

Page 327. **"when I complain . . ."**: Zicree, *Twilight Zone Companion*.

Page 328. **"I wanted a series . . ."**: *Ibid*.

Page 330. **"Now I know why people keep scrapbooks . . ."** : Article by Dwight Whitney, *TV Guide*, June 3–9, 1972.

Page 330. **"not a helluva lot"**: *Ibid*.

Page 337. **"Poverty knows no pride"**: Column by Sylvie Drake, *Los Angeles Times*, Dec. 24, 1972.

Page 337. **"It's a thrilling . . ."**: *Ibid*.

Page 338. **"some honest snuffles"**: Review by Dan Sullivan, *Los Angeles Times*, Dec. 27, 1972.

Page 341. **"That's what I anticipate death will be . . ."**: "Serling's Last Interview," *Writer's Yearbook*.